ON MATRICIDE

AMBER JACOBS

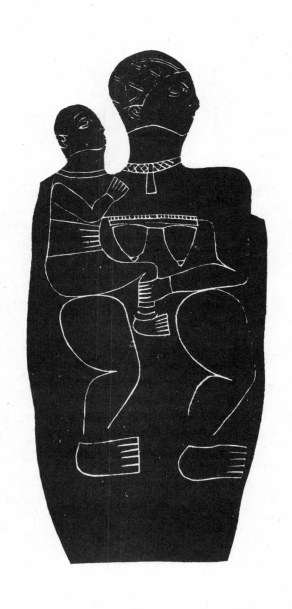

ON
MATRICIDE

Myth, Psychoanalysis, and the Law of the Mother

COLUMBIA

UNIVERSITY

PRESS

NEW YORK

COLUMBIA UNIVERSITY PRESS
Publishers Since 1893
New York   Chichester, West Sussex
Copyright © 2007 Columbia University Press
All rights reserved

Library of Congress Cataloging-in-Publication Data
Jacobs, Amber.
On matricide : myth, psychoanalysis, and the law of the mother / Amber Jacobs.
   p.   cm.
Includes bibliographical references and index.
ISBN 978-0-231-14154-3 (cloth : alk. paper) — ISBN 978-0-231-51205-3 (electronic)
1. Parricide—Psychological aspects. 2. Parricide in literature. I. Title.
HV6542.J33   2008
150.19'5—dc22
   2006036864

Columbia University Press books are printed on permanent and durable
   acid-free paper.
This book was printed on paper with recycled content.
Printed in the United States of America
c 10 9 8 7 6 5 4 3 2 1
Designed by Lisa Hamm

References to Internet Web sites (URLs) were accurate at the time of writing. Neither the author nor Columbia University Press is responsible for URLs that may have expired or changed since the manuscript was prepared.

For my daughters, Maisie and Beattie

Contents

PART III

Preface

THEORIZING MATRICIDE, IN my argument, means making a feminist intervention into classical psychoanalysis via structural anthropology.

I argue that matricide, unlike patricide is untheorized in psychoanalysis. What this means is that there is no place within psychoanalytic theory for a maternal subject position that could function as a site of structuring power leading to a mode of symbolization that does not refer automatically to the paternal law. The key question with which I am concerned is whether the mother can be theorized within the terms of the underlying cultural laws that determine sociosymbolic organization.

The most ambitious aim of this book is to contribute to the creation of a symbolic organization that would counter the situation whereby femininity assumes its status as the limit of representation. My position is based on the feminist hypothesis that the present organization of the dominant symbolic order is not inevitable.

My specific strategy of sociosymbolic intervention will be through contemporary reworkings of ancient Greek mythology and tragedy. Ultimately, I pursue an analysis of the complex intersection of myth, phantasy, and culture and offer a strategy of feminist intervention into the dominant current Western symbolic organization through identifying what I will term the "(re)structuring power of myth."[1]

My rereading of ancient mythology and tragedy in this context aims to develop new insights and interventions into current psychosocial realities. In this way, I am not concerned with what Aeschylus, Sophocles, and Euripides meant but with how they have been or might be read, used, and interpreted today.

These rereadings of Greek mythology in contemporary terms enable me to interpret the unconscious phantasies that remain operative in our present sociosymbolic organization. Specifically, I use a rereading of the matricidal myth of the *Oresteia,* as dramatized by Aeschylus, Sophocles, and Euripides to question the status of matricidal phantasies within the terms of the underlying human laws that inform and determine our contemporary dominant symbolic organization and discourses.

Looking back to myth is part of a strategy that aims to modify our existing sociosymbolic organization. Using Greek myth in what I term its "restructuring capacity" is my specific strategy for combating the present symbolic hegemony that feminist theorists have persistently diagnosed.

Considering myth in terms of its structuring power requires addressing the question of its role with regard to the transgenerational unconscious transmission of sociocultural bonds. I am concerned with cultural receptions of mythology: how it has been and may be used today with respect to the question of sociosymbolic reorganization. Psychoanalysis is an exemplary instance of the recycling of Greek myth in contemporary discourse. I suggest that psychoanalytic feminism needs to address the implications of this particular mythical inheritance if it is to be able to intervene into psychoanalysis for the purpose of working toward the theorization of unconscious structures that are not reducible to the structure of Oedipus alone.

I work from translations of the Greek tragedies. In analyzing myth and tragedy, I do not concentrate on the language of the plays. I am not undertaking a materialist reading of ancient texts but rather am following Lévi-Strauss in adopting a structural approach; I am concerned with the processes by which myths "operate" in people's minds "without their being aware of the fact."[2] More precisely, I want to address the question of using myth as an instrument to establish a new order of values within the thinking process itself. In this sense, working in translation is not an intellectual or methodological problem since I concentrate on cultural receptions of myth in the present and in the future, rather than on what the ancient Greek dramatists might have meant in the context in which they wrote.

The key conceptual operation underlying my argument is to use myth in order to theorize an underlying cultural law that is not reducible to the structure of Oedipus. In this way, one can begin to posit the possibilities of other fields of desire and meaning and their symbolic representation. Such a position takes as its premise an understanding of the symbolic that differs from Lacan's. Rather than holding to the Lacanian view of the symbolic as static and monolithic, the post-Lacanian position espoused here considers the symbolic as a dynamic order that can be expanded and reorganized to accommodate different economies of desire and meaning. Rethinking the definition of the symbolic in this way introduces the possibility of including femininities as active participants in the symbolic network and arriving at an understanding that proposes a *dynamic heterogeneous symbolic* with openings allowing for potential reorganization and transformation.

What is in question is a symbolic economy that does not solely refer, in the first instance, to the paternal symbolic function but instead resurrects the mother from the so-called imaginary, presymbolic primitive realm and places her within the social arena of language, representation, and history. Such a move immediately upsets and destabilizes the structure of the oedipal phallic paradigm through which patriarchal power relations are secured. As soon as the symbolic function is dislodged from its automatic reference to the father as the third element functioning to break up the mother-infant imaginary dyad and thus creating a position from which to think and speak,[3] the armatures of a new theorization concerning symbolic sexed subjectivities are necessarily suggested.

In summary, the backbone of my argument comprises three interrelated aims: first, to postulate a nonmonolithic theory of the symbolic; second, to theorize a maternal subject position that would lead to a reformulation of the crucial differentiating function of the symbolic; and, third, to bring matricide into theory as a structural concept.

Acknowledgments

M Y DEEPEST GRATITUDE to Margaret Whitford, who provided invaluable and inspiring intellectual engagement and
support during the process of researching and writing this
book. For important discussions about this work I want to thank Ulele
Burnham, Helen Carr, Matt Cook, Sara Flanders, Susanna Jacobs, Vicky
Lebeau, Allegra Madgewick, Juliet Mitchell, Vincent Quinn, Nick Royle,
Naomi Salaman, Alan Sinfield, and Estela Welldon.

Thanks also to my parents for their constant support—especially How-
ard Jacobs for his generous editorial help. Finally, to Gordon Hon, whose
brilliant mind has challenged me throughout and whose love and humor
have sustained me.

PART I

1 🐛

Postpatriarchal Futures

FEMINISMS' FRAUGHT DIALOGUES with psychoanalysis, post-structuralism, and contemporary French philosophy have brought the current debate to an abstract level where everything from identity and collectivity to biological sex and the possibility of social change have been problematized, deconstructed, or put "under erasure."[1] We seem to be living in the intellectual era of the "post" and the "beyond." I have inherited feminism's complex dialogues with psychoanalysis and French philosophy, and this intellectual situation throws up the most difficult question: namely, what a so-called third wave or stage of feminism is. It is a reality now to think back through one's intellectual mothers and receive a rich tradition with which to engage. Yet thinking back through our theoretical feminist mothers is not always a straightforward practice. The so-called third wave of feminist scholars has the privilege of a vast inheritance: a theoretical labyrinth in which there is no single point where all routes converge.

The multiplicity that characterizes contemporary feminisms in the academy at once subverts any assumptions of a shared or collective feminist agenda. While the essentially interdisciplinary and plural nature of feminist studies promotes the making of new intellectual links, academic feminism faces the constant danger of short-circuiting the commitment to the fight for social change. Oppression of women is a concept that cannot now be uttered in the academic context without acknowledgment of the homogenizing impulse that such a concept implies. It is no longer viable to speak of women as a homogenized group, and neither is it viable to speak of change without paying due attention to the masculinist humanist ideology inherent in such a notion. In the current intellectual climate, a feminism that claims to be committed to social change necessarily confronts complex theoretical problems, problems that feminist theorists themselves have brought to light. Speaking of social change, the oppression of women under Western patriarchies, and the transformation of our society as we know it has been disclosed by poststructuralist feminisms as risking complicity with a humanist masculinist view of subjectivity and history. Such a view posits the subject as autonomous and unified, in charge of his conscious aims, and committed both to a teleological view of history and to ideas of a progressive perfection of a complete, knowable. and stable (Enlightenment) self/identity. The poststructuralist and postcolonial critique of identity that certain feminist writers have taken on board has necessarily both problematized and enriched the feminist debate. The current poststructuralist emphasis on difference, on unstable "decentered," "fluid," and "performed" identities means that to speak of women and their oppression is invariably to be charged with collaboration with an imperialist and totalizing gesture. To my mind, the most urgent question for contemporary feminisms is how to constitute a viable collectivity that avoids the neglect of difference and thus the somewhat coercive impulse that desires to speak of and represent "women" as if this was an unproblematic category. What is required now is to follow through the implications that the poststructuralist critique of identity has had on the feminist project, while still retaining a link with the project of social change.

One consequence of the necessary confrontation of feminism with the implications of the "split" or decentered subject of poststructuralism or contemporary French philosophy is a polarization within feminism of feminism as politics, on the one hand, and feminism as discourse, on the other. The poststructuralist celebration of difference, multiplicity, and fluid unfixed "identities" renders feminism a heterogeneous discourse of textuality that is set against a materialist feminist politics committed to a campaigning "movement" based on the idea of a common cause.[2] It is as though the latter project no longer tallies with the intellectual positions of the currently flourishing critical theories, which can sometimes appear (ironically) as a new canonized orthodoxy. No feminist position can afford to display any complacency in the face of the complexities that writing about "women" or "femininity" will entail. Yet, at the same time, in doing feminist research one must resist collaborating with this split within contemporary feminisms. In the poststructuralist new orthodoxy, any appeal to collectivity and the concept of oppression is declared to be a case of "logocentric imperialism,"[3] while the countercharge against poststructuralist feminism concerns its absolute divorce from the reality of social relations and the project of combating social oppression on the material level. To negotiate these seemingly incompatible positions within feminism is, to my mind, a necessity.

What is required is a rethinking of the implications of textuality and the deconstruction of the "subject" with a view to preventing the latter's transformation into a new metaphysical dogma that undercuts the project of social change and so relegates feminism solely to discourse. If there is to be a third wave of feminist thought and practice, then its point of departure needs to be based on the attempt to overcome the splitting within feminisms wherein theory, discourse, and textuality are pitted against, or declared to be antithetical to, politics, collectivity, and social transformation.

J. Whitebrook refers to the intellectual climate after the critique of the subject as being witness to a "general slide into groundlessness" and contends that the critical debate has become polarized, such that the only two theoretical alternatives seem to be a "violent synthesis or no synthesis at all."[4] Whitebrook suggests that the contemporary theorist needs to explore the possibility of a nonobjectionable synthesis.[5] In this way, coherence, standpoint, and strategy are not sacrificed for groundlessness, instability, and the vertiginous unknowability of the decentered subject but rather reformulated in order to undo the current equation of synthesis with coercive totalizing gestures of mastery, an equation that contemporary critical theories continue to maintain.

It is for this reason that the work of Luce Irigaray has been crucial in allowing me to think feminisms into its so-called third wave. The originality of Irigaray's work, as I see it, is precisely in its potential to overcome this split and provide us with a powerful feminist strategy of radical sociosymbolic change thorough interventions at the level of discourse and representation. Her work, in my view, comes closest to Whitebrook's notion of a nonobjectionable synthesis. Irigaray has a standpoint and a strategy, as she is committed to radical sociosymbolic change while simultaneously foregrounding the workings of language and the unconscious, with its radical undercutting of mastery and telos; she both deconstructs and constructs, describes and prescribes. In my view, Irigaray's works can offer us a poststructuralist feminist position that does not compromise

feminisms' commitment to social change; her work can be used as a starting point for a poststructuralist strategic praxis that prioritizes radical
social transformation.[6]

The multiplicity of feminisms together with their often irresolvable internal conflicts necessarily means that any idealization of a feminist tradition operating through a collaborative and nonhierarchical dynamic is
no longer credible. To look back through one's feminist "mothers" is no
simple strategy; it may bring as much conflict as support.

While "sisterhood" and collectivity characterized the women's movement of the early seventies, and the "liberated" anger belonging to women
was directed at "patriarchy" as the unquestionably culpable oppressive re-
gime, we now have a situation wherein the rage has returned or resurfaced
within feminisms, manifesting itself between feminist "sisters," "mothers,"
and "daughters." "Patriarchy," as a term, has been problematized in relation
to its "universalizing" thrust. It is no longer viable to point to "patriarchy"
as the bad object without problematizing such a gesture. Certainly, Western patriarchies continue to exercise their power, but the emphasis within
feminisms has shifted into a deconstructionist self-reflexive vein, and the
limitations of the earlier feminist theories of patriarchy have been revealed
by an antihumanist feminism that aims to move beyond homogenizing
categories. Such a shift in emphasis comes hand in hand with a fragmentation within feminisms leading to internal contests over what is and is
not radical or what is and is not conservative. It is not enough to unify
feminisms through an appeal to a common and clearly identified enemy.
Through the established body of transgenerational feminist thought, its
mutations, developments, and internal conflicts, together with the inevitable transference relationship among feminist mothers, daughters, and
sisters, the analysis of and the theorization of a between-women symbolic
paradigm becomes something of a necessity.

By turning attention to the (absent) status of between-women relations
in the context of the human/cultural laws that underlie symbolic life, we
can see that the dominant (patriarchal) symbolic order is founded on the
exclusion of the subject-position of the mother and, further, the foreclosure of a symbolically mediated mother-daughter relation. Under this kind
of symbolic organization, Irigaray has argued that women remain in a state
of "immediacy" and "affectivity," a "too close proximity" to one another
that is reflected in the current dynamics in contemporary feminisms, and
urgently need a "means of distancing."[7]

Rather than reinforcing the logic of classical psychoanalysis that emphasizes the absolute necessity for the "paternal third term" to interrupt

this "immediacy" in relation to the mother, could there be an alternative process that would provide the crucial differentiating function but without cutting the daughter off from her mother? What is needed, I suggest, is the theorization of different underlying cultural laws that are not reducible to Freud's Oedipus complex so that we are not forced to choose between the (paternal) prohibition on incest and psychosis. What I am arguing for is the possibility of a culture in which there is more than one mode of symbolization.

How radical this project of producing new unconscious structures in the context of a conception of a nonmonolithic symbolic becomes evident when one considers it in the context of recent psychoanalytic debates in which theorists *inside* the psychoanalytic feminist debates consider the conception of more than one symbolic economy as (by definition) impossible.

It is for this reason that I identify with Irigaray's description of her own position: "I am [therefore] a political militant for the impossible, which is not to say a utopian. Rather I want what is yet to be as the only possibility of a future."[8] It is this commitment to facilitate the "yet to be" that characterizes the kind of feminist theory to which my argument belongs. Third-wave feminism, I suggest, needs to construct ways of reconciling an academic approach with a political desire for "what is yet to be as the only possibility of a future."

Getting Beyond Lacan

In the cultural void of today, it is tempting to hang on to someone who speaks in his own name and who develops a theory that provides answers to the most complicated questions. In doing so, however, one transforms Lacanian theory into a new ideology.

—FRANÇOIS ROUSTANG, *DIRE MASTERY: DISCIPLESHIP FROM FREUD TO LACAN*

We have, I suggest, finally broken free of the impasse in feminist theory caused by the split between those feminists who defended Lacan's theory of the symbolic and those who argued for the possibility of finding alternatives to the phallic dominance implied by Lacan's symbolic law.

The conflict between these two positions concerned the question of a feminist politics of social transformation. Lacan's theory describes the ways in which the founding scene of the symbolic order is the repudiation of the feminine that assumes its status as the limit of representability. That is to say, the representation of the feminine becomes, in Lacan's schema, that which phallic culture makes impossible. Focusing on the implications of the exclusion of the feminine as the primal scene of symbolic structuration forms the basis of feminist reformulations of Lacanian psychoanalysis. The argument against Lacan reads his theory as a manifestation of and a promotion of social conservatism. It is proposed that his particular theorization of the symbolic law-of-the-father brings any attempted intervention for change in direct confrontation with the threat of psychosis. Here we witness a slippage between description and prescription whereby the situation Lacan describes becomes set in stone, impervious to intervention because psychosis is posited as its only alternative.

The debate moves toward questioning the ways in which it may be possible to make changes in the symbolic while also remaining alert to the implications of the Lacanian position that argues for the inevitability of the present symbolic law and in this way tends to accept the patriarchal symbolic structure as both universal and uncontestable.

Whatever view one takes concerning Lacanian theory, there is an identifiable consensus that contemporary psychoanalytic feminism takes the symbolic as its point of departure. The assumption that the symbolic order is a condition of sanity is generally accepted, and any attempt to call on a presymbolic realm to recover an unmediated "femininity" before the law is now thought to be untenable, not simply because of its essentialism but because of the understanding that the alternative to the symbolic order is psychosis. It is generally agreed that it is not in the interests of feminism to hark back to a concept of a pre-given femininity belonging to an undifferentiated space before the mark of sexual difference and the law, since the consequence of such an appeal would be to position women outside language and history, in a psychotic realm in which thought and action are rendered impossible. It is, then, in the area of symbolic life that any viable feminist position belongs.

For Lacanian feminism, emphasis on the sociolinguistic construction of the radically decentered sexually differentiated subject successfully combats assertions of biological determinism/essentialism. Yet the adherence to the antihumanist implications of Lacan's always-already-divided subject—where femininity is theorized as empty of content, thus as a nonbiological construct—means that the feminist agenda of social transformation becomes compromised.

The desire to explain the psychic origins of sexual difference whereby subjectivity is created through a single major division led Lacanian feminists to confirm and tighten the tie between sexual difference and phallic domination. "One thing is needed to differentiate the sexes," said Juliet Mitchell.[9] But that "one thing" turned out to be the phallus, so some other way of creating distinctions was a question that Lacanian feminism did not address. The phallus as the central structuring signifier of difference, around which the subject takes his/her position, is a principle to which Lacanian feminists hold; to have or to be the phallus becomes the pivotal split determining the position one can take within culture. This contention, which announces the absolute impossibility of theorizing femininity outside phallic binary logic, becomes the bulwark that prevents any mobility away from the oppressive structures that feminist revisions of Lacanian theory so eloquently describe. Psychoanalysis, for Lacanian feminists, can only describe the discontents of becoming a subject under patriarchy; it cannot offer any ways out.[10] For many feminists, such a position is gravely detrimental to a feminist politics of social change.[11]

Jessica Benjamin contentiously asks: "Might not the demand for such a central structuring principle have to be suspended, or for that matter analysed?"[12] As the French psychoanalyst François Roustang has effectively shown in his critique of the Lacanian system,[13] once inside its logic, the force of its rigid theoretical systematization can have a profoundly tenacious hold, preventing the possibility of independent or innovative thought.[14] Roustang comments that: "if one is a Lacanian, one has to swallow it all; otherwise one is not a true Lacanian. . . . Psychoanalysis, which was supposed to liberate speech, soon ends in silencing it."[15]

Roustang's thesis is so convincing precisely because he criticizes from the inside and thus is not proposing a rejection of the discipline outright (he is a psychoanalyst) but instead warns against the seduction of systematic thinkers and the danger of unknowingly embracing dogma through an unanalyzed transference to the so-called Master theory. As a feminist working with psychoanalysis and committed to its indispensable insights—while also retaining a commitment to paradigm shifts—one must avoid being subject to the hold of a systematic theory.[16]

In terms of feminist uses of psychoanalysis, there must be stages subsequent to the initial descriptive strategy in order to avoid such ossification and thus prevent what began as a critical intervention from becoming a confirmation and reinforcing of the description that psychoanalysis offers. As Judith Butler asks: "Is this structure of feminine repudiation not *reinforced* by the very theory which claims that the structure is somehow prior to any given social organization, and as such resists social transformation?"[17] To move beyond the static conclusions of Lacanian feminism—without rejecting its invaluable insights—is to make considerable headway in breaking out of the so-called Lacanian impasse.

Psychoanalytic feminism in the post-Lacanian mode foregrounds symbolic necessity and uses Lacan's work for the analysis of the processes by which femininity functions in sustaining the present symbolic, with its patriarchal bias. Having used Lacanian theory for an account of the mechanisms of the phallic cultural law that inaugurates sexual difference and symbolic subjectivity, the debate then moves toward two issues. The first concerns the very possibility of interventions into the organization of the symbolic order with a view to modifying its patriarchal structure; the second concerns the problem of how actually to effect the modification. Lacan is no longer the central theorist for psychoanalytic feminism, and this, I think, is significant in terms of breaking out of the stagnation in which feminism was necessarily trapped when it could not go beyond the parameters of Lacan's theory.

From the Static to the Fluid: On the Limits of "Performativity"

Whilst Lacanian feminism posited femininity as empty of content and emphasized the necessity of taking up a position in relation to paternal law, some theorists such as Judith Butler took the debate in a different direction by positing a theory of "gender fluidity" as constituting psychosexual reality. Butler-type theories attempted to avoid an overinvestment in Lacan's emphasis on the limitation before the law and instead used the notion of the sociolinguistic construction of sexual difference to theorize multiple fluid cross-identifications as the "truth" of sexual identity. Sex and gender were not only theorized to be "empty of content" but were fundamentally a matter of shifting performed positions. An essential fluidity of gender was seen to be particularly liberating and subversive in that it rendered any normative biological model of sexuality redundant and maintained that every sexual identity was a performance that could be literally played with to explode normative stereotypes and constraining models. Gender as performative practice meant that the being/having, identification/desire oppositions outlined in the Lacanian schema were disclosed as inapplicable. According to this theoretical position, psychoanalysis did not necessarily have to be read as a static theory of the symbolic with its absolute imperatives dictated by the paternal law; there was far more mobility available within the terms of symbolic life than Lacanian feminism would have allowed us to believe. Performativity replaced stasis with fluidity. Yet, as I shall suggest, while claiming to be a subversive and radical theory of gender and identity, this position remains finally conservative in relation to feminism in its inability to intervene on a structural level in the present phallic hegemony underlying the dominant symbolic organization.

During the radical retheorizing of fluid identification processes, the question of social transformation via symbolic intervention was neglected. Pleasure and play replaced oppression and pain; the pleasure of performance, humor, and irony became, in these theories, the new so-called strategy through which to refuse patriarchal imaginary projections and the restricting frames of compulsory heterosexuality. Statements like the following from Finzi illustrate the optimism some feminists found in this new model of gender fluidity: "Whereas the hysteric of the past expressed her discomfort in the contortions of the body, like a butterfly on a pin, the woman of today attempts to free herself from the immobilizing hold of the 'female position' with a myriad of identities. She approaches and distances, identifies with and opposes. By evading every possible identification, she interweaves autonomy and authenticity, and recaptures a sense of possible wholeness."[18]

Now that sexual identity had been disclosed as essentially indeterminable—not necessarily slave to the oedipal structuration Freud posited as a condition of sociality but instead free to wander through multiple identifications—the "hysteric of the present" was called upon to become somewhat of a gymnast. There she apparently was, cartwheeling and dancing around different sexual positions, changing costumes and blowing apart stereotypes, ironically inhabiting conventional constructions of femininity in order to show up their fabricated nature. The "masquerade" was to be celebrated and appropriated with the ease and the humor of the performing acrobat.[19] Rather than being paralyzed by the imperatives of the paternal law, the former hysteric was rendered supple and double-jointed,[20] and what is more she was apparently now able to choose which particular version of femininity to inhabit from day to day. Queen of parody and performance, the new hysteric was supposed to represent a politically empowering position in her dexterous juggling, her mimicking and repetitions, which always pertained to the subversion of dominant codes.

The vicissitudes of oppression are excluded from this feminist post-structuralist discourse. Instead of oppression, we have play, pleasure, parody, reappropriation, and choice. Patriarchal structures, instead of being heralded as oppressive and needing to be radically reorganized (or overthrown), could now apparently be satisfactorily negotiated via the sophisticated performative gimmicks of the postmodern circus. With grandiose conviction, Braidotti tells us what we feminist women are apparently doing: "Feminist women who go on functioning in society as female subjects in these postmetaphysical days of the decline of gender dichotomies, act 'as if' Woman was still their location. In so doing, however, they treat femininity as an option—a set of available poses, a set of costumes rich in history and power relations, but not fixed or compulsory any longer. They simultaneously assert and deconstruct."[21] There is a strong element of omnipotent wish-fulfilling fantasy going on here, in which any kind of conflict, loss, mourning, or limitation is whisked away with the wave of the poststructuralist magic wand that says you can be everything, have everything, and lose nothing—just so long as you possess the sense of humor, the precarious skill of the performing artist and vigilantly maintain a critical self-reflexive consciousness. And just so long as you can turn your pain into laughter: "We need more complexity, multiplicity, simultaneity. Irony and self humour are important elements of this project—our collectively negotiated Dionysian laughter . . . to cultivate a culture of joy and affirmation."[22]

My critique of this type of feminist poststructuralist polemic draws upon the language of psychoanalysis with its constant reminder of the reality of limitation and loss. It is my contention that there is a complete lack of theorization of conflict and pain in this Dionysiac celebration of poststructuralist psychosexual acrobatics. The idea of a "collectively negotiated Dionysiac laughter" skims over the social and psychic realities that may prevent such an empowering fluidity of subjectivity from being part of a culture of joy and affirmation and leads to the complete neglect of the problem of oppressive social structures. In some elite sectors of the academic world, or in some academics' fantasies perhaps, it may be true to say that we are living in "post metaphysical days of the decline of gender dichotomies," but this is only a tiny enclave of society that can sometimes seem as if it has blinkers on.

What is lost in the "performative" feminist theoretical position is a political agenda of social transformation. Instead, early Butlerian theories promote a voluntarism that, in my opinion, does not do justice to the extent of the entrenchment of oppressive structures in the individual psyche and in the cultural imaginary and, further, does not acknowledge the slow and complex process through which social change can be achieved. There is no project of working toward the relinquishing of the dominance of patriarchal symbolic structures in favor of the expansion of the symbolic economy to give structural support to sexed subjectivities, sexualities, meanings, and desires that are organized around a structural center different from that of symbolic castration. Without symbolic intervention and change, the feminist poststructuralist celebration of fictive identities, fluid sexualities, and parody/mimicry as political strategy is, to my mind, rendered superficial.

In exploring Rosi Braidotti's promotion of the metaphor of Dionysian laughter, we must remember Dionysiac rapture's close proximity with violence. It is a kind of manic laughter that defends against an unbearable reality. The point at which the joyful rapture of Dionysian manic laughter switches into screams of despair is perhaps where the conflict can be located in Braidotti's project. There is a precarious line between laughter and pain, joy and terror. In Euripides' *Bacchae,* at the point at which the mother of Pentheus comes charging down from the mountain in a rapture of Dionysiac ecstasy, triumphantly holding the mutilated head of her son yet believing it to be the head of a beast, we witness the conflict between excess and limitation, laughter and pain. Once the intoxicating Bacchic mania has faded, she sees that in fact she has murdered her son.[23] Such is the cost of Dionysian frenzy, whose mania functions to obliterate distinctions and limitations. Yet the severed head she holds becomes a powerful emblem of a loss that cannot (however much one laughs) be denied.

The question at issue is the political potential in, on the one hand, disavowing/laughing at limitations or, on the other hand, recognizing and suffering them. Psychoanalysis relentlessly reminds us of the painful realities of limitation and loss. It is crucial to consider at what point such a clinging to a sense of limits remains conservative and at what point it can become allied with change. It is as though there is a pessimistic psychoanalysis with its language of loss, on the one hand, and, on the other, an optimistic feminism that must oppose the language of loss in order to break out of the limitations imposed by patriarchy. Yet feminism must be able to theorize loss and limitation without condoning or idealizing psychoanalysis's complicity with the logic of patriarchal oppression. When Judith Butler accuses Lacan of romanticizing and idealizing humility and limitation before the law, she is right to identify the tendency toward the idealization of limitation as ideologically suspect: "There does seem to be a romanticization, or, indeed, a religious idealization of 'failure,' humility and limitation before the Law, which makes the Lacanian narrative ideologically suspect."[24]

Idealization of the essentially split subject is an instance of the conservative use of description, discussed earlier, that pervades the majority of Lacanian feminist arguments. But it is not necessary to idealize limitation before the law, or the "failure at the heart of identity,"[25] in the process of theorizing it. It is also not necessary, however, to deny loss and embrace a manic Dionysiac position in order to break out of phallic binarism.

Both Lacanian and early Butlerian-type theories cannot, in my view, contribute to a feminist politics aiming for symbolic reorganization. The limitations of both approaches lie in their inability to theorize alternative structures that are not reducible to the phallic law. The Lacanians elevate limitation before the law to a static universal truth and performative Butler-type theories promote a kind of voluntarism that skims over the question of the entrenchment or internalization of unconscious structures. In both cases, there is no ground from which to work toward the construction of a symbolic organization that could accommodate more than one structural law and thus more than one mode of symbolization. Whilst Lacanian feminism and Butlerian "performativity" have made crucial advances within poststructuralist feminism, the question of alternative modes of symbolization cannot be developed within the terms of their theoretical horizons. More precisely, the question of theorizing a different cultural law whose underlying prohibitions may allow "yet to be" unconscious structures to enjoy symbolic expression cannot be addressed within the parameters of Lacanian feminism or early Butlerian theories. It is my view that the engagement between academic feminism and psychoanalysis needs to enter a new stage. Instead of being paralyzed by the charge of utopianism or ego psychology, I argue for a third-wave poststructuralist psychoanalytic feminism defined by a commitment to the creation/theorization of a structural alternative to the phallic hegemony that characterizes our present symbolic organization.

2 🐌

Myth, Phantasy, and Culture

> *In the great mythological figures one sees the structuring of the imaginary system.*
>
> —LUCE IRIGARAY

> *Myth is a form of knowledge about delirium and symptoms. The myth reveals psychiatric knowledge.*
>
> —JEAN-JOSEPH GOUX

THE PROJECT OF analyzing the complex and multiple relations among myth, phantasy, and culture in the context of feminism is driven primarily by the conviction that such an unraveling of interconnected and interdependent registers can contribute to change at a symbolic level. I will begin by using a working definition of the (Western) symbolic, namely, as primarily a register of structuring whereby the material world is mediated through a structural hierarchical dualism so that it can be thought about, represented, and in turn reproduced.[1]

My consideration of the symbolic is intellectually located at the point at which the movements of structuralism, poststructuralism, and feminism have established in their different ways the distinction between the symbolic as a cultural mediating phenomenon and material economic realities. Structuralism attempted to identify the underlying structures determining symbolic products (e.g., language, kinship systems, and so on); poststructuralism in its deconstruction of Western philosophical discourses identified the entrenched dualism determining symbolic phenomena; and feminism revealed the hierarchical nature of these structures in relation to sexual difference. Thus the symbolic can be defined as a process of structuring whereby the material world is organized according to a hierarchical dualism: the projection of an order onto the material world to enable thinking about it.[2]

In thinking about the symbolic, then, we are primarily considering the concept of and process of structuring. Structure will always leave a residue, something is always left over; structure functions through the dynamics of inclusion and exclusion: the residue is that which exceeds the structure. The question posed here concerns the possibilities of *re*structuring: rather than posing a (utopian) vision of an all-inclusive symbolic, my concern is to question what can and cannot be included through the process of re-structuring. Psychoanalysis is indispensable to the methodology adopted here, but it is crucial to emphasize that while I depend wholly on a theory of the unconscious and a structural psychoanalytic methodology, this does not mean a commitment to a particular model. The question I am posing is: *what can and cannot be structured?* This is my fundamental question, a complex one that holds within in it further questions, including: what can and cannot be *theorized?* And, finally: what can and cannot be *symbolized?*

Already, then, I have adopted a model whereby structure, theory, and symbolization are interrelated but also distinct from one another. If theory and symbolization are dependent on structuration—leaving aside for the moment the difference between theorization and symbolization—what is it that I am asking of the work of structuration? What importance has this process for feminism?

In this chapter, I present the question of structuration in relation to the most ambitious aims of this book, namely, those concerning the possibilities of creating new structural constellations as part of a feminist project of sociosymbolic change. I subsequently introduce and explain the particular strategy I have chosen, which is to engage with certain Greek myths and tragedies with a view to elucidating, first, *the structuring power of myth* and, second, the ways in which a feminist writer can use myth in a constructive if not radical manner to facilitate sociosymbolic intervention and change.

The work of the French structural anthropologist Claude Lévi-Strauss informs my use of myth in fundamental ways. While I discuss my use of Lévi-Strauss's work further in later chapters, it is necessary here to emphasize a few points relating to the structural analysis of myth in relation to my proposed intervention into the dominant contemporary symbolic organization. Lévi-Strauss, like Freud, assumed that myths "get thought in man unbeknownst to him" and that behind the manifest sense of the stories in myth, there must be a "message wrapped up in a code."[3] Lévi-Strauss proceeds by "disregarding the thinking subject completely" and works on the hypothesis that the thinking process itself takes place in myth.[4] Myth, for him, is a complex set of codes with a high degree of internal organization that, under structural analysis, reveal the "unconscious truths" that "make ... man aware of his roots in society."[5] Lévi-Strauss contended that beneath the heterogeneity of myth underlying "universal" unconscious structures are at work that can be decoded by organizing the mythical variants into sets of paradigmatic relations and units that reveal a latent structure that can disclose the universal mental formulations that determine sociosymbolic realities. To speak of the meaning of myth, for Lévi-Strauss, is to speak of its underlying "rules" or "laws." Where Lévi-Strauss's work is essential for my feminist context is in his key point that myth needs to be read like an "orchestral score"; each mythical sequence is considered as a variant, whose underlying unconscious structures or underlying rules/laws can only be revealed if they are analyzed in relation to other mythical variants: "Exactly as in a musical score, it is impossible to understand a myth as a continuous sequence. We cannot read myth as we would read a novel, i.e., line after line, left to right. We have to understand the myth as a totality and discover that the basic meaning of the myth is not conveyed by the sequence of events."[6]

This fundamental point is crucial to my argument. If we take seriously the implications of Lévi-Strauss's statement about the necessity to read myths together as interrelated variants, then we can begin to see how differential myth analysis (which came out of structural anthropology) can be used to challenge psychoanalysis's unilateral approach to myth. It will suffice to say here that I am using Lévi-Strauss's point that one cannot read any myth in isolation to reinforce my question: what can and cannot be structured/included in the symbolic economy? In this way, I use his model of myth—that is, the orchestral score—in order to comment on the Oedipus model in psychoanalysis with a view to postulating the idea of a symbolic that can accommodate more than one structuring operation.[7]

Lévi-Strauss's work on myth is not an object of study here but rather serves as a methodological starting point. I draw on his extensive analysis of how myths work in order to consolidate my specific feminist strategy of symbolic intervention, which, though not structuralist in the orthodox sense, is nevertheless structural. Additionally and crucially, while Lévi-Strauss wanted to find the universal structures underlying myth, my project is to change or reorganize those structures. Thus I am not committed to structuralist orthodoxy but am indebted to aspects of structuralist methodology.

Initially, then, one must interrogate more specifically what is actually meant by "structure." Psychic structures? Symbolic structures? Social structures? Analysis of myth, phantasy, and culture is precisely an analysis of different but overlapping structural systems operating at various levels in the mediation of experience.

Central to my argument is the emphasis on the determining power of the symbolic order: the order of meaning to which all human beings are subjected if they are to become part of the social world. Moving on from my earlier definition of the symbolic as a register of structuring through hierarchical dualism, I can now engage with Irigaray's analysis of this structuring principle, leading us to the fraught question of sexual difference and the position of women in relation to the dominant symbolic order.

For Irigaray, it is the symbolic that structures the imaginary,[8] that is, the symbolic organizes or gives structural form to the embodiments of the unconscious phantasies of the dominant order. And that dominant order is not neutral but masculine, so that, for Irigaray, the symbolic order, in which we must all take a place, is essentially the male imaginary, structured and in turn endowed with the status of law: "The symbolic you impose as a universal innocent of any empirical or historical contingency, is *your* imaginary transformed into an order, into the social."[9] The phantasies of the male imaginary are therefore systematically supported, represented, and confirmed by social institutions through the operating structuring principle of the dominant symbolic order. Irigaray states that the present symbolic order is in fact completely imaginary—which means that the so-called present patriarchal symbolic order is an *effect* of the male imaginary; projections of male unconscious phantasy achieve the validity and the weight of a powerful and determining symbolic order.[10] She goes on to say: "The symbolic order is an imaginary order which becomes law. Therefore it is very important *to question the foundations of our symbolic order in mythology and in tragedy,* because they deal with a landscape which installs itself in the imagination and then, all of a sudden becomes law. But that only means that it is an imaginary system that wins over another one. This victorious imaginary system is what we call the symbolic order" (my emphasis).[11]

A feminist rereading of myth and tragedy, then, is part of a strategy that seeks to disclose the underlying phantasies that constitute this "victorious imaginary system." Engaging with myth allows the feminist critic to identify the phantasy structures that inform the symbolic. It is a process of *undoing* the imaginary constructions of the dominant symbolic order and thus carries with it the demand that contemporary culture confront the phantasies that dominate and determine its social and political realities. While these phantasies remain unanalyzed, their systematic institutionalization and endowment with the status of moral and empirical "truth" goes unchecked; ideological systems of oppression such as Western patriarchies continue to exercise power while remaining blind to their subjection to their own imaginary and to their unconscious motivations.

Irigaray's interventions into Western philosophy and psychoanalysis have powerfully demonstrated the ways in which the masculine symbolic economy sustains itself through the exclusion of the "feminine." Her use of the psychoanalytic method together with the practice of deconstruction unravels the logic of these dominant cultural discourses in order to expose the structure that allows this logic to appear as neutral and universal.

Irigaray's specific mode of intervention often involves the insertion of her own voice at particular moments in the text under scrutiny while also employing modes of mimicry and parody, so that the manifest coherence of the original discourse is radically destabilized. The excluded or the latent of the text returns to haunt, so that Irigaray's interventions work to produce writings that bring back the *delirium* (a term further elaborated below) that the master discourse has defensively and successfully expelled. It is as though she is analyzing Western philosophical texts as if they were dreams. That is, rather than being satisfied with the manifest content, she interprets the latent material, working to put the "male subject" of philosophy back in touch with his delirium. The delirium I refer to brings us back to the Jean-Joseph Goux statement quoted at the beginning of this chapter: that "myth is a form of delirium and symptoms" that reveals "psychiatric knowledge." As Irigaray states, "Our imaginary still functions in accordance with the schema established through Greek mythologies and tragedies."[12]

I will be engaging with the schema established through the Oresteian matricidal myth in relation to both the analysis and the potential restructuring of the imaginary that has become law. In chapter 4, I discuss in detail my reasons for choosing to work with the *Oresteia;* it suffices to say here that the Oresteian myth is organized around the question of matricide, a theme that I argue is untheorized in psychoanalysis and feminism. Working with a matricidal myth with a view to theorizing the cultural laws belonging to the mother can lead to the possibility of the emergence of more than one mode of symbolization.

My work on this particular myth is an attempt to theorize the underlying (structural) laws belonging to matricide, which neither Irigaray nor any other psychoanalytic or feminist theorist, to my knowledge, has attempted. One could work with many myths in the attempt to deconstruct the male imaginaries and, further, to begin the project of restructuring. It is through the Oresteian myth, however, that I have been able to address the specific theoretical questions relevant to my particular psychoanalytic feminist context. This is not to say that different myths could not also be instrumental to structural reorganization.[13]

In myth, then, we witness what is left of the delirium of the (male) imaginary once it has been structured and "installed in the imagination."[14] It is precisely this delirium that gives us "psychiatric knowledge" about the *social* world. The delirium and symptoms expressed through myth allow us to glimpse what could be described as a kind of cultural dreaming.

What I am suggesting in my feminist strategy is to reread a myth in contemporary terms and then interpret the rereading in order to use the myth to effect change. In some senses, using myth in this way is to be involved in a process similar to that of Freudian dream interpretation in order to present the latent phantasy content of the dream to the dreamer with a view to reorganizing the underlying psychic structures.

Myth is a riotous and sprawling web of inexhaustible meanings, fueled by violence and filled with absurd juxtapositions. Like dreams, myth is always dynamic, engaged in working something out, always transforming, eluding, regressing, and transgressing. Dreams and myths are both symbolic products with primitive content, that is to say, they are simultaneously regressive *and* symbolic.[15] Their content may belong to a regressive primitive register, yet at the same time something has been symbolized and worked over. In contrast, in regression proper, there is no psychic elaboration, because the psychic apparatus is inadequate or nonfunctional. My conflation of the dream and the myth in terms of their symbolization of primitive regressive phantasy content is a working hypothesis that can be thought of as part of the heuristic gesture of this book.

To enter into the register of myth is to engage with the content of the imaginary register, interpreting the phantasies that are the "productions of the subject's 'madness.'"[16] The subject's "madness" relevant to the analysis of the social imaginary is the madness or delirium of the male subject of knowledge.

That the symbolic order reinforces aspects of the social imaginary through its embodiment in social institutional organization is indicative of a form of acting out. What this means is that the source and repetitive nature of unconscious phantasies and wishes are not analyzed or thought about (worked through) but rather acted upon and transformed into a so-called rationalization that determines or underlies the social organization.[17]

Carol Kohn's powerful article "Sex and Death in the Rational World of Defence Intellectuals" lucidly demonstrates an aspect of the lethal results of the social embodiment, or the acting-out, of unanalyzed phantasies belonging to the male imaginary.[18] Writing the article after attending a workshop on nuclear weapons, nuclear strategic doctrine, and arms control conducted by distinguished "defense intellectuals," Kohn shows how the "rational" language of nuclear strategic analysis is blind to its source in unconscious phantasies arising from a male wish for parthenogenesis. It is worth quoting some of her observations here in order to give a striking example of how the phantasies of the male imaginary can become embodied or acted out in the social world:

> There is one set of domestic images that demands separate attention—images that suggest men's desire to appropriate from women the power of giving life and conflate creation and destruction. The bomb project is rife with images of male birth. . . . This idea of male birth and its accompanying belittling of maternity—the denial of women's role in the process of creation and the reduction of "motherhood" to the provision of nurturance—seems thoroughly incorporated into the nuclear mentality. . . . In light of the imagery of male birth, the extraordinary names given to the bombs that reduced Hiroshima and Nagasaki to ash and rubble—"Little Boy" and "Fat Man"—at last became intelligible. These ultimate destroyers were the progeny of the atomic scientists—and emphatically not just any progeny but male progeny. In early tests, before they were certain that the bombs would work, the scientists expressed their concern by saying they hoped the baby was a boy, not a girl—that is, not a dud. . . . The entire history of the bomb project, in fact, seems permeated with imagery that confounds man's overwhelming technological power to destroy nature with the power to create—imagery that inverts men's destruction and asserts in its place the power to create new life and a new world. It converts men's destruction into their rebirth.[19]

I cite Kohn here for two reasons. First, the area of nuclear strategic doctrine is the most extreme example of the destructive results of the acting-out or rationalization of unconscious phantasies in the social world, and, second, the phantasy of male parthenogenesis that Kohn identifies as operative in the "nuclear mentality" is a phantasy that I later engage in my rereading of the Oresteian myth. Interpreting the register of mythical delirium in the embodied social (patriarchal) world aims to put that world back in touch with what has been split off, disavowed, and repressed—with a view to countering the effects of those unconscious mechanisms that result in the denial of women's ontological status, if not the destruction of the planet.

But what of the other dreams, that is, the imaginaries that do not find support in the social symbolic world, those that have not been subject to structuration but remain on the level of unsymbolized delirium?

These questions are fundamental to the feminist project since to effect symbolic change requires the structuration of the *female* imaginaries that can only be found in the leftovers or remnants after the dominant structuration has occurred. It is not as if a buried realm called the female imaginary sits waiting to be structured; if such were the case, then this project would not be so profoundly difficult. The female imaginary does not yet exist but is constantly in process.[20] By definition, then, describing or theorizing this realm is not straightforward. We are in no position to say what it is, what it might look like or mean. Additionally, it is unlikely to be benign and more likely to be full of primitive rage and similar affect.[21] One can only observe and report the symptoms—the failed repressions that relentlessly return to haunt in the form of hysterical somatic complaints, for instance. We are thus in the realm of dream and affect.

It is one thing to refuse the imaginary male projections and attempt to behave toward the masculine symbolic as the analyst acts toward the patient—that is, giving back to the patient his projections in order that he may identify them and acknowledge them as his own. But the more complex strategy concerns the attempt to structure something that does not yet exist as such and can be felt only as unsymbolized pain, trauma, or affect.

The challenge for contemporary psychoanalytic feminism is to go beyond critique and analysis into the realm of creating new thought—alternative structures that may counter the effects of an alienating patriarchal imaginary. Feminisms are left with a profoundly difficult challenge—*how* to structure the female imaginaries.

This challenge necessitates different faculties from that of analysis and critique. It demands that we attempt to think the unthinkable or realize something that does not yet exist. This is not always an easy place to inhabit; it is like being at the level of the navel of the dream that Freud refers to in drawing attention to the blind spot in his Irma dream and, more generally, to the "unplumbable" unconsciousness of the unconscious: "There is at least one spot in every dream at which it is unplumbable—a navel, as it were, that is its point of contact with the unknown."[22]

My placing of third-wave feminist thinkers (who are attempting to structure the female imaginaries) at the level of the navel is not only to indicate the inevitable confrontation with the unknown in such a project. More than that, Freud's using the navel as signifier or metaphor for the blind spot of the unconscious is of great significance when we think about the navel as the scar that signifies the cutting of the umbilical cord. It is the point of connection and disconnection with the maternal body—that is, it is the point of contact and severance with the unknown. To structure the female imaginary, to create alternative symbolic productions to counter the effects of the male imaginary *precisely* involves working at the level of the navel, working to give symbolic expression to the maternal body—that body whose very unknowability functions to sustain the illusory omnipotence of dominant bodies of knowledge—and will necessarily force a significant reorganization of the symbolic economy.

If we accept that the symbolic function is essentially one of structuring, then we now need to examine what is involved in this structuration process. That is, *how* do the imaginaries achieve transformation into the symbolic—what is the nature of the process of structuration? More fundamentally, what is the relationship between the maternal body and structuration?

I now want to introduce the work of the contemporary French psychoanalyst and writer André Green. Green's work is not concerned with feminism, yet, as I hope to show, his work can be used productively in a feminist context. His work, to my mind, challenges psychoanalytic theory from within, so that a feminist engagement with Green's work brings feminism into a new dialogue with psychoanalysis, which allows new and far-reaching questions to be posed.

Green articulates the question of structuration in a particularly precise way in his essay "Conceptions of Affect." While Green's questions do not concern gender and are located in a purely psychoanalytic clinical model, he raises some deeply challenging questions that are of particular relevance here: "What can be structured, by what, by whom? to arrive at what type(s) (in the singular or plural) of structuring? Is it necessary to finish up with a more general structure, a place to accommodate the diverse structurings—or should one, on the other hand, accept the juxtaposition of structures which do not communicate with each other except by intermittent links? What is the meaning of pragmatic, if not theoretical, reference to the notion of integration in psychoanalysis? Is it only a question of a meeting between the subject and his structure, or is some new functioning installed?"[23] This quotation is so rich and suggestive, I want to consider each question he asks in relation to my own feminist context.

What can be structured, by what, by whom?

If we agree that the symbolic order constitutes the structuring of the male imaginary, then what is structured are the imaginary projections, which after structuration attain the status of symbolic law. Irigaray argues that the female imaginary is yet to be structured. The structuration of the female imaginary would, then, allow for the creation of an alternative female symbolic. Yet Green is questioning *what can be structured, by what, by whom?* To reformulate his question in my context would be to ask: *how and by whom can the female imaginaries be structured?*

To arrive at what type(s) of structuring (in the singular or the plural)?

For my purposes here, the type of structuring to arrive at would be the structuring and symbolic representation of the maternal position and, further, a structurally mediated mother-daughter and between-women relationship. Oedipal structuration radically denies the daughter a symbolically mediated relation to her mother. Psychoanalytic feminist research has repeatedly described the ubiquitous pathological organizations operating within the mother-daughter relation. Clinical accounts of the symptoms specific to the mother-daughter relation tend to describe the psychosexual difficulties in this relation as resulting from collapsed identifications, lack of boundaries, and murderous and suicidal phantasies deriving from primitive anxieties about engulfment inside the mother and separation from her.[24] Separation-individuation between mother and daughter seems to be an area of acute difficulty leading to (at best) a flight to the father and an acceptance of his law as an inevitable defense and escape route from a psychically dangerous symbiotic fusion with the mother.

Descriptions of pathological organizations between mother and daughter seem to confirm and reproduce the (oedipal) model of subjectivity that represents the relation to the mother as essentially devouring and threatening of psychosis. In this way, while the relation to the mother and the mother-daughter relation have undoubtedly achieved considerable attention in contemporary (object-relations) feminist psychoanalysis, accounts of the problematic proximity between mother and daughter do not in themselves go beyond phenomenological description. The descriptive material does not tend to be critically considered in relation to the social symbolic paradigm that produces it. What I mean to indicate here is the necessity to move from producing description to creating theory.

Descriptive material alone does not open the way to innovative thought or research; it remains in the area of phenomenology, which cannot contribute to the expansion of psychoanalysis as a structural discipline.[25]

Irigaray manages to extrapolate from clinical descriptions a diagnosis of what is dysfunctional (for women) in the present symbolic order. She thinks about the voluminous clinical descriptions of pathological mother-daughter dynamics (with which Irigaray, as a clinician, has herself some direct acquaintance) in relation to the structure that produces them, rather than endowing them with the status of a so-called raw material, a foundational empirical "truth."

The necessity of the flight of the daughter from the dangerous maternal proximity—while hard to avoid in the present symbolic organization—points to a situation that leaves women in a state of "dereliction."[26] The daughter is "derelict" because she is cut off from her origin and sequestered in a position in the patriarchal economy that denies her the possibility of achieving a sexed subject position outside the powerful structure of phallic binarism. Her "dereliction" renders her susceptible to the systematic projections of the male imaginary, which, according to Irigaray, lead to the denial of her ontological status. While I do not dispute the reality of the situation that clinical psychoanalytic material describes, I maintain that this is all the more evidence of a symbolic organization that does not work for women.

In order to avoid limiting my argument here to the realm of description, I suggest that it is the patriarchal symbolic economy that is at fault, not the mother. That is, I want to challenge the status quo within psychoanalysis that perpetuates the view that there is something intrinsically psychically dangerous about the primitive relation to the mother and instead reposition the problem in relation to the effect of the dominant symbolic organization. It is the lack of structural symbolic mediation between mother and daughter that produces the ubiquitous pathologies. So long as there is no possibility of giving symbolic expression to the mother-daughter relation, the latter will inevitably remain an area of pathology. The ubiquitously reported symptoms belonging to the mother-daughter relation are, I suggest, a cultural problem, in that the lack of symbolic mediation between mother and daughter is a result of the present structural configurations underlying the patriarchal symbolic. If psychoanalysis does not wish to reproduce such a structural configuration and instead attempts to use its powerful methodology to throw light on what is not yet known, then it must be able to identify the ideological impetus at work in its adherence to a particular theoretical model or structure that depends on the absence of the construction of the maternal subject and in turn the absence of the construction of a symbolically mediated mother-daughter bond.

Contemporary psychoanalytic object-relations theory from Klein to Bion certainly positions the mother as central to the process of the psychic development of the child. The partially occluded mother in Freudian and Lacanian theory is resurrected, and her power and significance in terms of the development of the infant is nowhere more fundamental than in the theories of Klein, Bowlby, Winnicott, and Bion. Yet, as a considerable amount of psychoanalytic feminist scholarship has argued,[27] the mother is only ever described as an object in these theories, whether object of phantasy, need, and/or blame. Her status as symbolic sexual subject is nowhere raised. In this way, psychoanalytic theories that focus on the mother have not moved out of the framework of phallic binarism. Moreover, feminist critics such as Doane and Hodges have dismissed those psychoanalytic theories that appear to be theorizing the mother as counterproductive for an interventionist psychoanalytic feminism.

In my view, the fact that the object-relations tradition does not theorize the relation to the mother in terms of her structuring power creates the major problems for its use in a feminist psychoanalytic theoretical intervention. Its invaluable descriptive insights therefore become part of a closed circuit fed back into a confirmation of the logic of phallic binarism. Rather than using its descriptive insights to break the circuit of a dysfunctional model of subjectivity and desire, it can be convincingly argued that object-relation theories remain wedded to a structure that can only reproduce the pathologies they describe.[28]

Jessica Benjamin, who uses object-relations theory but through a poststructuralist frame, criticizes the concentration on the relation to the mother in Kleinian and object-relations theory: "The mother's mental work is so essential to the construction of the mind, and yet the mother's own mind was not represented. As long as psychoanalysis could not theorize maternal psychic work *as an aspect of subjectivity*, it could not formulate a mother who is more than merely a mirror to the child's activity" (my italics).[29] In my view, as long as the relation to the mother is merely described and attention to the mother's place within the structural laws of the human order is neglected, psychoanalysis remains complicit with the reproduction of a model that relegates the mother to the realm of the imaginary. The project of structuring the female imaginaries necessitates a radical paradigmatic shift, since to give symbolic structuring power to the mother means to dislodge the paternal monopoly on symbolic functioning and conceive of coexistent structures that produce a variety of unconscious phantasies and modes of symbolization. The mother must be able to be theorized as a sexed subject whose relation to filiation and generational transmission is given expression in the symbolic economy. My positing a theory of matricide is contingent on the maternal site as a possible site of structuring power, rather than a site of deathly fusion leading to psychotic undifferentiation.

In concentrating on the position of the mother, my approach will be structural, that is to say, it takes the dream as the true paradigm of psychoanalysis so as to avoid, in André Green's words, moving "backwards into phenomenology and psychology."[30] Green contrasts the model of the dream with the model of infant observation (a model often foregrounded in British psychoanalysis), which he contends does not lead to a topological formulation. I follow Green in preferring the structural model of the dream to that of the developmental mother-baby paradigm.

Creating a structural theory of the maternal raises serious conceptual problems, since it demands a complete reconceptualization of the structural function itself. For some theorists, a maternal structural function is impossible by definition. With this, we begin to understand the threat such an exercise will pose.

Structure protects from psychosis; it allows for differentiation and the capacity for thought. Structure protects from the fusion of a too-close proximity; it creates space to think. The consensus within psychoanalytic feminism concerns the evident lack of symbolic mediation between mother and daughter that leads to a situation of foreclosure when there is no structural element to break up the imaginary dyad. The need for a third element, a structuring principle to interrupt the dyad, is a necessity widely recognized as the condition of psychic survival. On this point, there is little productive controversy. It is at the next step of the argument that the divergences and the complexities begin.

The classical psychoanalytic model (the oedipal structure) claims that the daughter must turn to the father as her only possible defense against psychosis; the father as the symbolic third element becomes the only possible route away from the dangerous immediacy of maternal proximity. Psychosexual structuration depends on the phallus as central structuring principle. In the thinking of the French psychoanalyst Janine Chasseguet-Smirgel, the phallus serves to "beat back the mother."[31] While Chasseguet-Smirgel is not making a critique of this process but is rather, in the classical psychoanalytic vein, foregrounding the intrinsic dangers associated with the omnipotent devouring preoedipal mother, she inadvertently brings to view the somewhat defensive function the phallus represents in the classical model. Her famous phrase "beating back the mother" brings into view quite explicitly a paranoid and defensive violence underpinning the phallic model, which is, to my mind, quite an accurate observation. This situation is inevitable as long as there is no structure other than the phallic to provide the mediating structural function.

Feminist thinkers who attempt to find alternative strategies to mediate the imaginary relation to the maternal body differ from the more traditional classical psychoanalytic writers in adding to the phallus a different structural process that would serve the function of differentiation while avoiding cutting the daughter off from her origin, her maternal genealogy, and her symbolic, ethical, and ontological status. The point is to move away from the notion of a central structuring principle toward a less rigid conception of the structuring process.

At this point, we can return to André Green's questions concerning structuration, a questioning that by definition implies a different conception of the symbolic from that of the Lacanian schema: "Is it necessary to finish up with a more general structure, a place to accommodate the diverse structurings . . . or should one, on the other hand, accept the juxtaposition of structures which do not communicate with each other except by intermittent links? What is the meaning of pragmatic, if not theoretical, reference to the notion of integration in psychoanalysis?"[32] Green's questioning as to the possibility of "diverse structurings" allows the debate to move on from a somewhat rigid adherence to the one and only structuring principle outlined in the Lacanian theory of the symbolic to the possibility of different structures existing side by side, thus suggesting a structural heterogeneity.

Such a radical questioning of the symbolic from within psychoanalysis confirms the exciting and productive ways in which feminism can engage with contemporary psychoanalytic theory to further its own aims. In considering what Green is asking here in relation to feminist strategy, the first step would involve the acceptance of structures that "do not communicate with each other except by intermittent links." The attempt to symbolize potential female imaginaries through the establishment of a maternal structuring function would allow for the superimposition or juxtaposition of different psychic structurings that would not necessarily need to be integrated into an overall structure. Instead, there would be a network of diverse structurings that did not aim toward overall integration, equilibrium, or reducibility. In this way, Irigaray's conception of the possibility of the structuration of more than one specific sexed subjectivity becomes more easily realized. At the same time, Green's question concerning the subject "meeting" his/her specific structure (with inevitable mobility and cross-identification) can be used to develop the idea of a structural economy that could accommodate more than one mode of symbolization.

In discussing the creation of structures specific to female psychosexuality, Irigaray refers to the work of Prigogine, who uses the term "dissipatory structures" to describe structures that function "through exchanges with the exterior world, which proceed in steps from one energy level to another, and which are not organized to search for equilibrium but rather to cross thresholds, a procedure that corresponds to going beyond disorder and entropy without discharge."[33] Green's question concerning the "pragmatic, if not theoretical, meaning of the notion of integration in psychoanalysis" could merit a whole thesis, but here the notion of integration belongs to a theory that attempts to reduce all modes of symbolization to a coherent whole. To conceive of heterogeneous diverse structurings means necessarily to dispense with the notion of integration.[34] That notion, to my mind, is associated to a theory of the Symbolic with a capital letter. An analogy will illuminate the meaning of integration in this context: The notion of an integrative structural system is like a jigsaw puzzle where every piece fits together to create an overall static image/coherence that can be undone again and rendered fragmented or in pieces. The jigsaw can come apart and be put together again, but the pieces will only fit together in one way. Additionally, the completed jigsaw allows the edges of each piece to be seen so that *meaningless fragmentation, on the one hand, and meaningful wholeness/integration, on the other, form the underlying opposition through which the jigsaw can operate.* In contrast, a heterogeneous system of diverse structures that does not operate through the either/or fixed binary of fragmentation/integration functions more in accordance with the model of a kaleidoscope. In the kaleidoscope, integration is disclosed to be a temporary illusion. The patterns of the kaleidoscope are in perpetual mutation where there is an unlimited variation of patterns that cannot be predicted. There is no one way for the elements to connect for the creation of a pattern, and, as the kaleidoscope moves, the illusory distinction between a meaningful integration and a meaningless fragmentation disappears. Rather, we have a diverse and unpredictable dynamic sequence of constellations that are not predetermined or programmed to result in an integrative master pattern. There is far more room for the unknown, for the multiple, for possibility and openness in the kaleidoscope (which pertains to a symbolic without the capital letter) than there is in the jigsaw.[35] In using this analogy, I am following Jacques Derrida in his critique of phallogocentrism, which undermines the notion of a transcendental signifier or a monolithic Symbolic. The model of the kaleidoscope could be thought of as related to Derrida's *"différance"* or, to put it another way, his idea of a "structure without a centre,"[36] whereas the jigsaw is analogous to Lacan's phallogocentric model of the Symbolic. The notion of integration belongs to a monolithic Symbolic (jigsaw) and is not operative in the heterogeneous (kaleidoscopic) symbolic with which I am concerned.

What of Green's query, "Is it only a question of a meeting between the subject and his structure, or is some new functioning installed?"[37] First of all, the use of the word "only" at the beginning of his question somewhat underestimates the complexity involved in the very idea of a subject meeting with his structure—especially when we think about it through the issue of sexual difference. Green uses the nongendered subject here, which we can assume refers to the masculine subject, but when it comes to the *female* subject meeting *her* structure, then it is evident that in order for this to happen there is indeed the necessity of the installation of "some new functioning."

The female sexed subject's meeting with her *specific* structures is precisely the situation that would counter the domination of the patriarchal symbolic economy and provide her with a position within the social-symbolic world which would not reduce her to the state of dereliction that Irigaray has persistently diagnosed. Such is the logic of Irigaray's thesis, and thus I will attempt to synthesize Irigaray's theory with Green's theoretical innovations to posit a theory of a heterogeneous symbolic allowing for the installation of "some new functioning" that is concomitant with the reorganization of the present symbolic hegemony. The question of how to "install some new functioning" is, however, the more complex and controversial point. We cannot say what this "new functioning" will be, we cannot predict what constellations it will create; the point is to facilitate the possibility of more than one by theorizing the maternal as an alternative site of structuring power leading to alternative and as yet unknown modes of symbolization.

Raising the possibility of more than one structural function certainly implies the conception of a symbolic realm that can accommodate multiple and coexisting structuring processes. Thus questioning the processes and possibilities of structuration allows for the conception of a symbolic realm that does not yet exist or at best is in nascent form. This is extremely important, because it implies a retheorization of the concept of the structural function and in turn the relation between the symbolic and the social—an extremely troubled area that opens up the most urgent challenges for contemporary feminisms. What is at stake is the possibility of moving beyond the model of culture that understands the symbolic as "a field of normativity that exceeds and structures the domain of the socially given."[38] While the determining power of the symbolic is not denied here, it must not be taken to be absolute, as this would foreclose the possibility of its reorganization. To imply that the structure is prior to social organization renders social transformation impossible and moreover keeps the repudiation and exclusion of femininity as the inevitable founding moment in the creation of the symbolic itself. The worthy hypothesis of feminist theory supposes that the exclusion of the feminine is *not* inevitable.

Green's positing of the question of a structural heterogeneity opens up profound questions with regard to a reconsideration of the limits of representation and thus of the relation among structuration, the symbolic, and the social. What is at stake is a rejection of the idea of the symbolic as static and instead the positing of a less rigid model that conceives of a symbolic that is essentially *dynamic.* Such a notion of a dynamic symbolic realm can be inferred from Green's questions, enabling us to begin to consider this aspect of his work as valuable in relation to Irigaray's project. Once we accept a theory of a dynamic symbolic then the project of working toward the reorganization and expansion of the symbolic becomes more easily conceivable. On this point, in a recent interview, Judith Butler appears to agree: "In my view, the hetero-pathos that pervades the legacy of Lacanian psychoanalysis and some of its feminist reformulations can be countered only by rendering the symbolic as increasingly dynamic, that is, by considering the conditions and limits of representation and representability as open to significant rearticulations and transformations under the pressure of social practices of various kinds."[39]

The kind of social practice with which my argument is engaged concerns the attempt to formulate a *maternal structural function* that would allow for a symbolization of potential female genealogies and thus work toward the creation of a sociality, inheritance, and transgenerational transmission between women. Contrary to the logic of Theseus, who believes there to be only one correct way through the labyrinth/Symbolic, Ariadne's thread in this book contains no preconceived knowledge of a unique path. There could be a multitude of paths to explore within the labyrinth, each creating its own specific structural constellations. Rather than wanting to get out of the labyrinth with the desire to solve/kill its riddle/sphinx/Minotaur and reduce the multiplicity and complexity of the labyrinth into a single meaningful route, I am more interested in exploring multiple dynamic processes leading the subject into symbolic life. The crucial point is to change the labyrinth, not to find a way out of it.

3 🦢

Matricide in Theory

I in my turn wish to point out the censure of the dead mother: the mother of silence as heavy as lead.

—ANDRÉ GREEN

In reflecting recently on matricide, I thought that, for me, Oedipus is a repetition of Orestes: it is in fact a repetition of matricide.

—LUCE IRIGARAY

I F ANDRÉ GREEN'S conception of the symbolic can be interpreted as pertaining to an increasingly dynamic and potentially heterogeneous system of structuring, his work begins to appear (however indirectly) theoretically allied to that of what I am calling third-wave feminism. In identifying further the ways in which Green's work could be productively used in conjunction with a feminist project of social symbolic transformation, I now intend to pursue my own attempt to formulate a theory of matricide in relation to Green's postulation of diverse structurings and Irigaray's project of constructing potential female imaginaries.

By proposing diverse structuring and allying Green with Irigaray, I am challenging Irigaray by arguing that there is the possibility from within contemporary psychoanalysis to theorize alternative symbolic economies that are not reducible to oedipal castration.[1] So far, I have argued that where Irigaray and Green's theories meet productively is in the conception of the dynamic and diverse possibilities within the process of symbolic structuration. Now I will show in more specific terms how aspects of Green's essay "The Dead Mother" can be interpreted as even closer to the concerns of Irigaray. "The Dead Mother" is a profoundly suggestive work containing within it some far-reaching implications that prove to be relevant to the feminist context. My reading of Green's essay will be linked to Irigaray's ideas about matricide and alternative symbolic organizations.

Irigaray's reference to the Orestes myth (in the quotation cited at the beginning of the chapter) immediately brings the Oresteia into the oedipal debate. I interpret the reference to Orestes as an attempt to draw attention to the occlusion or censorship of matricide in psychoanalysis and to suggest that matricide constitutes an unacknowledged and untheorized underlying phantasy structure that is excluded from Freud's structural theory of Oedipus. The Oresteian myth is a symbolic expression of a constellation of phantasies that has been marginalized or overshadowed by the primacy of the oedipal patricidal structure. I see it as an omission that sustains the father's monopoly of filial generative transmission.

Psychoanalysis has not made a primal phantasy out of the Orestes (matricidal) myth. The significance of this omission is fundamental, since to make a primal phantasy of a myth is essentially to posit it as a universal structure operating and determining the psychic economy of the subject and of the unconscious transmission of the culture or social bond that produces that subject. My own engagement with the Oresteia (in part 2) involves an attempt to identify its potential as a structural model accounting for a constellation of phantasy whose underlying prohibitions have been written out of psychoanalytic theory. In this way, I will be exploring the potential of using the matricidal Oresteian myth in contributing to the theorization of a maternal structural function. For, although patricide is a concept in psychoanalytic theory, matricide is not.

I begin the theoretical interrogation of the nonconcept status of matricide in psychoanalysis with quotations from both Green and Irigaray that when considered together indicate the precise area of my investigation:

Psychoanalytic theory, which is founded on the interpretation of Freudian thought, allots a major role to the concept of the dead father, whose fundamental function is the genesis of the superego, as outlined in *Totem and Taboo* (Freud, 1912–13). *When one considers the Oedipus complex as a structure and not merely as a phase of libidinal development, this is a coherent point of view.* Other concepts derive from this: the superego in classical theory, the Law and the Symbolic in Lacanian thought. *This group of concepts is linked by the reference to castration and to sublimation as the fate of the instincts.* On the other hand, *we never hear of the dead mother from a structural point of view. . . . Matricide does not involve the dead mother as a concept,* on the contrary; and the concept which is underlined by the dead father, that is to say the reference to the ancestor, to filiation, to genealogy refers back to the primitive crime and the guilt which is its consequence [my italics][2]

What is now becoming apparent in the most everyday things and in the whole of society is that at a primal level, they function on the basis of matricide. When Freud describes in *Totem and Taboo* the murder of the father as founding the primal horde, he forgets the more archaic murder, that of the mother, necessitated by the establishment of a certain order in the polis.[3]

Considering these two quotations together, we can identify the theoretical crux of this debate as concerning the question of generative loss. That is, filial inheritance and symbolic genealogy have hitherto been theorized as contingent on patricide and its vicissitudes. With the possibility of alternative and diverse structurings, the status of matricide as a nonconcept, that is, the denial of its structural function in psychoanalytic discourse, begs for close attention. In the above quotations, Green and Irigaray are both commenting on the occlusion of matricide in psychoanalytic theory. Irigaray suggests that Freudian psychoanalysis reflects the situation wherein matricide forms the blind spot of Western patriarchal civilization. Green addresses the same problem but more ambiguously. It is not clear whether he is saying that we ought to hear about the dead mother from a structural point of view, or if he is implying that there are good reasons why we do not.

In the first instance, what we can ascertain is that oedipal theory has patricide as its central concept in its conflation of generative loss with murder of the father. I have two fundamental questions with regard to this schema. First, what is it about matricide that denies it concept status? That is, why do matricide and its vicissitudes (unlike patricide) not give way to the generative structural loss that allows for symbolic genealogy? Second, in the attempt to formulate matricide as a concept, which means attributing to it a structural function, is it necessary to adhere to the conflation of generative loss with murder? That is, can we theorize a matricidal structure that organizes a different kind of loss that may not necessarily involve the loss proper (murder, castration) outlined in the oedipal paradigm? Or, in other words, must the conception of a structural maternal genealogy follow the same logic that dictates that symbolic generative inheritance be absolutely dependent on the particular version of loss (the gone-forever loss) that the patricide/castration model describes? Might there not be an alternative model of loss that can be both structural and generative but involves a different mode of symbolization? Can matricide be a new concept referring to a structural loss that is not reducible to the logic of patricide?

In these questions, I am suggesting the conception of a different structural paradigm organized around a different structural center whose underlying constellations may produce a variation of unconscious processes, a different set of desires that are not reducible to the oedipal and castration structures. From my understanding of Green, it appears that he, too, proposes the possibility of some such a move, which would be consistent with his questions about the potentiality of diverse structurings in his "Conceptions of Affect" essay, discussed earlier. In "The Dead Mother," Green boldly criticizes the situation within contemporary (French) psychoanalysis whereby the castration model is referred to as the one and only structure to which all varieties of psychic phenomena—symptoms, anxieties, and pathologies—are reduced. Green complains of Freudian successors "castratizing" all forms of anxiety,[4] that is, systematically reducing diverse types of anxiety to castration fears and conflicts. He also makes the same complaint in relation to Lacanian thought and its systematic reduction of all varieties of anxiety to the concept of lack. Green seems to be implying that insofar as the French successors of Freud take on fully the structural character of Freudian thought, an unfortunate result of this adherence is a certain limitation and reductionism that, in Green's words, entails "doing violence as much to experience as to theory to save the unity and generalization of a concept."[5]

Green then goes on to dissociate himself from this particular structural point of view (that is, the monopoly of the castration paradigm) and proposes a structural conception organized around "at least two" centers or paradigms.[6] The "at least two" is highly significant for my context and refers back to his ideas in "Conceptions of Affect" about diverse structurings and the juxtapositions of different types of structurings "which do not communicate with each other except by intermittent links."[7] What begins to emerge in Green's essay is the suggestion of a variety of symbolic organizations programmed by different phantasy structures: "What I would propose, instead of conforming to the opinion of those who divide anxiety into different types according to the age at which it appears in the life of the subject, would rather be *a structural conception* which would be *organized not around one center or paradigm, but around at least two,* in accordance with a *distinctive characteristic, different* from those which have been proposed to date" (my italics).[8]

Green emphasizes that departing from the structural point of view that has castration as its one and only reference does not mean embracing a developmental descriptive model. That is to say, proposing more than one paradigm or center does not necessarily entail dispensing with structural thought. Green then begins to distinguish his idea of the two centers/paradigms or the two groups of anxieties deriving from two types of phantasy structures that pertain to different types of loss.

The first center or paradigm that Green describes concerns the (familiar) castration model. The loss involved in all the varieties of castration fear is always to do with a "bloody mutilation." It concerns the phantasy of an act of destruction that is "always evoked in the context of a bodily wound associated with a bloody act."[9] The castration model refers to the phantasy of a gone-forever loss whereby the detachable thing has been cut off and permanently lost. The lopped-off bodily part cannot be recovered; in its final severance, it produces a generative loss that will deliver the passage to filiation, ancestor, and genealogy. Green calls this "Red" anxiety. The bloody context of the loss entailed in the phantasy of castration gives way to the transmission of the father's name and symbolic fertility.[10] The bloody context, involving the actual lopping-off of something in phantasy underlies the organization of symbolic generativity in the "Red" paradigm.[11] Green's "Red" paradigm refers to the paternal structural function whereby the phantasy of castration that always belongs to a bloody context sets in motion the process of symbolic generational transmission.

If matricide is not a concept, that means (initially) that it does not function structurally. Unlike patricide, in classical psychoanalysis, matricide in its status as nonconcept does not give rise to a generative loss. That is, it does not figure in the psychical order as a moment at which symbolic organization is born. While patricide forms the key moment in Freud's structural theory of the oedipal complex in its relation to castration—it allows for ancestor, filiation, and genealogy—matricide proves to be less fertile or perhaps less possible. Matricide remains as an ambiguous nonconcept excluded from the economy of loss and generation and cannot figure in the "Red" paradigm because it does not (like patricide) involve the phantasy of a bloody mutilation. The loss of the mother or the breast does not function in a "bloody context." The breast is taken away or disappears, but it is not chopped off, never truly gone, always subject to reappearance. The loss of the breast and the anxieties and phantasies related to this loss lack the generative bloody context, the absolute goneness that would merit its entrance into Green's "Red" paradigm.

The color of the loss of the maternal breast is not red. Its loss is of a different kind from that of a chopping-off. One could, at this point, conclude that in that case it cannot function as a structural organizing moment of loss that in turn delivers filial symbolic transmission. But to make this assumption would be complicit with the idea that I (with use of Green's suggestive essay) am contesting: that the only generative loss would be that belonging to the "Red" model. Now the question becomes more specific and concerns different kinds of losing. How is it that the dead father allows for a symbolically generative loss but the dead mother can only ever deliver a symbolically sterile loss? Is it a matter of matricide being an interminable unfinished process, never giving birth to the loss proper that determines symbolic generativity? If matricide does not concern the dead mother from a structural viewpoint, then does this mean that there is something in the nature of her death that is somehow not dead enough?

Matricide as a nonconcept would seem to constitute the essence of disavowal: the mother is dead, and she is not dead—simultaneously. In her improper death, she is both lost and not lost. She dies a death that will not deliver. Matricide as a nonconcept means a death without structural loss. In the Freudian schema, as I have noted, structural loss refers to an irrecoverable, irreversible, gone-forever loss. Thus matricide as the improper death—the dead and not dead (nonconcept) will not (according to Freudian structural theory) yield structural generativity.

What is at stake here is the question of whether or not structure is categorically dependent on this particular "Red" type of loss proper. To posit the notion of a maternal structural function necessarily means to rethink the relation between loss and structure. Why should the notion of a maternal structural function have to mirror the process of the paternal structural function? *Would it not be true to say that a different type of loss will produce a different kind of structuring?* If, as Irigaray persistently states, "our culture is built on matricide,"[12] then we have to interrogate what matricide actually means, that is to say, what does it signify, how does it function, and, more important, what are its underlying laws. If matricide is not reducible to patricide and is programmed by a different phantasy and a different kind of loss from that of patricide, then it will necessarily produce different modes of mourning, of remembering, of symbolizing.

There is, to my mind, no reason why only one kind of loss can produce a generative structural symbolic function. The problem is that matricide has not, as yet, been theorized in psychoanalysis or feminism, even by Irigaray. To make matricide a concept, that is, to theorize it, means to identify its specific place in the order of the symbolic laws. Irigaray has analyzed the matricidal phantasies operating in the male imaginary, but she has not addressed the problem of theorizing the specific underlying matricidal law that prohibits these phantasies.[13] Addressing the question of a matricidal law allows us to formulate a different configuration of loss and structure that does not adhere to the particular conceptualization that informs the patricidal structural "Red" economy.

In "The Dead Mother," Green introduces a second paradigm or center that he describes as "Black and White." Black and white are for Green "the colours of mourning," linked to the loss of the maternal breast. In a highly complex section of "The Dead Mother," Green, as I understand him, argues that the loss of the breast is metaphorical in that it is part of the retrospectively established phantasy of the primal scene. That is, the loss of the breast functions as a fundamental determining moment signifying the "symbolic mutation of the relation between pleasure and reality" that is linked to the prohibition of incest. He then goes on to discuss different psychoanalytic versions of the loss of the breast, distinguishing two mutu-ally exclusive approaches. The first concerns the breast as metaphorical: the loss of the breast is theorized synchronically and thus structurally. Green identifies this conceptualization of the lost breast in Freud's es-say "On Negation": "Freud talks about it as though it implies a unique, instantaneous, basic event—decisive, it goes without saying, because its repercussion on the function of judgement is fundamental."[14]

The second approach concerning the lost breast identified by Green is "less theoretical than descriptive." Green contends that, in "An Outline of Psychoanalysis" (1940), Freud departs from his earlier theoretical for-mulation of the loss of the breast and embraces an approach more akin to observation. This approach is based on a narrative form describing loss as a "process of progressive evolution that advances step by step."[15] Such an approach does not theorize or conceptualize since it favors a diachronic phenomenological perspective rather than a structural synchronic ap-proach based on memory and retrospective reconstruction. For Green, these two approaches are mutually exclusive. In order to follow through Freud's initial structural approach to the loss of the breast, it is essential to "retain the metaphor of the breast, for the breast, like the penis, can only be symbolic."[16] To theorize is always to reconstruct retrospectively; the theorized lost object will always be mediated through the retrospec-tive conceptualization. The breast in theory, then, for Green, is always a metaphor: "It is in the aftermath that this theory of the lost object is formed and acquires its unique, instantaneous, decisive, irrevocable, and basic characteristic."[17]

For Green, psychoanalytic accounts of the relation to the breast such as that of the object-relations tradition are not theorizing, they are describing a process of loss that does not use metaphor, structure, or theory. In this way, Green is suggesting that there is no structural theory of the metaphorical lost breast in psychoanalysis, despite the voluminous accounts of the infant's relation to the breast in the Kleinian and post-Kleinian tradition. But when he sets up the second center—the "Black and White" model—he begins to complicate this whole trajectory.

In my reading, the main theoretical knot or ambiguity in Green's essay concerns the question of whether he is using the "Black and White" model to distinguish the descriptive approach from the "Red" structural metaphorical approach or whether he is introducing it as another potential structural metaphorical center that is not "Red" but still pertains to generative loss. Does the metaphorical breast belong to the "Black and White" paradigm, or is it subsumed retrospectively by the "Red"/castration model? The question of whether it is only "Red" loss that can be symbolically generative is ambiguous in Green's essay. In other words, he might be suggesting that the phantasy of loss related to the mother has the potential of being schematized into a structural theory despite the absence of a bloody mutilation and is therefore not reducible to castration/"Red" loss. I want to discuss the question of the potential of the "Black and White" model with regard to the conception of a matricidal structural center that can deliver a generative symbolic loss.[18]

In the conference "A Celebration of the Work of André Green,"[19] Juliet Mitchell, through her reading of "The Dead Mother," addressed precisely this ambiguity in Green's essay. From my understanding, it seems that Mitchell's reading categorically stated the impossibility of matricide as a concept within the terms of Green's two paradigms. She made the distinction between loss and absence. This subtle and crucial distinction clarifies the debate considerably. In the "Black and White" model, for Mitchell, there is no loss; there is only absence. And absence is distinct from loss because it always implies a return, so that presence is never far off. The breast, for Mitchell, is never truly lost; it rather exists as either absent or present/black or white. It is never truly gone, lost, irrecoverably lopped off, and, as a result, Mitchell suggested that it is no coincidence that the turning to the mother in object relations produced description rather than theory.[20] She is, I think, saying something to the effect that it is not possible to theorize the maternal realm within Green's "Black and White" paradigm since theory depends on loss rather than absence. The maternal realm in Mitchell's reading of Green can only ever be described, since the loss of the breast is an irresolvable process to do with appearance and disappearance. Only death can be handed down and internalized as a reminder of limits, of mortality, of generation. The mother cannot serve this function according to Green's reading, since for Mitchell, you cannot theorize out of absence. In Mitchell's reading of Green, it would seem that matricide will remain as the nonconcept or that which cannot be structured because the mother's absence creates a presence that forecloses the mourning of a proper death that would allow for generative symbolization. Matricide, according to my interpretation of Mitchell's lecture on Green's essay, belongs to the "Black and White" paradigm and in this way can only describe an absence evoking a presence; it cannot theorize a loss. I will return to this interpretation in a moment.

After the conference dedicated to celebrating the work of André Green at which Mitchell presented her paper, a book came out called *The Dead Mother: The Work of André Green* (1999), a collection of essays by practicing psychoanalysts engaging with the particular essay of Green's that I am discussing here. The emphasis of the book is on the clinical uses that psychoanalysts have made of Green's essay. None of the essays in this book addresses the aspect of Green's essay that challenges the theoretical paradigms of psychoanalysis; none of the contributors refers to the beginning of Green's essay, where he sets up his thesis of the two structural centers. In the preface to the book, however, R. Horacio Etchegoyen makes some bold statements concerning Green's theoretical innovations in "The Dead Mother" that deserve close attention here. He states that "the concept of the dead mother is a structural concept—even though it is found in the concrete experience of the subject's childhood. While in Lacan's theory there is the concept of the dead father, which represents the continuity of previous generations through the superego (the law-of-the-father), the concept of the dead mother (although not a transgenerational phenomenon) comes to re-establish a balance between the two parental figures in psychoanalytic theory."[21]

Etchegoyen is implying that matricide *is* a structural concept in Green's formulation and thus reestablishes the balance in psychoanalysis between the parental figures. Yet he is careful to add that there is a difference: matricide is a structural concept, *yet it is not a transgenerational phenomenon.* What then is he concluding? A structural function for the mother, but one that does not represent the continuity of generations? What kind of balance does Etchegoyen perceive in this interpretation of Green? It appears that his reading wants it both ways: the dead mother is a structural concept but not structural enough, it would seem, to involve transgenerational continuity. That function remains solely and safely secured with the father. The ambiguity in Green's essay becomes even more apparent. Now, according to Etchegoyen's reading, we can have a maternal structural function that does not concern the continuity of generations. In this reading, the mother even in her structural death still will not produce a generative loss. There is something serious at stake in pursuing the idea of matricide as a structural concept whose underlying laws may figure in the structuring and the transmitting of an alternative symbolic economy. Etchegoyen is perhaps aware of this in his willingness to interpret Green as giving the dead mother a structural function but not linking this function with transgenerational symbolic transmission.

Increasingly, it becomes apparent that there is a conceptual problem in using an untheorized notion of matricide especially when attempting to think about it in relation to structure. Etchegoyen's comments are a witness to this problem; he gives matricide structural properties yet denies it the possibility of yielding the results that these properties would normally secure. In my thinking, you cannot have a structural function that does not partake in the process of unconscious transgenerational transmission. But Etchegoyen seems to place matricide in a somewhat obscure zone that makes matricide both structural and not structural, thus reproducing the structure of disavowal in relation to the mother. We can see that the meaning of matricide shifts problematically from theorist to theorist and within each theorist's work, so making urgent the necessity of formulating a specific theoretical definition.

Mitchell's response to the ambiguity in Green's essay concerning whether Green's "Black and White" model can be conceived of as a structural paradigm that organizes a matricidal generative (symbolic) loss leads her (as I understood her) to decide that it cannot. But in the process, what I infer from her reading is an implicit or nascent definition of matricide as absence. This formulation proves highly relevant to the argument I present in part 2. In making the distinction between absence and loss, Mitchell then places matricide within the absence/presence binary (that can only generate description not structural theory) that she considers characteristic of Green's "Black/White" model. We can interpret and develop this further by suggesting the following formulation: *untheorized matricide means absence and will therefore always elude structure.* What I shall propose in later chapters is a definition of untheorized matricide, arrived at through a reading of the Oresteian myth, as *incorporation* rather than *introjection* or, to put it another way, as *presence* rather than *loss*. At this point, such a formulation will not yet be clear, but for now it suffices to say that Mitchell anticipates my own later formulation when she places matricide on the side of absence/presence rather than in an economy of loss. Incorporation is fundamentally a phantasy that functions to deny loss and belongs, in my formulation, to the presence/absence binary, to which

Mitchell referred. Additionally, Etchegoyen's paradoxical formulation of matricide as a structural concept that does not function transgenerationally can be read in the light of my later argument, as a manifestation of a symptom of the phantasy of incorporation to which matricide belongs. So long as matricide belongs to the absence/presence binary and to the phantasy of incorporation, then it cannot function transgenerationally. To theorize matricide will mean, in this argument, to postulate matricide as a structural center that can deliver a transgenerational generative loss that is not reducible to Green's "Red" paradigm and moves beyond the descriptive "Black/White" paradigm. In this way, I am suggesting that there is a difference between untheorized definitions of matricide and a theorized definition or a matricidal law.

Green himself said of his essay: "The interesting thing is that when I wrote 'The dead mother' I was not fully aware of what I was saying."[22] My intention is to follow through the suggestions in Green's essay in order to arrive at a specific definition of matricide as it functions in the male imaginary and then go on to theorize matricide in relation to its underlying cultural laws. In this way, I will move from absence to loss and from description to theory. Through using Irigaray's ideas concerning matricide in conjunction with Green's suggestions, I will depart from the tradition that states that theory, structure, and representation can only be born of a "Red" loss. Matricide will be proposed as a concept that structures a different type of loss, a different type of limit, the internalization of which may lead to the production of imaginaries that can lead to a generative social bond representative of the continuity of generations of women—mothers and daughters. I will suggest that in theorizing matricide, the daughter who can never properly lose her mother can have this not-quite-lostness mediated and structured so that she may be able to experience difference as well as sameness in relation to her mother. In this way, the mother-daughter relation could be mediated, creating a different site for a between-women symbolic space of exchange, transmission, and transgenerational genealogical inheritance.

To create a covenant or a social contract different from the "Red" patricidal one certainly transgresses psychoanalytic theory as we know it, but this does not exclude the possibility of further exploration of Green's work in conjunction with Irigaray's project. We need to hold on to two key points: the possibility of a heterogeneous system of diverse structurings and the possibility of theorizing matricide as a generative loss (rather than an absence) that has different properties from that of the "Red" patricidal law. In this way, we can take a significant step further in the conception of a maternal structural economy.

My own engagement with symbolic intervention, as previously stated, involves the register of myth and its relation to phantasy and culture. In this way, I will be introducing the Oresteian myth as it is reworked in Aeschylus's trilogy and the matricide plays written by Sophocles and Euripides, in an attempt to demonstrate how this myth can be analyzed and used in the context of conceiving of alternative structural systems. Irigaray states: "It is idle to revive old myths if we are unable to celebrate them and *use them to constitute a social system,* a temporal system. Is this in our power? Let us imagine that it is possible: will Gaia or Demeter be enough? What shall we do with Kore? Persephone? Diana?" (my italics).[23] It is the ambition of this project to explore the possibilities of using myth in its structuring potential to constitute an alternative social bond.

Finally, to close this chapter, it is crucial to reiterate and clarify that in my argument the return to ancient myth is not a matter of an attempt to uncover and describe a buried matriarchal structure and neither is it an attempt to celebrate existing representations of goddesses for the purposes of fostering positive identifications or processes of relating (for women). This would be to confuse identification with identity. I am concerned with the way in which myth contains evidence of imaginary structurations and, further, with using myth as a structuring device that can function to mediate the inclusion of previously excluded imaginary phantasy structures into the institutions of the social and symbolic order.

The methodology that is demanded here is double-edged. Initially, I will try to recover traces of the imaginary phantasies in the symbolic products that have taken their place, in order to think about the latent imaginary rather than being thought by it. Second, I will attempt a process of restructuring whereby myth is used as an organizing dynamic instrument that can contribute to the establishment of a social order that can structure specific economies that have hitherto escaped structuration. In other words, it is not only a matter of rereading myths and describing their constitutive underlying phantasies. It is rather a matter of considering the structural organizing potential of myth so that it can be utilized in the creation of theory and in symbolic innovation. To use myth in this way is to move beyond a descriptive approach; myth ceases to be considered for its narrative content alone and instead is interrogated for its structural properties and possibilities. It is only in its structural transformative potential that myth can be of any political use to feminism. Thus it is not so much the discovery of obliterated or displaced goddesses in the Western mythical corpus as the subsequent uses of these strategic discoveries that will determine the political force of a feminist engagement with myth. Jean-Joseph Goux claims: "There are no teachings more dense and powerful than those of myths, whose transmission ensures the reproduction of a social bond from one generation to the next."[24] It is this relationship between the transmission of myth and the reproduction of a generative social bond that forms the kernel of my feminist engagement with myth. In the next chapters, I will see what work we can do with myth to create and transmit a different social bond from this generation to the next.

4

Oedipus and Monotheism

I differ from Freud because I think again we must be able to work with two or three constellations. He wanted a unifying Oedipus complex; everything had to converge there. . . . There are other constellations.

—ANDRÉ GREEN

PSYCHOANALYTIC THEORY IN the post-Lacanian mode is increasingly concerned with expanding its theoretical field to accommodate the conceptualization of different psychic organizations and phantasy structures. Psychoanalytic theorists/clinicians such as André Green, Jean Laplanche, Jessica Benjamin, Carol Gilligan, and Juliet Mitchell in addition to post-Lacanian psychoanalytic feminists have, in different ways, begun to depart from sole adherence to the oedipal structure as the one and only clinical and cultural model and are seeking to expand their references to include different structural constellations and new theories. In this way, the unconscious is now, from within some sectors of contemporary psychoanalysis, being considered as a dynamic reservoir of the yet-to-be-known or yet-to-be-structured. Unconscious processes are no longer systematically reduced to one particular model or law, and thus psychoanalytic theory is beginning to adopt a less monolithic approach that enables a broader field of inquiry to be considered.[1]

It is from within this climate that I attempt to posit the Oresteian myth as an alternative structural model for understanding and theorizing living present constellations of unconscious phantasies on the level of both the clinical and the cultural. The Oresteian structure is not presented here as antithetical or opposite to the oedipal structure but rather as a different perspective, that is, a structural constellation alongside Oedipus that signifies another field of desire producing alternative systems of meaning. It is my contention that the Oresteian structure can be productively utilized to give us deeper insight into the male imaginary as it is legitimized and naturalized in the symbolic social world. More fundamentally, I will argue that use of the Oresteian structure creates potential for theorizing different constellations of unconscious phantasy belonging to the mother-daughter relationship, which the oedipal model excludes. In this way, the attempt to explore an Oresteian structure is linked to the aim of developing a structural theory that can include a maternal subject position and, further, the mother-daughter relation, *inside* the symbolic. In this way, my focus will remain on the relationship among myth, phantasy, and structure and, in turn, the relation between mythical structures and the feminist project of social transformation.

Concentration on the mother-daughter relation by psychoanalytic feminists, such as Nancy Chodorow, for example,[2] who wish to find a way out of the univocal Lacanian theory, have often, perhaps unwittingly, embraced psychology, sociology, or phenomenology and in this way have not contributed to an intervention into or a reorganization of psychoanalytic theory. Rather than moving away from structure and thus moving away from psychoanalysis, my own intervention is wholly concerned with thinking through the mother-daughter relation in a post-Lacanian mode that necessitates the postulation of a structural model that serves to theorize hitherto excluded imaginary phantasies. In my argument, the structural mediation of the mother-daughter relation cannot be achieved until the mother is theorized as a subject. As long as matricide remains as a nonconcept that cannot deliver a generative loss, the possibility of a symbolically mediated mother-daughter relation is foreclosed. In this way, the first stage of my work with the Oresteian myth concerns the attempt to establish a structural theory of matricide. Having posited the mother's structural and generative possibilities, I will then be in a position to concentrate on the mother-daughter relation (in part 3).

Freud's engagement with Sophocles' Oedipus tragedy led him to discover what he believed to be a universal structure of desire; certainly, his reading of Sophocles helped him understand (some of) what his analysands were saying. It is striking that, since Freud, psychoanalysis has not delved much further into the vast labyrinth of Greek myth, has not strayed away from Oedipus as the one myth that can teach us about the structure of desire. The enormous extent to which Greek myth and tragedy informed Freud's work might have led one to assume that the development of his theories would involve a further study of myth.[3]

That Oedipus has been singled out as the master myth and has sustained this master status for the century in which psychoanalysis has been alive is a phenomenon worthy of reflection. To posit Oedipus as the universal law of the unconscious, in Irigaray's terms, results in a reduction of the "yet-to-be subjected to the already subjected." The question, as I see it, is not so much *why Oedipus?* as *why only Oedipus?*

It is at this point that the work of Claude Lévi-Strauss becomes crucial to the development of my argument. Between 1964 and 1971, Lévi-Strauss wrote *Mythologiques* (Plon, 1964–1971), a work that comprised four volumes, entitled *The Raw and the Cooked* (1964), *From Honey to Ashes* (1967), *The Origin of Table Manners* (1968), and *The Naked Man* (1971). While Lévi-Strauss is an expert on the way myth works, Freud is not. It is my contention that we thus need to take Lévi-Strauss's theory of myth seriously with regard to questioning Freud's unilateral approach to myth. I noted in chapter 2 how the fundamental characteristic of myths, according to Lévi-Strauss, is their indeterminate nature. One cannot ever get a definitive understanding or a complete story in one myth alone since myths are fragments that need to be looked at together to achieve insight into their underlying structures. Levi-Strauss found that one needs to "read the myth as if reading an orchestral score. We should apprehend the whole page. Not only read left to right but at the same time vertically from top to bottom. . . . The basic meaning of the myth is not conveyed by a sequence of events."[4]

I want to ask, what happens to Freud's treatment of Oedipus if we introduce Lévi-Strauss's model of myth as an orchestral score into psychoanalysis? This question, to my knowledge, has not hitherto been posed.[5] More precisely, I want to ask, what happens to the encounter between feminism and psychoanalysis if we make use of Lévi-Strauss's theory of differential myth analysis? My hypothesis is that psychoanalysis's monolithic approach to myth leads to fixations of interpretation. Given this, my basic intellectual move will be to use Lévi-Strauss's structural anthropology in order to make a feminist intervention into psychoanalysis by postulating a multidimensional differential model of myth.

Lévi-Strauss insists that the units of myth make sense only in relation to other units such that myth, like language, acquires meaning only through the differential relation between terms. Isolated elements or units have no intrinsic meaning but achieve significance only from their relation with one another. In this way, for Lévi-Strauss, the context of each myth comes to consist more and more of other myths. Attempting to explain one event or sequence in a myth can only be achieved through considering that particular event in relation to both the other elements in that myth and also in relation to other myths that manifest a similar context. Additionally, analysis of a myth, for Lévi-Strauss, must involve all different versions of the myth so that there exists a "bundle of mythical relations" to be analyzed;[6] one cannot prioritize a certain myth or a certain version of a myth. Each mythical variant needs to be analyzed in relation to a "paradigmatic set" of mythical variants rather than isolated into a single "syntagmatic chain."[7] Through a differential analysis of mythical elements/variants, one can begin to understand their structure. *Some myths will present parts of the structure that others do not.*

To isolate a myth is to seal it off and block the open-ended paths that link it with other myths. To use one myth, as Freud did, as an armature for a structural system of the unconscious is to make a somewhat violent appropriation by severing one element from its context—that of an elaborate constellation. We can now ask, in the light of Lévi-Strauss's points, what happens to the feminist encounter with psychoanalysis if we decenter the Oedipus myth and reread it in relation to other mythical variants?

While Juliet Mitchell made use of structural anthropology to give a structural account of women's oppression,[8] my use of Lévi-Strauss differs from hers in important ways. I am taking a specific but fundamental point of Lévi-Strauss's, concerning how myth works, in order to subvert the monolithic approach to myth belonging to psychoanalysis. While Mitchell's use of Lévi-Strauss allowed us to understand the entrenchment of women's oppression, my use of structural anthropology allows me to expand the psychoanalytic frame of reference by reading Oedipus in relation to other myths with a view to theorizing more than one structuring possibility. Considering the relation among myths, their connections, superimpositions, repetitions, and variations, deepens and complicates each structure that we may perceive in them singularly.

Psychoanalysis has isolated the myth of Oedipus as if it were self-contained and complete, rather than considering it as part of a constellation of myths relating to other constellations. In so doing, psychoanalysis neglects the fundamentally heterogeneous and dynamic nature of myth and thus limits the potential of its own findings, listening to or reading only one register of the "orchestral score." Oedipus has hitherto managed to explain or describe one aspect of the psychic relation to social reality, that is to say, the singular history of Oedipus describes the *dominant* structuring process of the subject under Western patriarchy. Yet it is no longer convincing to refer to "Western patriarchy" as if this were a homogeneous static order that has not changed since the time Freud constructed the Oedipal paradigm.

In a recent article, "Sexuality, Psychoanalysis and Social Changes," Juliet Mitchell poses provocative questions concerning the relation between psychoanalysis and social reality that I think have significant implications with regard to the necessity for theoretical innovation inside psychoanalysis. She identifies the radical changes in family patterns and social organization that have occurred since the 1960s, commenting that:

> Our work as psychoanalysts in this area uses theories either as old as our discipline (one hundred years) or as old as the work emanating from the crises of the second world war and ending, at the latest, in the 1960s. Today as distinct from the periods of our dominant theories, there is in the Western world, by-and-large, a decline in the rate of marriage, an increase in the rate of divorce, a decline in family size to less than two children, an increase in the number of children born outside marriage, an increase in single-mother families, in paternal absenteeism, in cohabitation, in serial monogamy and in a range of living arrangements including homosexual couplings with or without children. Although all these phenomena have been witnessed in other historical epochs or in other societies they were not dominant practices at the time—or times—of the creation of psychoanalytic theory.[9]

Freud's model did not and could not anticipate such radical social changes, and Mitchell implies that it can no longer adequately account for or explain the changing psychic relations to diverse social realities. She identifies a sociological trend concerning the marginalization of the father together with clinical evidence suggesting the growing absence of the castration complex in male heterosexuality, the waning power of the "symbolic father," and, more fundamentally, the annihilation of the existence of the father in the mind. This demise of the father is something Mitchell claims is reflected in psychoanalytic theory of the Kleinian and Middle School psychoanalytic groups, which continue to refer to the oedipal complex yet marginalize the role of castration. Concentration on the mother-infant relation in these theories and the concomitant diminishing of the importance of castration are for Mitchell evidence of "an unacknowledged reflection of these social changes." Mitchell then warns that psychoanalysis should not reflect social reality; it should explain it.

Theory should go beyond observation, beyond fact, beyond mirroring reality, and toward the construction of a model that can allow for an explanation of how the psychic and the social function in the construction of the subject. When Mitchell claims that Kleinian and Independent psychoanalysts mimic the social situation through stressing the centrality of the relation to the mother, she is, I think, suggesting that where their theories fall short is that they neglect to explain the processes by which the father is diminishing in both the psychic and the social registers as well as failing to analyze the implications or cost of such a situation. This has serious implications since psychoanalysis is the one place wherein the structure of psychosexual identities and their relation to social reality should be able to be thought about rather than acted out.

New paradigms are needed in order for psychoanalysis to retain its status as a theory—a metanarrative or tool—that can account for and explain changing psychic structures rather than unconsciously reflecting these changes. As long as there are no other models to explain new organizations of sexuality and social/familial relations, the psychoanalytic world, in my view, becomes susceptible to or unwittingly involved in reflecting the prevalent anxiety about these changes rather than attempting to explain or construct different models from which new theorizing could flourish. The situation wherein the growing manifestation of different substructures is complicating and disrupting the idea of a monolithic phallic symbolic law brings with it a powerful anxiety that can often lead to clinging to the established models. If Oedipus has the monopoly on sanity, then its erosion will inevitably be interpreted by a large part of the psychoanalytic community as catastrophic.

The problem, as I see it, concerns the present position within psychoanalysis whereby the negotiation of the Oedipus complex, with castration as its structural center, is equated with sanity or, more important, any deviation from Oedipus is systematically interpreted as rejecting or foreclosing sanity. There are no models available to account for or theorize symbolic positions achievable through different psychic processes other than castration, meaning that anything that eludes or subverts the parameters of the oedipal model is interpreted as pathological and on the side of insanity.[10]

This state of affairs is indicative of the monolithic approach to myth in psychoanalysis, an approach that urgently needs to be contested. We should be able to respond constructively to evidence that the old model is proving limited by attempting to theorize emerging alternative psychic constellations that negotiate a different (and not necessarily pathological) relation to sociosymbolic realities. That there are psychosexual substructures that cannot be adequately understood with reference to the dominant psychoanalytic theories but are becoming visible or audible as phenomena that challenge the dominant psychoanalytic theory suggests the necessity for the construction of new theoretical models.[11] Instead of reacting to beginning-to-be-articulated or yet-to-be-subjected psychic organizations by interpreting them as apocalyptic, (no Oedipus = undifferentiated chaos),[12] it is possible to think about new phenomena as indicating an increasingly heterogeneous and dynamic symbolic that can accommodate different unconscious psychic constellations, meanings, and representations. Freud himself acknowledged our need or tendency to arrange perceived unfamiliar material in accordance with the already-known or the "conditions of intelligibility," yet he warned that such a practice risks falsifying the perception. In discussing the motives generating the aspect of the "dream work" that involves the revision of the dream content, Freud comments: "As is well known, we are incapable of seeing a series of unfamiliar signs or hearing a succession of unknown words, without at once falsifying the perception from the considerations of intelligibility, on the basis of something already known to us."[13] Freud's comment should remind us not to submit to this common tendency and subsume or rearrange all unfamiliar phenomena into already-known constructed models. To see the unfamiliar or hear unknown words without immediately reorganizing or transforming those signs or words in order to make them fit into the frame of what we already know is to work at the level of the navel. To be able to see evidence of and then tolerate the unknown or that which exceeds or subverts the already-known models is genuinely to work toward the creation and expansion of theory rather than constantly and perhaps unwittingly reproducing the already-known.

The displacement of oedipal castration as the one and only structural center or universal law of the unconscious through the addition of different (coexisting) structures is less a sign of catastrophe and more a sign of the possibility of a nascent articulation of the full "orchestral score." If the voice of the oedipal father is getting quieter, then all the potential whisperings that have been hitherto drowned out or struck dumb by the univocal law can begin to be articulated and heard, allowing us to consider the diverse passages into symbolic sexed subjectivities. This is not to say that these other organizations or symbolic constellations are already there waiting to be acknowledged but rather that there may be an emergent space for the possibility of something not yet known to become.[14] It is the facilitation of this space that is in question here. To allow for a stage on which there could be more than one protagonist (Oedipus) means to imagine a stage with many different doors, a multitude of entrances. If Cixous, in her essay "Sorties,"[15] presented women with the possibility of finding the psychic exits, of finding the ways out of constructions of femininity that fixed them in a place that alienated them from the possibility of their specific desire, it is now time that we were able to theorize different entrances onto the symbolic stage: different doors, different ways into the realm of the symbolic.[16] Entering the stage from different doors means seeing the stage itself from different perspectives.

If psychoanalysis is to theorize new phenomena without turning into psychology or sociology and without merely reflecting social changes (Klein and the object-relation tradition) or the related anxiety about those changes, then it needs to resist and analyze the inclination compulsively to pathologize any different organization that transgresses its present systems or models. The need to construct new models with a structural center different from that of castration is a necessity if we are to be able to understand, explain, and represent alternative passages into the symbolic and different organizations of masculinities and femininities in a symbolic order organized around more than one structural constellation.

Using Lévi-Strauss's model of myth enables us to expand the psychoanalytic frame so that a consideration of other mythical constellations becomes a new psychoanalytic feminist question. We can then begin to broaden the theoretical field in order to explain new arrangements and give symbolic mediation to previously unsymbolized phantasy structures that have a different (but not psychotic) relation to the phallus. Roustang comments: "It is not so easy to produce what is truly theory, that is, to find a formulation that becomes operational and defines what are really general mechanisms that can undergo several combinations; it is not so easy to depart from pure description or projection in order to provide models that deconstruct the symptoms and make way for new arrangements."[17] Looking contiguously at myth will develop the psychoanalytic conceptual apparatus; we may enrich it by making audible the different tones, resonances, and chords in each mythical sequence, thus achieving a deeper and richer understanding of their interrelated structural properties. Oedipus is never only Oedipus; in him, we will find Orestes, even Athena. In Athena, we may glimpse Metis. We will see Phaedra in Jocasta and Jocasta in Clytemnestra; in Clytemnestra, we may see Demeter; in Iphigenia, we may find Persephone; in Electra, we may hear Antigone. In suicide, we may find sacrifice; in patricide, we may find an already committed matricide. In one law, we may find another concealed, one structure may be propped up by another, and so on. In myth, nothing will ever be only itself.

PART II

5 🐙

Oresteian Secrets

DECRYPTING METIS

ESCHYLUS'S *ORESTEIA* IS the oldest surviving tragedy. It provided the source for the later plays dealing with its themes written by the later tragedians Sophocles and Euripides. In total, ten ancient plays rework and elaborate the Oresteian myth leaving us with a rich corpus of material concerned with the house of Atreus and the bloody chain of murders that marks its transgenerational history.[1] The plethora of tragedies representing different aspects of this myth build up a complex map or grid charting the multifarious interweaving stories that surround the murder of Clytemnestra by her son, Orestes, and his subsequent acquittal in Athena's court of justice. Because of this, the theme of matricide can be examined synchronically through a study of the mutations, variations, repetitions, and exclusions existing in each ancient representation of this tragic theme.

It is necessary here to give a brief and condensed description of the Oresteian myth so that the reader can hold in her/his mind the basic structure, which will be considerably elaborated as part 2 progresses. While both Euripedes and Sophocles rework the many strands of the myth, at this point in my argument I am going to describe the myth as it is represented in Aeschylus's trilogy, which dramatizes the overall structure of the myth, whereas Euripides and Sophocles concentrate on and expand particular parts of the story.

Aeschylus's Oresteian trilogy opens in the royal palace of Argos, home of Agamemnon and Clytemnestra and their four children.[2] Agamemnon has been away for ten years leading the Greek army in the war against Troy, leaving Clytemnestra ruling in his absence. The first play dramatizes Agamemnon's homecoming after the Greeks have successfully sacked Troy. Clytemnestra, who had taken a lover in her husband's absence, murders Agamemnon on his return as an act of revenge for his murder of their eldest daughter, Iphigenia, at the beginning of the Trojan War.[3] The second play in the trilogy dramatizes the return of Orestes, Agamemnon and Clytemnestra's son, whom Clytemnestra had banished from Argos when he was a baby, afraid that he would avenge his father's death. Orestes' sister Electra has been waiting for her brother's return in a state of excessive mourning for her father and hatred for her mother, her only hope being that Orestes will return and kill their mother. Orestes returns, and Electra helps him plan the matricide, which Orestes has been ordered to commit by the god Apollo. Orestes kills Clytemnestra and is immediately hounded by the Furies (the mother's curses) and flees Argos in a state of insanity and guilt. He seeks help from the goddess Athena, who establishes the first court of democratic justice, where Orestes is put on trial. The court case results in a split vote, and Athena is given the crucial casting vote. She sides with Orestes, and he is absolved from his crime. Athena persuades the Furies to give up their cause of fighting for the mother's rights and instead become "the Kindly Ones" who will protect Athens and support Orestes' rule.

In view of the argument I have presented concerning the necessity to consider myths as inextricably linked rather than as isolated self-contained elements, it is crucial here to explain that my use of the *Oresteia* is not an attempt simply to isolate a different myth from that of Oedipus and position it as a competing master narrative. First, my rereading and use of the *Oresteia* is never in isolation. The *Oresteia* is never only the *Oresteia;* it is always already a complex reworking of other myths.

Second, I use the *Oresteia* here as a way to reread Oedipus so that, rather than competing with Oedipus, it functions to expand the horizons of oedipal logic, to add something new to the frame. In a sense, what the *Oresteia* does for Oedipus is to give him back his sight. Psychoanalysis becomes blinded at the moment that Oedipus gouges out his eyes; it closes its eyes at the point at which Oedipus's trajectory is complete. While Oedipus's blindness is supposed to represent his insight, psychoanalysis need not mimic their protagonist's truth by being satisfied with his insight as the only insight. In closing our eyes at the point of Oedipus's blindness, we shut out the possibility of seeing more, as if Oedipus has seen everything. Certainly, he has not seen his daughter/sister Antigone, and neither has he realized that in addition to killing his father and marrying his mother, he has also brought about the death of his mother and the Sphinx. Psychoanalysis, like Oedipus, needs the *Oresteia* so that it can cure the blindness surrounding the mother who is not only desired but desires, who is not only a suicide but murdered, and who has not only sons but daughters.

Considering my feminist context, the *Oresteia* as my focus functions to provide an alternative structural constellation that can go some way toward representing phantasies more specific to potential female imaginaries. This is not to say, however, that the *Oresteia* is *the* myth for women — as if such a thing could possibly exist. Instead, my argument is that it can function as an analytic tool for women in its capacity to act as a structure that can be used to both interpret and counter the projections systematically forced on women through the workings of the male imaginary. The *Oresteia* has the potential to be used to analyze the male phantasies surrounding the mother and matricide, so that those phantasies are not repeatedly acted out and projected into women. As Christina Wieland comments: "Freud chose the myth of Oedipus to describe masculinity and its pitfalls. However, it is apparent that the story of Oedipus cannot be used to describe femininity, and even for the boy the Oedipus myth does not tell the whole story. Had Freud chosen the Oresteian myth he might have uncovered some different aspects of masculinity, as revealed in the boy's dread of the omnipotent mother, the search for a male identificatory figure, and the boy's violent destruction of his attachment to his mother."[4] The Oresteian myth can function as a structure that theorizes aspects of the male imaginary that Oedipus omits so that women are no longer used as receptacles for unanalyzed projected phantasies related to matricide. The Oresteian myth may express significant parts of the structure of masculinity that Oedipus does not.

It could be argued that the aspects of masculinity that Wieland describes *are* available to be analyzed within the oedipal myth through the figures of the Sphinx and Jocasta. For example, "the boy's dread of the omnipotent mother" could be found in Oedipus's confrontation with the Sphinx, and "his violent destruction of his attachment to his mother" could quite convincingly be analyzed in terms of his relation to Jocasta. While suicide rather than murder is represented as the process by which the dead mother is created within the oedipal narrative, these suicides are precipitated directly by the confrontation between mother and son. Moreover, in myth, it is certainly not uncommon to come across what Freud described as an unconscious process at work in dreams and phantasies, whereby one element is converted into its opposite as part of a censoring device. In this way, the suicides of Jocasta and the Sphinx could convincingly be interpreted as belonging to a matricidal phantasy structure specific to the desire of Oedipus, the son.[5] If, as Schneider suggests, Freud's "reductionist" treatment of the Oedipus myth related to his failure to analyze the two matricides, then why not remain in the oedipal model by concentrating on the Sphinx/Jocasta problem and work to expand the oedipal frame from within? In other words, why complicate matters by examining a different myth when matricide is already present in the chosen and established myth of psychoanalysis?

I am going to answer this question in two ways. First, through recourse to Lévi-Strauss's contention that the meaning of one myth cannot be understood in isolation and, second, in relation to the question of femininity, more specifically, by looking at the position of the daughter in terms of matricide and its psychic vicissitudes.

The structure of Oedipus positions the mastery and destruction of the Sphinx as what made everything possible in terms of the unfolding of Oedipus's desire. In this way, the murder of the primitive mother, who is represented in the form of a monstrous riddle (the Sphinx), acts as the gateway to the realization of Oedipus's trajectory. Jocasta, like the Sphinx, commits suicide after Oedipus has learned who she is. The two suicides occur in response to Oedipus's finding something out. He finds the answer to the Sphinx's question and finds out the identity of Jocasta, and this finding-out causes the two maternal figures to die. It is as though the Oedipus myth reworks Orestes' confrontation with Clytemnestra on the level of reason and intellectual mastery. Oedipus's wit functions to cause the death of these maternal figures rather than a more primitive visceral violence.[6] Orestes stabs his mother while Oedipus simply speaks. Orestes murders his mother while Oedipus causes suicides. Oedipus conceals the violence in relation to the mother and is given hands free of bloodstains and a head full of reason. The primitive register is eradicated from Oedipus, so much so that his response to his mother's corpse is to blind himself. He must not know his matricidal desire; his insight will only tolerate knowing his incestuous desire.

In this way, Oedipus repeats Orestes' act but in an oblique and sanitized manner. Words take the place of the knife and suicide takes the place of murder. What is radically eliminated from the Oedipus myth is blood, and, more specifically, female blood. While Orestes' hands are literally covered in his mother's blood, Jocasta's suicide by hanging is a blood-free affair, as is the Sphinx's leap from the mountain—she simply disappears. The blood on Orestes' hands is the blood that nourished him into being. Oedipus avoids both the violent proximity to and the identification with the mother's body. He knows the mother in terms of the pleasure principle, he knows what it is to *have* the mother. Orestes acts out the darker violent side of this relation; he must shed the blood of his mother, which is also his own blood. Orestes struggles with the more primitive conflict of identification with the maternal body so that the blood on his hands is the mark of both his attempt at differentiation from his mother and the inescapable reality of his being created from and nourished by the same blood.

To understand the matricidal phantasy structures in Oedipus, we need Orestes to bring back what Oedipus has expelled. The *Oresteia* gives us the opportunity to analyze phantasies related to the flesh and blood of the maternal body from which Freud, like Oedipus, steered clear.[7] If we superimpose Orestes' trajectory onto that of Oedipus, we expand the frame to include a complex mythical constellation that opens the way for a rigorous analysis of typical primitive *matricidal* phantasies that the myth of Oedipus excludes.

The question of the relevance of the *Oresteia* in relation to the potential structuring of female imaginaries is more complex. If the *Oresteia* is another structural constellation of phantasies belonging to the male imaginary, then how could it possibly function to symbolize a so-called female specificity/imaginary or genealogy?

The initial point about the Oresteian myth with regard to the question of theorizing a maternal structural genealogy is that, unlike the Oedipus myth, this one already represents mother-daughter structures. Additionally, in the *Oresteia, every* aspect of the action is generated or initiated by female figures. Structurally, the narrative is anomalous in that it is driven exclusively by female activity/will. Artemis, the goddess of hunting, orders Agamemnon to sacrifice Iphigenia at the beginning of the war with Troy, which is fought because of the adventures of Helen. Clytemnestra murders her husband to avenge her daughter. Electra urges Orestes to commit matricide. The female Furies drive Orestes to seek help from the goddess Athena. Athena sets up the court of justice and enables Orestes' acquittal through her determining vote. Every point of narrative development is achieved through the intervention of a female mortal or divinity. This is significant not only because of the numerous representations of active feminine subject positions but also because the myth positions the female protagonists against each other, thus representing a heterogeneous femininity that is far from harmonious. The representations of conflicts between the female positions means that matricide can be considered from the vantage of not just one daughter but four—if you include Athena as a daughter responding to the problem of matricide.[8] The myth thus structures a complex constellation of phantasies between women on both the vertical and lateral axis and in this way does not limit or fix these psychic relations to one particular model. Further, because of its complexity, it moves beyond the tendency either to idealize or to denigrate the relation.

The *Oresteia* allows matricide to be considered in relation to the daughter(s) as well as the son and the mother to be considered as both murderer (aggressor/subject) and murdered (victim/object). The crucial point, however, is that Clytemnestra is not the only murdered mother of the *Oresteia*. Metis, Athena's mother, haunts the *Oresteia* as the matricide that is hidden and unspoken, yet, as I shall demonstrate, this other matricide is disclosed precisely by the traces of the mechanisms of its exclusion from the manifest content of the myth. I suggest that the *Oresteia* can only be used to further the project of creating potential female imaginaries if we go beyond the analysis of its manifest content and work with what the "dream work" of the myth has succeeded in censoring.[9]

Decrypting Metis

The father can father forth without a mother.
Here she stands, our living witness. Look—
    Exhibiting Athena
Child sprung full-blown from Olympian Zeus,
Never bred in the darkness of the womb

—AESCHYLUS, *ORESTEIA*

Nowhere is the conflict between the sexes so violently depicted as in Greek myth. It is rare to discover a peaceful kinship relation. Our mythic imaginary remains a vivid and clamorous cacophony bearing witness to the psychic violence that underlies the constitution of the family, the social order, and human generation. The idea of a creative, complementary, and benign symbolic parental couple is nowhere to be found.[10] Instead, what is ubiquitous in our mythical heritage is the dramatization of the destructive dispute between the sexes over which sex has the power to engender. Phantasies of independent generation appear in myth as the most archaic and the most tenacious. The anxiety over the question of reproduction and the desire to appropriate and eradicate female generative power in favor of the male principle of agency and generative omnipotence forms a basic phantasy structure underlying the masculine mythic imaginary. Phantasies of male independent generation expressed in myth conceal within them the desire to subordinate the mother and appropriate her generative ancestry. Irigaray uses "matricide" as a term that describes these desires to subordinate or exclude the mother from symbolic generativity.

In discussing matricide as the concealed act on which our culture is based, Irigaray refers to the *Oresteia* as the founding matricidal myth: "The mythology underlying patriarchy has not changed. What the *Oresteia* describes for us still takes place. . . . The social order, our culture, psychoanalysis itself wants it that way; the mother must remain forbidden, excluded."[11] We can begin to see that there is a considerable slippage identifiable in the way that theorists define matricide. Irigaray, in the quotations cited above, moves swiftly from referring to the literal killing of the mother represented in the Oresteian myth to referring to matricide at the level of theory, where she describes the mother as being "forbidden" and "excluded." Likewise, Finzi refers to the "defeat" and "subordination" of the mother.[12] We are confronted with a plethora of different terms that are linked to matricide yet have different meanings. The conceptual problem of using matricide as a definition is not examined by the theorists who refer to the killing of the mother as a metaphorical/theoretical and social/cultural phenomenon. Consequently, we find a chain of related words that all refer to the murder of the mother but are not sufficiently differentiated. Matricide as represented by the murder of Clytemnestra in the Oresteian myth will quickly be rearticulated as "exclusion," "taboo" "obliteration," "annihilation," "defeat," "subordination," "seizure," or "appropriation," according to different theorists. The interpretation of the literal matricide (as represented in the myth) in metaphorical terms remains unclear when we observe how the meaning of matricide shifts not only from theorist to theorist but even within one theorist's work.

The metaphorical results of the interpretation of the literal matricide of the *Oresteia* have not been sufficiently thought through. Desiring the mother's exclusion, for example, is not the same as wanting to kill her, and neither is desiring to incorporate her the same as wanting to appropriate her generative function. It is crucial to point out this ubiquitous slippage since the question I address concerns postulating the meaning of matricide *in theory*. We cannot begin to conceptualize matricide before we have a more or less clear definition of what it is we mean when we refer to it. On the one hand, we have the matricidal myth that is equivalent to the

oedipal patricidal myth, and, on the other, we have the metaphorical interpretations, which are extremely variable. If patricide in the oedipal myth
has been interpreted as the name-of-the-father allowing for symbolic loss,
matricide in the Oresteian myth has not yet been translated into such clear
conceptual and theoretical terms.

Irigaray uses matricide loosely as a way of describing the mother's nonstatus under the current patriarchal organization. In order to move from
describing to theorizing, we need to think about matricide in relation to
its underlying cultural laws. In my argument, citing the murder of Clytemnestra as the descriptive reference point in discussing the place of matricide in the cultural imaginary and Western discourses will not suffice. I am
not using the term "matricide" as Irigaray uses it. Instead, I am attempting
to define the meaning of matricide in relation to its underlying prohibitive
functions, which, in my hypothesis, cannot be subsumed by the law-of-
the-father. Irigaray interprets matricide as a necessary but unacknowledged condition of the dominant patriarchy; in so doing, she announces
that dominant order as essentially pathological in its appropriation and
exclusion of the mother. In this way, Irigaray reads matricide into Oedipus,
and consequently it remains a descriptive term that indicates the process
of the relegation of the mother to the imaginary in the Freudian/Laca-
nian model. Matricide, then, for Irigaray is a term that functions to articulate a particular operation underlying the patriarchal order and thus
remains as a descriptive tool to further her deconstruction of the male
imaginary.

In order to arrive at a specific *theoretical* definition of matricide, I want
to discuss what I consider to be the prototypical patriarchal myth representing the obliteration and appropriation of the mother's capacities in
the service of the masculine project of the colonization of knowledge and
generative power. It can be read as a story of the origins of patriarchy. By
introducing the famous myth of Zeus's parturition into the discussion of
the *Oresteia,* I suggest that that an examination of the links between the
phantasy of male parthenogenesis and the phantasy of oral incorporation
will bring us closer to a theoretical understanding of the subordination of
the mother in Western discourses and the cultural imaginary. In analyzing
the myth of Zeus and Metis in relation to the *Oresteia,* I will argue that
we can reach a position from which to *theorize the cultural law underlying matricide* and so bring the term into theory. The myth is linked to and
anticipates the *Oresteia;* it provides us with a striking depiction of the male
phantasy of generative omnipotence and sets up the logic with which the
matricidal Oresteian myth engages and negotiates.

Athena, Zeus's daughter—born miraculously out of his head—will be the determining party in the "resolution" of the Oresteian conflict. It is she who will decide the fate of Orestes, the matricidal son, and in turn it is she who will declare that Clytemnestra, the murdered mother, will neither be mourned nor avenged. Athena, the literal brainchild of her omnipotent father, Zeus, has a very special relation to matricide. It is her birthright. That is to say, her unique status as her father's daughter, born from the head of the god of gods, came about through a brutal act of violence against her mother (Metis), whose name neither she, nor Zeus, nor Freud (who was very interested in Athena, as I shall discuss later) will ever mention. The myth runs as follows:[13]

Zeus took as his first wife Metis the Titaness, priestess of all knowledge and wisdom. In Hesiod's words, "Zeus lusted after Metis who did not reciprocate his feelings. In order to escape his advances, Metis changed into all different forms but was unsuccessful and was subsequently caught by Zeus and got with child." Before she gave birth to Athena, Zeus, "with slippery words, coaxed Metis on to a couch and there and then swallowed her whole. In his belly Metis then gave him council, spoke to him from inside of him giving him all her knowledge and wisdom."[14] A few months later, when Zeus was taking a walk, he was suddenly overcome with a most terrible pain in his head. From his roars of pain, the whole world shook, and finally his head split open, revealing Athena, who sprang from his head with a shout, fully armed. And that is the end of Metis. She is never heard of or referred to again. She will remain in the belly of Zeus, source of his knowledge and wisdom, incorporated and digested into the lining of his stomach.

In his comments on Zeus's incorporation of Metis the Titaness, Hesiod explains that "Zeus put her away inside his own belly so that this goddess should think for him, for good and for evil, then from his head, by himself, he produced Athene of the gray eyes."[15] Zeus achieves his power through rape, incorporation, and appropriation of the woman/mother. He cannibalizes Metis in order to rob her of her knowledge and wisdom, together with her reproductive capacity. From then on, she is silent and invisible, an internal source of power that Zeus will claim as his own. Her existence is obliterated so that not even her daughter will ever know of the maternal body in which she was originally conceived. Zeus, in his violent operation, succeeds in taking total possession of the (m)other, whose power he both envies and desires. His initial lust or desire for Metis quickly turns into aggression that results in rape, followed by incorporation. He moves the womb of Metis into his brain.

Incorporation of the mother and her subsequent disappearance/destruction form the process by which Zeus establishes his power. With the incorporation/swallowing of the pregnant mother, Zeus not only achieves the appropriation of the female reproductive capacity together with the "wisdom" of Metis but also effectively swallows and obliterates the mother-daughter relation. First, his incorporative act effects the merging of the mother into the daughter. Both mother and daughter are taken inside his body, such that Metis becomes infantilized: she now takes on the position of fetus inside the male womb/brain. The appropriated gestation achieves the fusion of the mother into the daughter with the final product of Athena. Through his incorporation of Metis, Athena is born the motherless daughter, who will never become a mother herself but will remain a virgin daughter forever: an asexual, aggressive virgin, veiled, armed, synthetic, all artifice, seduction, and defense, a femininity created from the mind of Father Zeus.

The myth of Zeus's parturition functions to foreclose the question of the scar of the navel, the one indelible mark of the connection to and disconnection from the original maternal body. Athena becomes the precious proof that the father is the prime author of identity. She will represent this grandiose logic/phantasy and devote her work to endorsing and institutionalizing it as law in her court of justice, as dramatized in the *Oresteia*. Unaware of the story of her own mother, Athena will condemn Clytemnestra and declare that the mother will not be mourned. The murdered mother will signify no loss, and Athena's culture will collectively deny that there has been any loss at all. It will become a buried loss that cannot be mourned, experienced, or represented. The name of Metis is shrouded in silence along with the eradication of the navel as a symbolic mark of the generative link to the mother. Eradicating Metis via incorporation functions to sustain the parthenogenetic phantasy on which Zeus's order is based. Athena, as Zeus's perfect abstraction, represents this radical divorce of the patriarchal sociosymbolic order from its roots to the flesh of the maternal body and the violence committed against the mother. Metis the Titaness is ransacked, raped, pillaged, and eaten. She will then be eradicated from representation in the moment that Zeus's order of democratic justice is established through his perfect creation: Athena and her court of law.

To demonstrate the significance of Zeus's incorporation for my argument, I want to reiterate Lévi-Strauss's point, discussed earlier, that in order to understand the meaning of one myth we need to explore its relation to others. The Metis myth is a matricidal myth that is inextricably related to the *Oresteia* yet is only visible in the latter through the figure of Athena, whose motherless status functions to secure her loyalty to Orestes. In this way, the Oresteian myth conceals within it the story of the incorporation of Metis. If we reread the *Oresteia* in relation to the myth of Metis, we are able to discover what I consider to be the defensive function of the Oresteian myth. That is to say, the Oresteian myth distorts and reworks the myth of Zeus's rape and incorporation of Metis in such complex ways that it functions to keep it concealed beneath its manifest content. The Oresteian myth, as I interpret it, conceals this matricidal myth of Metis as part of the desire of the masculine cultural imaginary that seeks to eradicate the process and the memory of the mother's exclusion.

The Oresteian myth, I argue, effects a type of censorship of the Metis myth for the purpose of consolidating and sustaining a paternal law that depends on the foreclosure of a generative matricide. Yet the myth, like the dream, reveals the traces of its censoring process through distortions, blanks, and alterations, which if analyzed can lead to the reconstruction of the original censored element. Rereading the *Oresteia* in relation to the myth of Metis serves to restore a vital link between these two matricidal myths, whose severance hitherto has resulted in an incomplete analysis of the Oresteian myth and, further, has led to the situation in which matricide becomes a nonconcept that cannot deliver its underlying structural law.

What is striking about the myth of Zeus and Metis is its representation of the violent primitive process of oral incorporation as the means by which what is desired and envied is appropriated and taken to be one's own. To demonstrate the significance of this incorporation for my argument, I refer to Abraham and Torok's distinction between incorporation and introjection. In their essay "Mourning *or* Melancholia: Introjection *Versus* Incorporation,"[16] Torok and Abraham identify incorporation as a phantasy and introjection as a process; both are psychic mechanisms that attempt to negotiate the loss of the loved maternal object. The psychic mechanisms of introjection and incorporation both pertain to taking something inside, but incorporation is not a process, for Abraham and Torok; it is a phantasy that blocks the possibility of transforming loss into symbolism. Incorporation defends against introjection. In the process of introjection, the loss of the loved object is acknowledged and mourned, allowing the loss to be converted into words. It is through the process of introjection that loss becomes generative. Incorporation, however, is a phantasy that functions to deny the fact that there has been any loss at all: "Failing to feed itself on words to be exchanged with others, the mouth absorbs in fantasy all or part of the person—the genuine depository of what is now nameless. The crucial move away from introjection to incorporation is made when words fail to fill the subject's void and hence the imaginary thing is inserted in the mouth in their place" (p. 128).

Incorporation, for Abraham and Torok, is the refusal to introject loss. The mechanism of filling the mouth with the object or "imaginary thing" functions to eradicate the idea of a void to be filled with words. Incorporation results from *"those losses that for some reason cannot be acknowledged as such"* (p. 130). In this way, the incorporated object is rendered unspeakable, unknowable, unable to be mourned or replaced with a substitute. Incorporation functions to deny loss and in this way forecloses the generative properties of mourning: "The crucial aspect of fantasies of incorporation is not their reference to the cannibalistic stage of development, but rather their annulment of figurative language. . . . Incorporation entails the fantasmic destruction of the act by means of which metaphors become possible: the act of putting the original oral void into words, in fine, the act of introjection" (p. 132).

The phantasy of incorporation functions in "the active destruction of representation" (p. 132). Torok and Abraham term the incorporated object the "anti-metaphor," that which destroys the "very capacity for figurative representation" (p. 132). This active destruction of metaphorization via incorporation is a phantasy that Torok and Abraham contend is characterized by a necessary secrecy: "Incorporation is an eminently illegal act: it must hide from view along with the desire of introjection it masks; it must hide even from the ego. Secrecy is imperative for survival" (p. 134). The incorporation of Metis becomes the secret concealed within the Oresteian myth. Metis becomes the "anti-metaphor"; she cannot be spoken of or speak—precisely because she is never lost or mourned (introjected). She cannot be replaced by another, she cannot create a generative symbolic loss, because she is taken inside, swallowed whole as the nameless imaginary thing, her alterity radically obliterated. She is neither absent nor lost. That is to say, she does not belong to Green's "Black and White" paradigm, which signifies an absent/present goneness, and neither does she belong to the "Red" paradigm, whereby a gone-forever loss is signified through a bloody lopping-off. Metis, the pregnant, swallowed mother who is not lost or mourned vanishes to the invisible inside. Her incorporation means that there will be no gap, no void into which a stream of symbolic products can flow, to stand in for and master her absence. Instead, this incorporated mother becomes irreplaceable: no substitute is possible. In this way, she will constitute the resistance to representation, to interpretation, to theory—eradicated from memory and history—the mute grounding from which the paternal metaphor with its sole claim on meaning takes off in all its (defensive) grandiosity.

Zeus's incorporation—the founding prototypical act of the patriarchal order—situates Metis, the pregnant mother, as the navel of thought, that is to say, the unknowable, the unspeakable: the antimetaphor/nonconcept that cannot be structured. Zeus, in his claim to generative omnipotence, manages to establish his power over the crossed-out no-name of the mother, whose incorporation ensures that no acknowledged loss will ever come of her disappearance and that the possibility of her symbolic ancestry is obliterated. The name of Metis signifies the eradicated; she is the limit of representation, the negative, the empty foundation of meaning—the point at which knowledge reaches its blindness.[17] The implications of this process for women's ontological status are profound. As Irigaray explains: "The problem is that, by denying the mother her generative power and by wanting to be sole creator, the Father, according to our culture, super-imposes upon the archaic world of the flesh a universe of language and symbols which cannot take root in it except as in the form of that which makes a hole in the bellies of women and in the site of their identity."[18]

The matricidal myth of Metis that is inextricably linked to the *Oresteia* is mysteriously overlooked, even by Irigaray. Irigaray has persistently argued that the mother is both unrepresented and unrepresentable under our present symbolic organization. The exploration of the Metis myth that I have introduced allows us to explore Irigaray's argument further and examine the reasons for and the mechanisms by which the mother is rendered unrepresentable. In identifying Metis as the incorporated object concealed within the Oresteian myth, we can examine the process by which the mother is positioned as the "anti-metaphor." Even myths such as the *Oresteia*, which manifestly appear to be representing the murder of the mother and its consequences, function (in complex ways that I will later interrogate) paradoxically to keep matricide as the nonconcept that cannot deliver a generative loss leading to the introjection of an underlying cultural law that does not refer to the law of castration.

In the cultural receptions of the mythical figure of Athena, it is Zeus's parturition that has received most attention, while the means by which Athena got into his head in the first place appears to be rarely referred to, although this is not because of any inaccessibility or obscurity of this part of the myth. In the "Rat Man" (1909) case, Freud states: "A great advance was made in civilization when men decided to put their inferences upon a level with the testimony of their senses and make the step from matriarchy to patriarchy. The prehistoric figures which show a smaller person sitting on the head of a larger person are representations of patrilineal descent: Athena had no mother, she sprang from the head of Zeus."[19] "*Athena had no mother,*" says Freud. The prehistoric representations of the establishment of patrilineal descent depict Athena's birth. The earlier part of the myth is banished, and Freud, who, as I describe below, took a significant interest in Athena, either does not know (represses?) or decides not to know (disavows?) the story of Athena's mother. When Freud states "Athena had no mother," he discloses the exact point at which he begins his momentous interpretation of Western culture: the point at which the perfect idea is born from the head of the father of fathers and the violence against the mother has been successfully transformed into the sterile silence of the "anti-metaphor." In her book *Tribute to Freud,* H.D., the American poet who was analyzed by Freud in the thirties, tells of an interlude in her interaction with Freud during which he showed her his precious collection of ancient statues. He picks up his statue of Athena, and (I quote H.D.), "'This is my favourite,' he said. He held the object towards me. I took it in my hand. It was a little bronze statue, helmeted, clothed to the foot in carved robe. One hand was extended as if holding a staff or rod. 'She is perfect,' he said."[20]

Athena is Freud's favorite—his perfect daughter created from the father's mind. Athena, like his brainchild, psychoanalysis, reveres the father as the prime author of identity and human generation. With Athena, Freud can forget the scar of the navel and can reinforce the effect of Zeus's founding incorporation of the mother *by not telling the whole story*. That is to say, Athena is "perfect" for Freud precisely because she represents the triumph over the mother yet simultaneously erases the nature of that triumph. In loving Athena, Freud will not know Metis. He will be dazzled by Athena's perfection and simultaneously blinded to the violence of her genesis.[21] To love Athena and to disavow the part Metis played in her creation is to hold to a parthenogenetic phantasy that the "motherless" Athena embodies par excellence.

It is not only Freud who overlooks the story of Metis. As I shall show in a later section, every subsequent psychoanalytic examination of the *Oresteia* repeats this omission and continues to confirm Athena's status as father's daughter. While Irigaray argues for the reexamination of the *Oresteia* as a myth that describes the matricidal logic that underpins our contemporary sociosymbolic order, she does not uncover the truly concealed matricide in the *Oresteia*. Instead, she concentrates solely on the already represented (manifest) murder of Clytemnestra that, in my reading, screens the founding matricidal myth of the incorporation, rape, and appropriation of Metis. Introducing Metis into the Oresteian myth allows us to work toward a more specific definition of matricide, namely, its relation to a male parthenogenetic phantasy.

In an interview concerning his work "The Dead Mother," André Green asks: "Why isn't there a dead mother like there is a dead father? The problem with the mother is entirely different. If we wanted to postulate the mother in a similar way, it wouldn't be the same; it wouldn't be a succession of mothers—the mother plus the mother of the mother etc."[22] It wouldn't be a maternal genealogy, Green says; that would not be possible, he implies. It is my contention that until we dislodge Metis from the position of "anti-metaphor" that provides the foundation of the paternal filial order, then it is true *there could not be a succession of mothers.* Green is right in his claim that "the problem with the mother is entirely different." To postulate the mother as part of a structural genealogy entails a complex strategy of restructuring our cultural imaginary. "Only myth," says Finzi, "allows us to glimpse what remains invisible in us."[23] Returning to the myth of the incorporation of Metis and tracing its relation to the Oresteian matricidal myth allows us to begin to piece together the omissions in our cultural imaginary and examine the complex relationship among symbolic laws, knowledge, and mothers. The Metis myth read in conjunction with the *Oresteia* allows us to rethink the cultural problem concerning the impossibility of knowing the mother and of the mother knowing herself as a subject with an unconscious, a subject of history, desire, ethics, and genealogy.

The Metis myth allows us to glimpse how the female generative capacity was (and continues to be) written out of our dominant mythologies and traces the process whereby the cultural laws underlying the maternal function are expelled from symbolic mediation in order to keep intact the male phantasy of independent generation. To return to Irigaray: "Yet it is not a matter of simply returning to the goddesses of the earth, even if this were in our power. We need to keep hold of them and establish (or re-establish) a social system that reflects their values, their fertility."[24] All we know of Metis, priestess of wisdom and knowledge, the only glimpse of her desire in the myth that remains after her radical exclusion, is that she resisted Zeus's advances, changing into all different forms in order to escape: we know about her *resistance* and *transformation.* Metis's fluidity, her capacity to change into different forms in the face of Zeus's desire to capture/fix/incorporate her, resonates with Irigaray's notion of a femininity that is always already becoming, that is to say, a femininity that is in constant movement/flux. Zeus's incorporation serves to banish the representation of such a psychocorporeal mobility and swallows up its indeterminate creativity/jouissance.

First, we need to "keep hold of" Metis and her capacities: resistance, fluidity, and transformation. Second, we need to rectify the Zeus-type operation that transforms her active (creative) political resistance into the immovable resistance/navel of thought. We need to allow her to have her (political) resistance rather than to embody the psychoanalytic notion of (pathological) resistance to interpretation and give her back her transformative capacity with all its concomitant phantasies of generation and becoming, which neither begins in gestation nor ends in childbirth but is "a creative act at every moment."[25] The mother's ethical role, her part in the unconscious transmission of cultural laws and prohibitions, has been systematically erased by patriarchal incorporative operations that are motivated by the phantasy of paternal parthenogenesis. Removing Metis from the position of navel of our culture (the unthinkable) and representing navel phantasies means to include the maternal body inside a symbolic field of representation. In this way, we work toward the possibility that the mother may be able to think about and represent her desire as a woman and as a mother, an ethical sexed social subject of desire, rescued from the invisible depths of Zeus's stomach. Only then will we be able to posit a viable model of a female genealogy, since there cannot be a succession of mothers until maternal subjectivity becomes a psychosocial symbolic reality whose underlying cultural laws are acknowledged.

If matricide is to create a generative loss that can function to transmit social bonds and thus cease to be the "anti-metaphor" or the nonconcept, then the process of the mother's sociosymbolic exclusion needs to be interrogated and reconstructed by finding the traces of the violence committed against her that still remain in our mythologies and our discourses. Before the mother can find her identity as a woman and give an identity to her daughter, she needs to disentangle herself from the imaginary incorporative act of theory and discourse that seeks to keep her as the mute ground of an order that denies her subject status.

Keeping Metis in mind, as we move through the labyrinth of our cultural imaginary to the Oresteian myth, we will witness a repetition of a matricide, condoned by Metis's daughter, Athena. As we enter the world of Aeschylus's Oresteian trilogy, we must hold in our minds this swallowed mother and watch how the daughter, Athena, cut off from her maternal origin, becomes the agent that sanctions and institutionalizes the phantasy of male parthenogenesis that depends on the annihilation of the mother. Athena will endorse the murder of the mother and exclude her from the polis, unknowingly repeating her father's crime and speaking in his murderous language. We must remember that Athena does in fact have a maternal genealogy. In reuniting Metis and Athena in our minds, we will heal the amnesia of Athena's maternal ancestry, which will allow us to reread the *Oresteia* in a different light.

6 ๑๏

The Blind Spot of Metis

MYTH TRANSMITS SECRETS as well as narratives, and these secrets become entrenched in and determine social organization and practice. The secret of Metis, Athena's mother, is transmitted with the Oresteian myth in the form of a silence or exclusion that functions to sustain the dominant symbolic organization that positions the maternal body as the limit of thought/representation. In this way, the *Oresteia*, as I read it, functions in the service of the antimetaphor by virtue of its concealment of Metis behind the manifest representation of Clytemnestra.

The *Oresteia* has the potential to allow us to analyze the very conditions from which it may be possible to theorize a maternal structural function based on a generative matricide that produces a different set of unconscious laws from that of the law of Oedipus/castration. A different set of laws will necessarily create a different organization of culture; reading the *Oresteia* via the Metis myth allows us to theorize a different unconscious structure, which in turn can lead to the possibility of the representation and symbolization of heterogeneous diverse structurings of the mother-daughter relation(s). But we can only use the Oresteian myth in this way if we read it in relation to the myth of Metis, which, in my argument, functions as the silent substratum of the Oresteian situation.

How can the Oresteian myth function, or what *use* can it have, with regard to the expansion of the psychoanalytic theorization of femininity and the structuring of potential female imaginaries? In the first instance, it is important to state what I am *not* asking of the *Oresteia*. That is, I am not looking for a myth that can uncover an uncontaminated "femininity" since I do not believe such a thing to exist. I am also not suggesting that through analyzing the mother-daughter structures available in the Oresteian myth women will be given an immediate and miraculous access to symbolic representations that will give them access to their specific desire. This would be to assume that the vicissitudes of the mother-daughter relation are all already symbolized in this myth and that it is just a matter of drawing attention to these structures in a kind of consciousness-raising gesture. There are no such assumptions underlying this project.

Instead, I am concerned with using the *Oresteia* to create a space from which different imaginary and symbolic products can at least have the potential to come into being. It is, in a sense, like embarking on what Anna O. (Freud and Breuer's first "hysterical patient") called "chimney-sweeping,"[1] but on the level of the cultural imaginary, clearing out or analyzing the content of the myth (the male imaginary) in order, first, to return the phantasies/projections to the masculine and, second, to identify the structures existing in the myth that can then be reworked for the purpose of constructing a different space or possibility for diverse imaginaries to come into being.

It is not a matter of merely pointing to Clytemnestra and promoting her as a symbolic mother since that would be a somewhat arbitrary move—I could as well point to Jocasta or Phaedra as other mothers that are symbolically represented in our mythic imaginary. The point is that these mythical mothers—Clytemnestra, Jocasta, Phaedra—are all aspects of a constellation of phantasy whose meaning has not been sufficiently analyzed. In my argument, they are to be interpreted as repetitions or screens that continue to conceal something unthinkable. In this way, they are not symbolic; rather, they symbolize the limit of thought or embody the point at which thought becomes blind. In a paradoxical way, these simulacra of mythical mothers function to represent the failure of representation, or, to put it another way, they function to destroy, erase, or defend against the psychic reality of the relation to the radically excluded mother, Metis. The represented dead mothers of our mythic imaginary are an obstacle to our thinking about the mother. As long as they remain intact, they prevent change by sustaining a phantasy structure that functions to defend against an unthinkable anxiety in relation to the violent incorporation and rape of the mother, sacrificed in the name of the father and the father's daughter.

Clytemnestra, in my reading of the *Oresteia*, functions to conceal the traumatic mise-en-scène of thought and patriarchal "civilization"—the incorporation of the raped and murdered pregnant body of Metis. The point about the murder of Clytemnestra is that *it is represented*, and thus the Oresteian myth, in its manifest form, allows matricide (and its justification) to be thought about in a digestible and bounded form. If, however, we are able to resist being satisfied by the manifest content of the myth while continuing to think about the complex relation *between* myths, what we find is that the represented matricide in the *Oresteia* serves to exclude or screen the founding matricidal myth (Metis) that must, for the maintenance of the dominant order, remain the navel of the symbolic, the absolute unknowable.[2]

I am arguing that what we are confronted with in mythological so-called representations of the mother and matricide is not the absence of representation but the *representation of the absence of representation*. Or, to put it another way, where representation should be, there are rigid phantasy structures or imaginary projections functioning in the service of defense rather than symbolism. Before we can even consider the possibility of new representations belonging to symbolism proper, we have to transform the antimetaphor (Metis) into an object that can be used for thinking. To do this, we need to analyze the simulacra of already "represented" mothers in their manifest form in order, first, to find out what they conceal (or are defending against) and, second, to diminish the defensive armor that these representations sustain in order to make way for a space for representations to emerge that are not in the service of the "anti-metaphor." In this way, Maria Torok's definition of the function of phantasy and myth proves useful for my argument: "I believe that phantasies like myths and religions exist solely to form a screen against a reality that is bitterly unpleasant and therefore unintrojectable. Phantasies use all their power of adornment to cover up the drama and dull its noise."[3]

The phantasies that exist in the Oresteian myth concerning matricide and the omnipotent mother serve to screen or conceal a reality that cannot be introjected and thus cannot be symbolized. Until we uncover (and therefore reduce) the power of the "adornment," we will be trapped, limited simply to repeating what the myth repeats by keeping the manifest Clytemnestra intact. In my own work with the *Oresteia*, then, Clytemnestra is *not* the dead mother who shall provide a maternal subject position or matricidal structural center. It is rather the destruction of Clytemnestra, as the adornment or phantasy, that is in question. Once she is dislodged as the screen that serves to cover up an unthinkable reality, we can begin to reconstruct that reality in a way that belongs to symbolic thought *proper*. In this way, my work with the Oresteian myth differs from that of Irigaray, who concentrates solely on the figure of Clytemnestra in her discussion of matricide and the *Oresteia*.

What I am attempting here is to instigate the transformation of the Oresteian myth from its present status as a symptom into a symbolic product proper. A myth acts as a symptom (on the cultural level) yet holds within it the possibility of the cure. In the same way, the dream functions (in the individual psyche) to conceal/censor the unthinkable thought, but by virtue of being dreamed it offers the potential for disclosing the unthinkable thought. Both the myth and the dream are at the same time conservative and radical, that is to say, they can function to prevent change through their power of concealment and yet can bring the possibility of change precisely through indicating that something is being concealed. In this way, I agree with Maria Torok when she writes:

> Myths are efficient ways of speaking by means of which some situation or other comes about and is maintained. We know how: by carrying out, with the help of their manifest content, the repression of their latent content. Myths, therefore, indicate a gap in introjection, in the communication with the unconscious. If they provide food for understanding, they do so much less by what they say than by what they do not say, by their blanks, their intonations, their disguises. Instruments of repression, myths also serve as a vehicle for the symbolic return of the repressed. Any study of myths, whether ethnological or psychoanalytical, should take this aspect into account.[4]

The Oresteian myth, to my mind, can expand and transform our symbolic frame only if we can go beyond its manifest content and begin to take apart the defensive phantasies that block the capacity for thinking and introjecting an unbearable reality in relation to the mother. Irigaray's reading of the myth remains on the level of the manifest, and for this reason she does not succeed in transforming the myth from symptom to symbolic structure. Consequently, Irigaray does not manage to use the myth as a tool that could contribute to the execution of her project of symbolic intervention. She uses the manifest content of the Oresteian myth to describe the symptoms of the masculine cultural imaginary. My own work with the myth aims to go beyond both the manifest and the descriptive, to move from the manifest to the latent and from the descriptive to the structural/theoretical.

It should now be clear that the characters as they appear in the myth are not my primary concern. It is not a matter of talking about "Electra complexes" or "Clytemnestra syndromes." The crucial point to reiterate is that if Metis is brought into the Oresteian frame as the concealed matricide in question, then the whole structure of the myth is necessarily altered. Bringing back or reintroducing an excluded element will necessarily shift and reorganize all the existing elements and their relations to one another. What it can mean to bring Athena and Metis together as the mother-daughter structure that has been so radically foreclosed will be my concern. It is my hypothesis that in bringing Metis back to the Oresteian myth, the whole constellation significantly changes and in so doing allows for the possibility of new ways of thinking, different possibilities, meanings, or outcomes, or, in Green's terms, "diverse structurings."

Psychoanalysis and the Blind Spot of Metis

The Oresteian myth has received scant attention from within psychoanalysis. Freud briefly mentions Aeschylus's trilogy in a footnote where he acknowledges it for its representation of the "transition from matriarchy to patriarchy" and indirectly in his various comments about Athena's birth.[5] The myth is known to Freud as one that charts the transition from one social order to the next, but he does not engage with the phantasies it may represent, and neither does he consider the problem of matricide that forms the organizing and determining structural center of the myth. The threads of this myth find their way silently into Freud's work—inasmuch as the disclosure of his attachment to Athena tells us that Freudian psychoanalytic theory takes as its point of departure the moment at which Athena has consolidated patriarchal and filial power in the final part of the last play of the Oresteian trilogy.

Melanie Klein's interest in phantasies surrounding the mother led her to reflect briefly on the *Oresteia* in a single unfinished paper, written just before her death, in which she uses the myth to illustrate the conclusions of her own work. Her reading is the most significant from within psychoanalysis, and there has been little discussion of it within psychoanalysis, despite the suggestive implications it contains.[6] Klein comments that "Aeschylus presents to us a picture of human development from its roots to its most advanced levels."[7] Going back to an older myth than that of

Oedipus is consistent with her concentration on earlier primitive phantasies than those described in Freud's oedipal model. As I will show in my detailed discussion of her paper, her use of the myth remains firmly within the Freudian paradigm. She uses it to illustrate the findings of her own theories while also somewhat paradoxically consolidating her loyalty to Freud. Klein did not use the *Oresteia* in an innovative way with regard to a feminist debate (she was not a feminist), but this does not diminish her interesting suggestion that the Oresteian myth may be relevant to psychoanalytic theoretical innovation. Her engagement with this myth at a mature stage in her professional life indicates her inclination to find another mythical structure to add to Oedipus. It would seem that she was seeking to find a parallel myth related to the oedipal patricide model that would effectively illustrate her description of primitive infantile unconscious phantasy in relation to the mother. The paper is unfinished, so we cannot know what she might have made of the myth if she had gone on to develop her first reflections.

My own use of the *Oresteia* both acknowledges and critiques Klein's reading with the aim of taking it further and marking out the Oresteian myth as an alternative structure signifying a different constellation of phantasies from that of Freud's Oedipus. I will also discuss more contemporary engagements with the *Oresteia* within psychoanalysis, found in the work of Luce Irigaray and André Green, reviewing and critiquing all three readings in order to distinguish my own approach to the myth from theirs, while also using their rich and often conflicting insights to build a theoretical setting/context or model from which my own distinct praxis can emerge.

Clytemnestra's Dream and the Paranoid Schizoid Position

She dreamed she bore a snake,
She swaddled it like a baby, laid it to rest
She gave it to her breast to suck
Blood curdled the milk with each sharp tug.

—AESCHYLUS, *THE LIBATION BEARERS*

Clytemnestra's dream of the newborn infant/snake devouring her breast could just as well have been the dream of Melanie Klein. The breast-devouring infant that Clytemnestra dreamed of anticipates the Kleinian construction of the infant driven by sadistic fury, devouring the mother's breast in phantasy. For Clytemnestra, this dream is an omen of the danger her own child is about to bring her. For Klein, the devouring infant was a psychic reality that she discovered through the analysis of very young children.

Melanie Klein claimed that her work should be seen as a continuation of the Freudian project. Though it turned out to depart from Freud's in radical ways, she never ceased to emphasize her loyalty to him. Klein's work takes up the most controversial and unresolved parts of Freud's later work, namely, the death drive and the role of the mother.

Innate destructiveness is the first experience of the Kleinian infant, who in the first months of life must resort to all sorts of complex mechanisms of defense against his/her own instinct for death. Development consisted of building defenses against this raging primitive hate. Thus death was given prime place in the primitive ego of the child. Klein then found that guilt, anxiety, and ambivalence, three concepts Freud had linked to the oedipal complex, were present far before the onset of the oedipal. The children she analyzed gave evidence of the existence of a cruel superego, intense anxiety, and persecutory guilt. The superego, then, could not be the heir to the oedipal complex as Freud had contended. It was the infant's relationship to the first object, the mother's breast, that provided the basis of the organization of his/her psychic life. With Klein, everything was moved backward. The breast took the place of the penis. The basis of subjectivity, rather than hinging on the entrance of the father, was constituted by an interaction between two things: innate destructivity and the mother/breast. It is here we must return to Clytemnestra's dream.

The devoured bleeding breast is the central motif of Clytemnestra's dream and the image that represents the essence of the object in Kleinian thought. That is, the breast is both gratifying and frustrating, comforting and feared, loved and hated. The relation to the breast is always already ambivalent. Ambivalence for Klein is the given condition of subjectivity, and the breast is the site at which this ambivalence is first worked out. It is the way in which the subject copes with the ambivalence that constitutes the major part of psychic life for Klein.

Primitive sadism reaches its height in the oral and anal phases, where the infant projects his/her hate on to the breast. This leads to phantasies of devouring the breast and later the whole of the mother's body. Overcome with hatred and envy of the breast/mother, the child phantasizes attacking the mother's body and stealing all the riches that s/he imagines it to contain. The body that the child is totally dependent on and is the source of all gratification and pleasure is destroyed in phantasy by the child itself. Unable to cope with his/her own destructiveness toward the thing it loves most, the child projects his/her sadism on to the mother, who now becomes the persecutory terrifying figure that wants to devour and destroy the child. The mother is now the feared figure, creating the most monstrous anxiety in the child. The introjected object then becomes so frightening it seems capable of annihilating the child. To ward off anxiety, the child in his/her earliest defense mechanism splits the object into a good part and a bad part. It is the first introjection of the persecutory maternal object and the subsequent defensive operation of splitting this object into a good part and a bad part that provide the basis for the primitive superego. This primitive superego is persecutory and savage in nature, consisting of the projected and introjected sadism of the child itself. It is this condition that Klein calls the paranoid schizoid position: paranoid fear of the devouring attacks of the mother and schizoid (splitting) defense mechanisms to cope with the anxiety generated.

Although Klein gestures toward the real, external mother, her central focus is on the phantasized mother. Further, the mother is always the object: the mother as subject with her own desire appears nowhere in Klein's work. While Klein gave us a mother-centered psychoanalysis, what we shall see is that her loyalty to Clytemnestra is precarious. Although we witness a shift from the father to the mother, matricide, it seems, is still a vital necessity.

Suffering Into Truth: Kleinian Catharsis and the Depressive Position

So far we have seen that in the first psychic position adopted by the child the picture is gruesome. The sadistic attacking child exists in schizoid mode, his/her prime motivation being to protect him/herself from the death instinct. S/he is in a condition of paranoid anxiety and defense. Love seems absent or irrelevant in the face of death. It is in the depressive position, however, that love plays a part and ambivalence and the dangers of aggression can be resolved. For Klein, resolution or truth can only be achieved through suffering and pain. And with this suffering comes wisdom. It is here that Kleinian theory comes to echo the philosophy of the Greek tragedians: "To have recognized and understood one's destructive tendencies directed at the loved parents makes for a greater tolerance towards oneself and towards deficiencies in others, for a better capacity of judgement and altogether greater wisdom."[8] The ability to suffer is a sign of mental health. Feeling pain is the first step in working through the paranoid schizoid position and entering the cathartic depressive mode. The primitive schizoid state is used to avoid or ward off pain. At this point, the pain is too overwhelming for the frail ego, necessitating splitting mechanisms. There is no pain, only defense. It is only when the child can cease splitting the object and hence his/her own ego that feelings are allowed to be experienced. The defensive child begins to be able to experience the mother as a whole person rather than a split part-object. The good and the bad become integrated; the object becomes whole. The child's ego is now strong enough to allow good and bad to meet. Ambivalence, rather than being denied through splitting, is now felt. The pain this provokes is both devastating and cleansing.

The child must now come to terms with the fact that the whole object, which is both gratifying and frustrating, is in danger from the child's own destructive tendencies. The introjected whole mother is exposed to the child's phantasized persecutors. His/her faith in its ability to protect the object is minimal because of the knowledge of his/her own sadism. This gradual suffering into truth entails a concern for the object, absent in the earlier schizoid mode. And with this concern comes guilt. Depressive guilt is of a different nature from the guilt of the paranoid schizoid position. In the latter, the guilt was experienced as persecution. It generated the fear and anxiety that urged the need for mechanisms of defense. It was guilt without insight. Now that the object is whole and the child has realized his/her lack of control over the object, the guilt s/he experiences is more like remorse. The child must face the fact that the object may be lost, that s/he cannot guarantee its safety. The loss of the object begins to be able to be experienced, and thus the child begins the painful process of relinquishing or mourning omnipotence. No longer resorting to schizoid defense mechanisms that function to deny the experience of loss, the child now has to confront his/her limits and begins to reposition him/herself in relation to the object that s/he can no longer control.

It is not simply the ability to feel pain and guilt that characterizes the depressive position; it is what that pain and guilt cause the child to do. Pain here is a motor for the mobilization of love and thus the next stage in development. The pain the child feels leads to phantasies of repairing all the damage it has done. Recognizing his/her capacity for destruction together with the feeling of remorse leads to the task of mourning, which in turn sets the way for the process of reparation. The child wants to mend the mother's body, to bring it back to the good state. This drive to reparation sparked off by depressive pain is vital in the future mental well-being of the child. Reestablishing the good object is the major aim of the depressive position. The strength of the love mobilized to carry out this work will depend on how far the child has allowed him/herself to experience the depressive pain. While it is unusual to describe Klein as an optimist (considering her relentless attention to the power of the negative and the irresolvable nature of coming to terms with loss), her seeming faith in the capacity for psychic reparation, evident in her reading of the *Oresteia*, marks her out as one.

As much as the depressive position seems the cathartic resolution of the struggle for development, however, it is crucial to reiterate that the boundaries between the paranoid schizoid and the depressive positions are not stable. Klein's using of the word "positions" rather than phases makes the point that oscillation between the two is inevitable. Regressions to the schizoid mode will be a constant danger. Defense may be used to ward off depressive pain, thus immobilizing love and stunting the important work of reparation. We are never safe from regression back to the paranoid schizoid mode; Klein's theory undoes any sense of completed psychic development. The primitive infant in the psyche is never totally surpassed, it may achieve some integration, but the psyche will periodically resort to employing its primitive mechanisms.

Klein's structure of development certainly echoes the structure of Greek tragedy: greed and destruction, followed by remorse and knowledge. The hero oversteps his mark (*hubris*), realizes the truth about himself, and then makes moves to repair and cleanse (*dike*). It is precisely this superimposition of her own account of the psychic positions on the structure of Greek tragedy that Klein practices in her "Reflections on the *Oresteia*." She relates the paranoid schizoid mode to *hubris,* where the child makes greedy destructive attacks on the mother's body, and the depressive position to *dike,* the suffering into truth, the relinquishing of the phantasy of omnipotence, leading to remorse, reparation, and integration. In her reading of the *Oresteia*, Klein finds Orestes' trajectory to represent the successful working through of her positions. For Klein, the *Oresteia* depicts a final resolution where integration and reparation have been gloriously achieved. To read the *Oresteia* as a structure of development that allows for a final resolution is, however, to miss its complexities and to overlook its more obscure insights. In the same way, to read Klein as offering the paranoid schizoid and depressive modes as describing a linear progressive development is to mistake her use of the term "positions" for phases. Klein in her treatment of Orestes ceases to be truly Kleinian since she refuses to see what is split off and denied in the so-called resolution that she claims to find in Orestes. If Orestes has worked through and negotiated the depressive position, we may well ask—*whatever happened to reparation?*

To my mind, in Kleinian terms, Athena helps Orestes to ward off depressive pain by allowing/endorsing the paranoid schizoid mechanisms to remain intact. In other words, reparation is what is radically *foreclosed* in the *Oresteia*, such that the question of the dead mother and her Furies remains interminably and dangerously unresolved. For Klein, matricide can only work, that is, deliver, if it is followed by reparation. Contrary to Klein, the *Oresteia*, as I will argue, describes a psyche and a culture wherein reparation is a distant country as far away as health.

7

Melanie Klein and the Phantom of Metis

K LEIN APPLIES HER theory of development to the character of Orestes, showing us the symptoms of the various stages of working through the positions. While she tells the narrative of development through Orestes, she also uses the other characters to show different symbolic roles. Klein uses Agamemnon, for example, to show an excess of hubris and the absence of guilt, pointing to regression to the paranoid schizoid position. Clytemnestra is used to symbolize the "bad breast," while Athena, for Klein, represents the reestablished "good internal object," the "good breast." I will return to this, but first I want to examine in more detail Klein's treatment of Orestes.

While Klein observes that Agamemnon shows no guilt over his actions, only persecutory anxiety (expressed in his fear of the gods), Orestes shows signs of guilt and a motivation to try and put things right. "This is why," Klein says, "I believe, in the end Athena is able to help him."[1] The guilt Orestes feels is symbolized by the Furies, who, for Klein, belong to the anal and oral sadistic phases. They are deformed part objects who are also female, and their persecution of Orestes causes him to descend into insanity. In Euripides' play *Orestes,* dealing with the period of time between the matricide and the court case, we are shown explicitly that the Furies symbolize an extreme disturbed mental state:

Mother! No, no! Don't set them at me
I implore you—
These female fiends with bloody faces
wreathed in snakes!

They have dog jaws and gorgon's eyes;
They'll kill me—priestesses of hell, dread goddesses.[2]

When Menelaus asks Orestes what disease it is that ravages him, Orestes answers: "Conscience. I recognise the horror of what I did."[3]

The state in which Orestes falls after the murder is what Klein calls the transition between the paranoid schizoid and the depressive position, a stage when guilt is experienced as persecution. It is the fact that Orestes shows signs of wanting to cleanse himself of his crime and return to his people that allows him to pass through to the depressive position: "These intentions point to a drive to reparation which is characteristic of overcoming the depressive position."[4] Orestes, then, has suffered into truth, his guilt has mobilized the drive to reparation, and it is this that breaks the vicious circle of crime and punishment. Orestes has supposedly reestablished his good internal object, while the Furies have been transformed into the Kindly Ones, that is to say, the primitive savage persecutory superego has given way to a milder, more benign, protective, and mature superego built around the good object (Athena). The circle of destruction has come to an end, and, for Klein, it would seem that they all lived happily ever after: "My interpretation would be that guilt and the urge to make reparation, the working through of the depressive position, breaks up the vicious circle because destructive impulses and their sequel of persecutory anxiety have diminished and the relation to the loved object has been re-established."[5]

Klein reads the play as a perfect rendering of her theory of development. Everything seems to fit into place. Yet toward the end of her reading, Klein comments briefly on the myth's depiction of the profound difficulty in achieving psychic unity, equilibrium, and peace. She acknowledges the crucial point in the *Oresteia* where the final vote for and against Orestes is split equally down the middle: "The opposing votes show that the self is not easily united, that the destructive impulses drive one way, and love and the capacity for reparation in other ways. Internal peace is not easily established."[6] The inaugural case in Athena's court does not result in a majority vote. The jury is split down the middle, so Orestes is trapped, he can go nowhere; still hounded by the Furies, still with his mother's blood on his hands, he stands before the court of justice *but with no final judg-ment:* his development is arrested. The split court mirrors the internal state of his mind.

The Oresteian myth offers no easy solution in its powerful depiction of ambivalence in relation to matricide, disclosed through the split court. But Athena has the decisive vote and is unique in her lack of ambivalence in terms of where her loyalty will lie. With a lucid candor she declares:

> My work is here, to render the final judgement.
> Orestes,
> I will cast my lot for you.
> No mother gave me birth.
> I honour the male, in all things but marriage
> Yes with all my heart I am my Father's child.[7]

A majority of one, and the case is closed. Orestes walks free crowned with laurels. A close call, but, for Klein, the "good breast" has won, and life has triumphed over death. While she recognizes the significance of the split vote in indicating the tenacity of psychic conflict, she nevertheless accepts Athena's solution with a surprising ease. Athena is, in Klein's reading, the "good breast" carrier of the life instinct, as opposed to Clytemnestra, the "bad breast" carrier of the death instinct.[8]

What does it mean to read Athena as representing the "good breast" in the light of her chilling justification, "no mother gave me birth"? Only the "father's daughter," implies Klein (echoing Freud), can bring peace and civilization—only the father's daughter is perfect. And Klein, like Freud, is seduced or satisfied by Athena's lie, "No mother gave me birth"—the great lie or misrecognition that has reverberated through the centuries again and again, wiping Metis out of the picture. If Clytemnestra is the dead mother of the *Oresteia,* Metis is its phantom, but Athena's logic is one of manic denial:[9] *There is no debt to pay to the mother; there was never any mother, anyway.* Love, guilt and reparation are not part of her repertoire. She is more familiar with the tactics of omnipotent coercion, denial, and splitting, as we shall soon see in her shrewd manipulation of the Furies. But Melanie Klein perceives a benign Athena who fosters reconciliation and integration.

It is fascinating that Klein, the major psychoanalytic theorist of negativ-ity, was able to see in Orestes a successful resolution. Reading Klein, it is rare to find any sense of the psyche's capacity to resolve primitive psychic conflict completely. Rather, her emphasis on innate destructivity precludes any notion of a subject free from the threat of return to the paranoid schizoid position. Her paper on Orestes, however, reads very differently from all her earlier work. Klein, whose theories suggest that psychic equilibrium or integration is always under severe threat from internal persecutors, strangely enough believed that Athena could finally bring peace, that internal psychic war could give way to stable psychic resolution. Major psychoanalytic theorist of the psychic relation to the mother, Klein, in one of the last papers she wrote, kills off the mother she had so powerfully resurrected. At the end of her life's work, Klein makes her final gesture to Freud by joining him in his love of Athena, the "father's daughter," whose work to obliterate the debt to the maternal body functions to sustain the amnesia surrounding Metis and so keeps operative the male parthenogenetic phantasy. The only convincing way I can understand Klein's treatment of Athena is to infer that Athena serves to reconcile Klein to Freud and helps her avoid the hostility (in the psychoanalytic "family") that she feared in digressing too radically from the father of psychoanalysis.

Klein's engagement with the *Oresteia* discloses her attempt to consolidate a psychoanalytic model that departed from Freud's. In a sense, it could be argued that she saw in the *Oresteia* a structure that could frame or theorize her clinical observations where Oedipus could not. In moving to a different myth, Klein was risking an explicit dissent from Freud— something that she constantly wished to avoid or else felt a need to deny. It is as though her coming to the *Oresteia* was the final move that could potentially set her overtly apart from Freud, yet she did not/could not take it that far. That is to say, Klein's work, despite her frequent protestations of loyalty to Freud, did take psychoanalysis in a different direction and into a different register from Freudian psychoanalysis, and her innovations led to different conclusions that are often not reconcilable with Freud's.[10] The controversial discussions held at the British Psychoanalytic Society in the years following Freud's death were concerned precisely with this question of Klein's divergences from Freud: "Was her work a continuation of psychoanalysis, the main lines of which had been first formulated by Sigmund Freud, or were her contributions based on such different assumptions that she could be considered as diverging from Freud's basic hypothesis enough for it to be said that she was founding another school of psychoanalysis, rather as Carl Jung had earlier?"[11]

Despite Klein's apparent dissent from Freud's "basic hypothesis" (castration), she still maintained the oedipal model as the dominant framework. Mitchell's critique of the Kleinian and post-Kleinian continual reference to the oedipal complex without attention to castration indicates that what Klein failed to do is to produce an adequate alternative structure that would firmly demarcate her theories from Freud through use of a different myth.[12] That she was beginning to engage with a different and *matricidal* myth is evidence that such a move was not inconceivable. But at the last moment she resorted to the father in making Athena (mouthpiece of the father who has murdered and appropriated the mother) represent peace.

In this way, what Klein did was to provide a powerful description of phantasies related to the mother yet without a structural model that would work to underpin a theoretical tradition wherein castration was not the organizing center/hypothesis. To do this would certainly have set her up as representing a dissenting school from that of Freud, and it is a move that she did not make, despite hinting at it in her last paper, on the *Oresteia*. Consequently, Klein's work had to be contained within the oedipal model despite the fact that it was often inadequate in relation to the phantasies she described. Klein did not use the Oresteian myth to theorize the mother whom she had so ceaselessly tried to bring onto the psychoanalytic stage. Instead, she joins Athena in her celebration of the obliteration of the mother, as if finally giving up the burden and strain of occupying the position of the rebellious daughter who has her own mouthpiece that speaks of the mother.[13]

Melanie Klein, Athena, and the Phantom of Metis

Klein's interpretation of Athena as the agent that allows for the capacity for reparation is, to my mind, the most puzzling moment in her essay. This is not only because my own interpretation of the myth differs so radically from hers: where Klein sees reparation in the *Oresteia*, I see its foreclosure. Instead, it is puzzling because of the striking and somewhat bizarre contradictions that Klein presents in her particular comments about Athena. What I want to suggest here is that Klein did *not* quite manage to sustain her attempted loyalty to Freud through keeping Athena "good" and that, given her specific receptivity or attunement to phantasies surrounding the mother, she was not so successful in her capacity to defend against the return of the secret of Metis. While Athena's mother, Metis, is never mentioned in Klein's text, we can find traces of the process of her exclusion at a particular moment in Klein's argument, a moment where, as I shall argue, her whole line of reasoning fractures, and the reparation that she so vehemently wants to find in Athena turns out to represent the very conditions of its failure.

What I want to pursue here is my argument that the Oresteian myth transmits a secret/concealed matricide that successive readings continue to keep intact or reproduce. The transmitted secret has an effect, "the phantom effect," theorized by Torok and Abraham in their work on "transgenerational haunting," that leaves traces of the incorporated trauma. Torok and Abraham's contribution to Freud's metapsychology concerns an attempt to account for or expand Freud's concept of phylogenesis: the idea of "archaic heritage" whereby the experiences of earlier generations are unconsciously transmitted to successive generations. The concept of the "phantom" attempts to describe a process whereby a subject inherits a secret belonging to an unknown ancestor. This inherited secret is received by its host as a gap in consciousness, or, in Abraham's words, a "crypt" in the psyche, from which the "phantom" exercises its haunting: "Let us note that the phantom is sustained by secreted words, invisible gnomes whose aim is to wreak havoc, from within the unconscious, in the coherence of logical progression. Finally it gives rise to endless repetition and, more often that not, eludes rationalization."[14]

The words used by the phantom to carry out its return "point to a gap, they refer to the unspeakable." In this way, the haunting of the phantom manifests itself in cryptic linguistic constellations that function to fragment and disrupt the psychic equilibrium and rational thought in the subject, who has no conscious knowledge or direct experience of the trauma suffered by the ancestor. Abraham comments: "It is crucial to emphasize that the words giving sustenance to the phantom return to haunt from the unconscious. These are often the very words that rule an entire family's history and function as the tokens of its pitiable articulations."[15]

While Torok and Abraham's theory evolved initially as a clinical tool, it has implications beyond the analysis of the individual and can be most convincingly applied to cultural phenomena. If we accept the definition of myth set up in part 1, wherein myth is inextricably concerned with the transgenerational transmission and structuration of the (male) imaginary that in turn determines or effects the organization of sociosymbolic bonds, it is also necessarily involved in the transmission of secrets, gaps, and omissions. In this way, I want to use the theory of the "phantom" in order to explore the transgenerational process through which the effects of a culturally transmitted incorporated secret surface in myth, and readings or receptions of myth, which in turn affect the organization of the social, symbolic, and political world. As Nicholas Rand contends: "The idea of the phantom has implications beyond the study of individual psychology or even familial psychology. Aspects of this concept have the potential to

illuminate the genesis of social institutions and may provide a new perspective for inquiring into the psychological roots of cultural patterns and
political ideology."[16]

I will now show how Klein's paper on the *Oresteia* is subject to the work
of a phantom. I will argue that the "nescience" of Metis appears in her text
in the guise of a particular word,[17] a word that powerfully disrupts the logical progression of her argument and brings to light the effects of the secret
or phantom that is entombed in the myth and is in turn entombed in subsequent readings of the myth. In detecting the effects of the phantom, we
come closer to dispelling the secret and in that way rescue the myth and
receptions of it from unwittingly and endlessly repeating the transmission
of a gap in consciousness.

I focus on the following paragraph in Klein's essay in this attempt to
demonstrate the unthought or unthinkable element in the *Oresteia* that
has never, hitherto, been analyzed: "We have seen Athena in many roles;
she is the mouthpiece of Zeus and expresses his thoughts and wishes; she
is a mitigated superego; she is also the daughter without a mother and
in this way *avoids* the Oedipal complex. But she also has another and
very fundamental function; she makes for peace and balance . . . symbolically representing the *avoidance* of hostility within the family. This atti-
tude expresses the tendency toward reconciliation and integration" (my
italics).[18]

Athena's motherless status means, for Klein, that she has avoided the
Oedipus complex and in this way brings peace, reconciliation, and the
avoidance of hostility within the family. Klein's diagnosis of Athena as
having avoided the Oedipus complex (by virtue of her unusual birth) is
provocative and suggestive because we begin to get a glimpse of Klein's
hinting at a more complicated reading of Athena. Yet she does not elaborate on this point and instead goes on to speak of Athena as representing
peace and balance, leaving the whole question of what it means to avoid
the Oedipus complex suspended.

"Avoid" is not a psychoanalytic or clinical term. It is extremely vague
in this context and has no place in Klein's system. To come across Klein
using this word is immediately jarring to the reader, who has necessarily
had to become accustomed to her unrelenting use of densely technical
language. Yet when discussing Athena, she suddenly lapses into ambiguity
by her peculiar choice of the word "avoid." How are we to interpret this
term? How does it relate to the more specific psychoanalytic terms that
it hints at, such as denial, disavowal, repression, resistance, foreclosure,
phobia—all of which have different and highly specific meanings relating

to particular psychic (pathological) structures? And, moreover, what is the significance of Klein's uncharacteristic resource to a generic term like "avoid" that belongs outside of the language of psychoanalysis?

In my thinking, this momentary leap out of clinical terminology, at this particular point in Klein's text, has enormous significance that warrants close analysis. It is, so to speak, the fault line in her text, the point at which the whole argument begins to fragment, disclosing Klein's acute ambivalence and conflict with regard to Athena and further with regard to her relation to Freud and the Oedipus complex and, finally, to the phantom of Metis. It is my contention that an unconscious conflict is compressed within this one word, "avoid," which would disrupt and erode the whole foundation of Klein's interpretation of the *Oresteia*. The word "avoid" in the context of Klein's text functions as a rupture or an opening through which the phantom of Metis returns.

Klein's use of the word "avoid" initially discloses her intention to keep Athena free of the pathologizing language of the clinic. While her whole paper on the *Oresteia* is full of clinical terminology, with most of the characters being analyzed in technical terms describing their particular pathologies, Athena escapes being subject to such diagnostic language and consequently achieves immunity from being pathologized. Klein manages to keep Athena "good" by *avoiding* subjecting her to clinical language. She simultaneously implies a most severe pathology in Athena, however, by saying that Athena avoids psychosocial reality (the Oedipus complex). In other words, the "good object" fails to fulfill the conditions of sanity that Klein elsewhere never fails to stress.

My own interpretation is that speaking of the "avoidance" of the Oedipus complex can only mean that Athena is immune from conflict and immune from desire—outside the circuit of the human passions. In this way, by virtue of avoiding, she is *devoid* of love, hate, and sexuality, knowing neither pleasure nor ambivalence, neither guilt nor shame. To my mind, Athena resembles a psychic state of aphanisis.[19] That is to say, she is much closer to death than life, much closer to the bad breast than to the good breast, in the service much more of annihilation than desire. Additionally, if we hold to the consensus established across all psychoanalytic schools that the Oedipus complex functions as the mechanism through which the socialization of the subject is achieved, then to avoid the Oedipus complex is either to refuse entrance into sociosymbolic reality and therefore embrace psychosis or it is to be nonhuman. Yet Klein maintains that Athena represents the "good breast" and the mitigating superego, in the service of the life instinct and the integration of reality.

It would be possible to interpret Klein's words as implying that Athena avoids oedipal and depressive negotiation through a manic denial of the mother, of guilt, pain, and conflict, and creates her law, her determining judgment, on the basis of that denial, with its concomitant splitting processes. But in her use of the term "avoid," Klein in turn avoids this interpretation (which would place Athena firmly in the paranoid schizoid register) and instead suggests that if you do not have a mother, you do not have an Oedipus complex: "She is also the daughter without a mother and in this way avoids the Oedipus complex."[20] Rather than saying that Athena is *deprived* of an Oedipus complex since she is deprived of a mother, Klein chooses to speak in terms of avoidance. To avoid something is to go out of one's way in order not to confront something; it is an active process of sidestepping that is associated with phobia. In fact, the only mention of "avoidance" in psychoanalytic literature, to my knowledge, is in relation to phobia: while "avoidance" is not a clinical term, its use in the description of the clinical concept of phobia links it to anxiety and defensive structures.[21] So Klein, instead of using the structure of deprivation in relation to Athena, implicitly gives her a phobic structure. In her discussion of the phantom, Maria Torok describes its relation to phobias: "The alien nature of the phantom resembles the indirect characteristics of phobia. For although phobic subjects actually speak and behave with the help of their own psychic apparatus, their phobias come from elsewhere. Phobia's stated intention of speaking amounts to no more than the impenetrable opacity of its genuine speech. However, the opacity does yield when specific phantoms are invoked; hence the concept of the phantom appears to be the key in understanding phobias."[22] I suggest that through using the word "avoid," Klein's text moves unconsciously toward phobia. In her avoidance, then, Athena discloses a phobia, and Klein begins to get nearer to the phantom of Metis, the split-off element in the *Oresteia*, the concealed object of Athena's phobia and, further, of Freud's phobia.

Klein makes a strikingly contradictory statement by linking Athena both with the good object and also with the process of avoidance. Athena can be the good object only in as much as she *avoids*. She functions to produce integration and reconciliation because she has no mother, which in turn allows her to avoid the Oedipus complex, giving her the capacity to represent integration. How can integration depend on avoidance, since in avoiding something (especially the Oedipus complex), one actively evades something, that is to say, one is intent on not letting something inside? Klein paradoxically seems to make integration depend on a figure who fails to integrate.

The word "avoid" means to evade or to shun, and its etymological root is "void," that is, empty space, containing nothing, null, invalid. It is necessary here to cite the definition of the *verb* "void" in order to pursue my argument. Since Klein is using the word "avoid" as a verb, as what Athena does, we need to interrogate what it actually means to (a)void: Void: to make vacant, to empty, to, clear, to send out, discharge, emit, to make of no effect, to nullify. What I want to point out is that *in avoiding something, one is actively involved in the process of making something absent*. It is as if there were something inside that is then discharged, so that void means both empty space (as a noun) and emptying out (as a verb). A void is only a void because it was once full and subsequently is emptied. Expulsion, then, is integral to avoidance. It is an act of making something into nothing. In this way, Klein's use of the word "avoid" unwittingly ends up being extremely precise and accurate in relation to Athena's function. Unconsciously, Klein, with an incredible acuity, allows us to glimpse exactly what Athena represents: the process of voiding Metis, her raped and murdered mother.

If Klein did really want to keep Athena as the "good object," then she would not have included this strange and opaque sentence about avoiding the Oedipus complex. She takes this interpretation (if you can call it that) nowhere. It seems to have no significance to Klein's argument other than to disclose her unresolved and ambivalent thoughts about Athena. She could have easily left out the whole question of Athena's "avoidance" of the oedipal complex, which would have made for a much more coherent and straightforward argument. Yet she was compelled to say something about Athena's relation to her absent mother, compelled to tell us that Athena, in her mind, is associated with (a)void. And that this void (her absent mother) that Athena avoids, Klein, too, is trying to avoid, but in doing so she paradoxically conjures up the phantom of Metis. Metis, who, as we have seen, has been voided/erased, is brought back precisely by the word "avoid" that Klein uses in relation to Athena. In this way, the very word that was used in order to keep the repression of Metis in place gestures toward the repressed element. What we see here is a powerful demonstration of the ways in which language can function to bring back the very thing that it is attempting to conceal. Metis continues to find her way back into the *Oresteia* and into the psychoanalytic celebrations of her daughter, Athena. Metis, the phantom, comes back to haunt in the form of linguistic slips or negations. If Athena managed to tame the Furies and silence Clytemnestra's ghost, Klein was obviously not entirely convinced, despite her manifest declaration of Athena's victory. We will never know if Klein was aware of the story of Metis, and in a sense it makes no difference. The point is that Klein did not refer to Metis directly, yet Metis nevertheless surfaces in her text. Such is the work of the "phantom" that, in Torok's words, comes to represent "the interpersonal and transgenerational consequences of silence."[23]

Klein's relation to Freud via Athena, then, is not so straightforward as her reading of the myth may initially suggest. Receptive to manifestations of unconscious phantasies surrounding the mother, Klein at some level was able to receive the effects of a void encrypted within the representation of Athena. Klein did not know what this void was; she just knew that Athena "avoids" and thus goes some way, unknowingly, toward bringing Metis closer to consciousness. While Klein, like Freud, refused to know Metis consciously, the language of that refusal encrypts within it the concealed matricide that constitutes the unthinkable or unintrojectable trauma: the rape, murder, and incorporation of Athena's (a)voided mother.

8 ཉྫྷ

Metis in Contemporary Psychoanalysis

I must not miss the opportunity to make a structural study of a theme of particular concern to the psychoanalyst, that of matricide.

—ANDRÉ GREEN

NDRÉ GREEN'S BOOK *The Tragic Effect: The Oedipus Complex in Tragedy* contains a significant contemporary psychoanalytic reading of the *Oresteia* of particular relevance to the discussion here.[1] This work was written considerably earlier than "The Dead Mother" and "Conceptions of Affect," essays that I have already discussed. While it is not my intention here to trace the development of Green's thought, it is of particular interest to this discussion to observe that Green is one of the few psychoanalysts to have written in some depth about the *Oresteia;* he is also one of the major theorists on whom I draw in order to posit the idea of heterogeneous structuring processes. Green's interest in matricide led him initially to consider the Oresteian myth. Years later, he returned to the theme of matricide in "The Dead Mother" yet did not bring the *Oresteia* into the later discussion. While Green questions the theoretical status of matricide in his "Dead Mother" essay and draws attention to its occlusion in psychoanalytic theory, he does not attempt to reconsider or incorporate his earlier work on the Oresteian matricidal myth in the light of his later theoretical exploration of the status and function of matricide in psychoanalysis. To undertake a parallel reading of Green's early essay on Orestes together with his later work "The Dead Mother" reveals a broken or overlooked connection in Green's thought. Green's theoretical innovations (discussed in part 1), bringing the question of matricide into psychoanalytic discourse in the context of positing more than one structural model, have hitherto been read in my argument as holding great potential for the feminist context with which I am concerned. His relevance to this discussion now becomes even more pertinent when we see that, predating these theoretical interventions, he was drawn to make quite a comprehensive reading of the *Oresteia*. It could be said that this early interest in the Oresteian (matricidal) myth anticipated his later return to the theme. Yet he himself does not retrospectively identify this connecting strand. It is of great importance to make this connection since my own approach is to work with the Oresteian myth in the theoretical context of Green's notion of a symbolic made up of more than one structuring process. This is something he did not do himself, since his reading of the *Oresteia* was very much dominated by the influence of Lacan early in his psychoanalytic career. That is to say, his thought was not yet at the point where he was moving away from sole adherence to the structure of the dead father, and thus in the earlier essay he reads matricide only in terms of the function of the father.

Green comments that interpreting the *Oresteia* gives him the "opportunity to make a structural study of a theme of particular concern to the psychoanalyst, that of matricide" (p. 43) and goes on to contend that: "Oedipus and the *Oresteia* constitute essential fundamental modes in which the problematic of all tragedy—and perhaps of all human endeavour is situated. Other themes and tragedies are joined to the common trunk of those primal situations" (p. 37). His reading of the *Oresteia* is based on the premise that the Oresteian situation "represents the other side of the Oedipal complex" (p. 37), and he pronounces that the two myths are "complementary" and belong to the same structure:

> The Oresteian situation is the tragedy of madness, in which the subjective position is attained only through a break with the natural bond that unites the subject with the mother. It is a necessary break, and involves murder, but is constituent of the subject. . . . In the case of Apollo and Orestes, matricide signifies the liberation from maternal power and the promise of a second birth, rendering the subject liable to the power of the father—for this is what the purification of Orestes amounts to. In the murder of the mother, the motive of this crime is by no means the animosity towards her, if it exists: it is part of the necessary passage that he must cross in order to call himself the son of Agamemnon. To deprive Clytemnestra of life is first of all to fulfil this programme, which lifts the silence from around his father's name and opens up to Orestes the status of subject.

(P. 56)

Green's reading locates the manifest phantasy in the myth, concerning the son's relation to the mother, where matricide is a necessity in its instrumental function, liberating the son from the imaginary narcissistic relation to the maternal body and delivering him into the social symbolic world of paternal genealogical transmission. Initially, it would seem that Green's interpretation is firmly located within the Lacanian schema. Matricide is subsumed by the law-of-the-father so that Orestes' murderous act functions for-the-father or is a correlation of the paternal third element that breaks up the imaginary dyad and delivers him into the oedipalized world. In this interpretation, matricide has no meaning in relation to the mother but is a contingent structural element or an agent of the paternal law.

I want to highlight two aspects of Green's interpretation. First, he oedipalizes the Oresteian myth and through a structural comparison of Orestes and Oedipus concludes that they are complementary; together, he claims, they form a binary pair constitutive of the two sides of the oedipal complex. Second, it is possible to read Green's interpretation not just as a confirmation of the inevitability and necessity of matricide but also as an identification of the "psychosis" that inhabits the oedipal subject. That is to say, according to Green, the Oresteian situation is one of "madness," and he goes on to state that it is also an impossible and irresolvable situation. Orestes kills his mother and is purified and delivered into his paternal genealogy, but the presence of the Furies, for Green, confirms the fact that the break from the mother is an "impossible break": "Yet it is an *impossible* break in that the separation from the maternal image is followed by the instantaneous reembodiment and its resurgence in the psychotic delusion that restores it to its *inalienable* place" (p. 57; my italics).

Implicit in Green's comments is the suggestion that the madness of Orestes will forever haunt the son who must radically sever his attachment to the maternal body (through phantasized murder) in order to add his name to that of his father's. He will never be free of the threat of a descent into madness, that is to say, the cost of his access to paternal lineage is the perpetual warding-off of psychotic anxiety relating to the feared retaliating mother. The situation in which the son is caught, then, is that of negotiating a primal conflict in which he has to destroy the means by which he came into life in order to acquire his filial right. Green inadvertently brings to light the pathological phantasy structure, represented in the myth of Orestes, belonging to the achievement of masculinity. Orestes, it would seem, for Green, represents the psychotic part of Oedipus, that is, Orestes is "the most shadowy" and the most "hidden" side of Oedipus (p. 36), which is neither eliminated nor resolved but instead haunts and threatens the symbolic world and the supposedly oedipalized psyche.

While Green is not explicitly proposing here that Oedipus as a psychic structure is always threatened with failure, my own interpretation of his reading of Orestes means to suggest that such a trajectory is implied in his text. My reading of Green is undoubtedly conducted through an Irigarayan lens. Reading Green in the context of Irigaray's work helps bring to light Green's own attention to the cracks or fault lines in the manifest Lacanian narrative that he interprets on the surface of the Orestes myth. His treatment of Orestes goes beyond a purely Lacanian interpretation, and, in fact, by thinking Oedipus through Orestes, Green begins to expand the model in order to disclose how the symptoms of the Lacanian oedipal (male) subject are constructed, bringing his reading close to the conclusions of Irigaray's critique. Orestes allows Green to find a latent pathological psychic structure of masculinity that complicates and problematizes the mechanisms of oedipal law. While Irigaray uses Orestes to draw attention to the pathological structures of a culture based on an unacknowledged matricide, Green uses Orestes to acknowledge matricide as the nucleus of impossibility that can *never* produce the deliverance that it is supposed or promises to effect. Green asks of Orestes: "How is he to acquire his filial right, and add his name to his father's lineage, yet also destroy the means by which he came into life?" (p. 80). In this question, Green opens up the profound problem that an instrumental matricide necessarily creates. In identifying Orestes' dilemma, Green's reading converges with Irigaray's critique. That is, matricide cannot only be thought about in relation to the father because it will always leave behind or never resolve an acutely disturbed relation to the mother, to the original body, to the first birth. The second birth promised by the paternal law will never properly cover or repress the obliterated first birth, and the guilt ensuing from the matricidal crime will resurface in the form of an anxiety or madness that will create a kernel of paranoia at the heart of the second-birthed (defensively organized) subject. Despite matricide, *the mother will never go away, she will remain in her inalienable place,* since the debt to her body, as that which gave life, will follow Orestes around in the shape of terrifying Furies echoing his primal crime and infiltrating every vicissitude of his now destructive and highly ambivalent relation to the body of woman.

The necessity of matricide for the accomplishment of manhood is (for Green, as I read him) an impossible trajectory that results in the mother's reembodiment in the shape of psychotic hallucinations. That is to say, it cannot give access to a loss proper, leading to mourning, reparation, and symbolization. In killing off the mother in order to gain access to paternal lineage, there is no digestive process that would allow for the working-through of the necessary loss. Matricide as the mechanism of separation from the maternal body is so radical a severance that what results is the relegation of the murdered mother to the unconscious as a bad persecutory object that is liable to return and wreak psychic havoc in the shape of violent reembodiments or delusions.[2]

The implications are crucial. Now we can see clearly the structure of the law that Orestes is enacting: matricide = severance = deliverance. Yet we can also see the failure at the heart of that law, that is to say, there is no possibility of deliverance because there is no possibility of a loss that is mourned and subsequently represented. Instead what results is *embodiment as opposed to representation.* The maternal realm for Orestes is fixed in the "inalienable place" of the realm of imaginary, wherein the mother is terrifying, devouring and retaliating. She remains in this *"inalienable"* place; that is to say, she cannot be transferred, transformed, replaced, or symbolized but can only return in the concrete phantasmic embodiments deriving from psychotic anxiety. Matricide creates no metaphorical loss: Orestes will overvalue/idealize his father in a passionate manner, justifying his crime against his mother by declaring his loyalty to his dead father as the only way forward. That is to say, the dead father will allow him to enter into the progression or succession of his genealogy—but just so long as he does not look back. The act of looking backward carries with it an intense danger. Behind him, there loom the monstrous Furies, those vampiristic dread goddesses who want to suck him dry. Orestes looks toward his "second birth" in hope that this will deliver him into a world where the Furies will be stamped into the earth and silenced by his father's name. But while matricide will effect the severance, *it cannot deliver the masculine subject position:* the hands of the matricidal son may be purified by Athena's court, yet the son, like Lady Macbeth, will always be haunted by the invisible stain on his hands that no court or law can ever completely wash away. The very possibility of masculinity, then, relies on the various defense mechanisms used either to ward off this terrifying mother or to act out an aggressive mastering of her.[3]

Green's reading of the *Oresteia* does more than merely confirm the Lacanian logic that states that matricide is necessary in order to achieve symbolic functioning.[4] Green, like Irigaray, problematizes this assumption in stating that matricide produces a madness that will not go away rather than a loss that can be generative. That Orestes walks free from Athena's court, apparently purified from his crime, does not lead Green to conclude that all is definitively well. Adding his name to his father's will be Orestes' reward but at the cost of a precarious subjectivity based on the most primitive defenses, perpetually fighting against the return of the imaginary, murdered mother, who cannot be represented but can only appear in concrete paranoid embodiments. Implicit in Green's reading is the sense that the masculinity that depends on matricide does not quite work. The question that Green inadvertently raises opens up the problem of whether Orestes can really commit matricide. That is, can the dead mother be laid to rest, without the return of phantoms? Can the dead mother be mourned, or, more important, can she be introjected rather than incorporated/embodied? While Green does not actually pose these questions directly in this early essay, he insists that, despite matricide and the subsequent deliverance to the paternal lineage, the mother is restored to her inalienable place through the hallucinatory resurgence of her image as vampiristic phallic mother. Considering this, my own conclusion about Green's reading of Orestes—a conclusion possible only through a retro-spective reading of his early essay in the light of his later work on matri-cide—is that he considers matricide as *presence:* a severance that can only operate within the binary of absence/presence, appearance and disappear-ance. Matricide in the *Oresteia,* for Green, can only produce a persecutory presence, not a loss: the dead mother is embodied; she produces no gap. In this way, Green's notion of matricide as embodiment/presence as opposed to loss/representation comes close to my own formulation of matricide as incorporation. But Green's matricide remains firmly in the realm of description, because, without the Metis myth, the parthenogenetic male phantasy that is concomitant with the phantasy of incorporation or em-bodiment is not disclosed. In this way, Green's reading *describes* a phan-tom presence that points to the problem of matricide with regard to the creation of the "oedipalized" masculine subject but does not identify the underlying phantasy that renders matricide as presence in the *Oresteia.*

The problem of matricide that Green articulates provides a powerful challenge to the standard (Lacanian) position. Green, as I interpret him, uses matricide (inadvertently) to produce a critique of masculinity. In this way, his interpretation (although it has no explicit relation to a critique of patriarchy) converges with that of Irigaray, who states that "Oedipus is no doubt re-enacting the madness of Orestes."[5] Irigaray refers to the *Oresteia* to demonstrate her diagnosis of Western culture: that it is orga-nized around the crime of matricide, obscured and concealed by symbolic patricide. She leaves the myth once she has made that point, adding that the *Oresteia* is still extremely contemporary and that "what the Oresteia describes still takes place."[6] Thus Irigaray identifies the *Oresteia* as a constellation of phantasy that operates and organizes contemporary culture in the form of the male imaginary that has become law. Her use of the *Oresteia* serves to intervene into the logic of oedipal discourse. She relates the two myths to demonstrate her contention that matricide is what Oedipus has already committed and then subsequently represses:

> When Oedipus makes love with his mother, it will in fact do him no harm to start with, if I can put it that way. On the other hand, he will go blind or become mad when he learns she was his mother: she whom he already killed in accordance with his mythology, in obedience to the verdict of the Father of gods. This interpretation is possible but it never happens.... Hasn't the mother already been torn to pieces by Oedipus's hatred by the time she is cut up into stages, with each part of her body having to be cathected and then decathected as he grows up? And when Freud speaks of the father being torn to pieces by the sons of the primal horde, doesn't he forget, in a complete misrecognition and disavowal, the woman who was torn apart between son and father, between sons?[7]

Both Green and Irigaray's readings of Orestes function to bring to light the matricide that precludes successful oedipalization. Both draw attention to Orestes' subsequent madness and the presence of the Furies as signifying the failure of matricide as an agent for enabling Orestes' transition to the status of the subject. Neither Green nor Irigaray is convinced by Athena's apparent resolution wherein the Furies are transformed into the "Kindly Ones" who will protect the walls of the new system of justice. For Irigaray, the Furies represent the madness associated with matricide, the ghosts of the mother who will forever haunt Orestes and his culture; for Green, the Furies are evidence of the mother in her inalienable place, the bad persecutory *present* object sequestered in the imaginary. Athena's taming of (or repression of) the Furies is not satisfactory for either Green or Irigaray. The conversion of the Furies into their opposite will not suffice. The psychic violence or madness associated with matricide (represented by the Furies) will find its way into the oedipal subject. Athena's resolution results in pushing the Furies underground, but they will return as symptoms that will break out and point to the silent substratum of oedipal law. Unlike Freud and Klein, who revere Athena and are (manifestly) convinced of her methods of acquittal, Green and Irigaray remain alert to the problem of the dead mother, alert to the phantom presence that pervades the shadowy parts of the psyche, our culture, and our discourses, and are not duped by the phantasy of resolution that forms the core of Athena's law. Nor are they convinced by a cured absolved Orestes, triumphant and saved in his "second birth."

However, while matricide, for Green and Irigaray, creates a pathological presence, this presence has not yet been theorized. That is, the phantom presence of Metis surfaces descriptively in their readings of Orestes but eludes theorization. Green and Irigaray are primarily concerned with the manifest symptoms that the myth expresses but cannot interpret the latent material that produces the symptomatic presence or phantom effect that matricide delivers. This is because they are oblivious to the Metis myth that is encrypted within the *Oresteia.*

From within psychoanalysis, then, it is Melanie Klein, André Green, and Luce Irigaray who have paid some interpretative attention to the Oresteian myth, identifying in it living phantasies operating, for Klein and Green, in the individual psyche and, for Irigaray, in our cultural imaginary. That such different theorists come to this myth is understandable when we reflect that both Klein and Irigaray's thought focuses on the figure of the mother—though from radically different and often antithetical perspectives—while running through Green's thought is a preoccupation with matricide and its meanings. Klein tries to interpret the *Oresteia* as a Freudian, Irigaray uses it to critique Freudian and Lacanian theory from a feminist perspective, Green interprets the myth in order to uncover the impossibility of matricide and thus problematizes Lacan's law-of-the-father.

Klein's treatment of the *Oresteia* sets her apart from Green and Irigaray in that she merely *describes* Orestes' relation to the mother in her own theoretical terms. This results in reinforcing the structure matricide-severance-deliverance and thus takes us no further than the Freudian-Lacanian position. While Irigaray and Green use Orestes to challenge and critique Oedipus, Klein considers Orestes' development as complete and thus adheres to the model whereby the mother is excluded from the symbolic. For Klein, Orestes' murder of his mother, his subsequent madness, and his final acquittal represent the successful working-through of the paranoid schizoid and depressive positions. Orestes has overcome his primitive sadistic relation to his mother, has made reparation, and thus emerges as a fully integrated mature subject. Matricide, for Klein, is not only a necessity; it is also *possible* and functions to free the subject into the psychic landscape of the depressive position where primitive psychic defense mechanisms of splitting and projection cease to dominate the workings of the mind. The transition of the Furies into the Kindly Ones, for Klein, marks the transition from the paranoid schizoid to the depressive position, and thus she reads the resolution of the *Oresteia* as depicting an optimistic picture of a psyche or a culture that has reached its most advanced level. In this way, it would seem that we should leave Klein here, since her reading of matricide provides no challenge to the standard position.

If, however, we go beyond Klein's particular essay on Orestes but keep hold of her theories, what we see is that there is another possible Kleinian interpretation of the myth that can contribute to a further articulation of the problem of matricide. It is my contention that Klein was unusually optimistic in her reading of Orestes, and what I will continue to argue is that, in Kleinian terms, Orestes in fact never reaches the depressive position and instead the *Oresteia* depicts a psyche or a culture operating in a primitive paranoid-schizoid mode wherein neither reparation nor integration has been achieved. While in this reading, the *Oresteia* represents matricide as that which precludes both oedipalization and the achievement of the depressive position, this is not where the story ends. Rather than resigning ourselves to the apparent fact that the dead mother cannot be mourned and in turn cannot be symbolized or lost, we need to employ a different model from which to rethink the relation between matricide and loss in the *Oresteia*, in order to come nearer to a structural theory of matricide.

Green and Irigaray do not use Kleinian terminology to describe the pathological solution that matricide delivers. We can, however, understand their descriptions of this pathology in Kleinian terms: as the inability to achieve depressive mourning. For both Green and Irigaray, matricide cannot produce a generative loss and cannot function as a mechanism that allows for a successful separation from the mother, who remains in her inalienable place. In this way, what is foreclosed in matricide is loss. If there is no loss, then, for Green and Irigaray, there can be neither symbolism nor genealogy and, for Mitchell, as I noted earlier, there can be neither structure nor theory. In Kleinian terms, symbolism depends on a successful mourning of the lost maternal object. Symbolism, in the Kleinian schema, is not used to deny loss but rather to overcome it. This working-through of loss through symbolism is dependent on reparation that can only be achieved if there is a capacity for depressive mourning. In Hanna Segal's words, "It is only if the dead person can be symbolically introjected and the internal object is symbolic of the lost person, that internal reparation necessary to overcome mourning can be achieved. . . . It is only with the advent of the depressive position, the experience of separateness, separation and loss, that symbolic representation can come into play."[8]

We have seen that the dead mother(s) of the *Oresteia* are not symbolic representations; they are concrete embodiments or psychotic hallucinations, ghosts or Furies or undead phantoms that threaten the psyche as bad persecutory objects fixed in the imaginary. There has been no symbolic introjection; rather, there has been pathological incorporation that, according to Torok and Abraham's theory, precludes mourning and symbolization. In this way, Clytemnestra can be read in Hanna Segal's terms as an example of "concrete symbolism," which she considers to be "at the root of pathological mourning" and prevails when paranoid schizoid projective mechanisms are in ascendance.[9] In this way, Green and Irigaray's conclusions, read in Kleinian terms, would be that matricide can only produce "concrete representations" belonging to the paranoid schizoid register, where symbolic functioning has not been achieved owing to the inability to introject and mourn the maternal object.

This view is echoed in a recent feminist psychoanalytic account. In a book addressing the psychic problem of matricide, Christina Wieland, following Irigaray, argues that "matricide has been the Western culturally sanctioned means by which separation of the mother has been achieved. However, this does not lead to a genuine separation from the mother or to the establishment of a parental couple in the psyche, but to a rigidly divided psyche where persecution reigns."[10] While Wieland does not refer to Klein, Irigaray, or Green's readings of the *Oresteia*, her position on the myth can be read as supporting Green and Irigaray's, yet her terminology or model is Kleinian and post-Kleinian. In this way, Wieland concentrates on mourning and reparation as that which matricide forecloses and argues that the dead mother remains as the "undead" mother, as the "bad present object" that cannot be used for thinking but can only be endlessly projected: "The present bad object has to be murdered, annihilated, or endlessly projected—yet in each of these 'solutions' the object refuses to die because it is never mourned."[11]

The *Oresteia*, then, is interpreted from different psychoanalytic perspectives as a description of the seemingly irresolvable problem of mourning in relation to matricide or, more specifically, as a description of pathological or aberrant mourning in relation to the mother. While the theorists I have discussed use different terminology to describe this situation, all of them arrive at a similar conclusion concerning the improper death that matricide delivers.

Wieland attempts to account for this situation by concluding that (psychic) "murder cannot be mourned": "That murder cannot lead to separation is obvious, since murder ties the murderer irrevocably to his victim.

More than love or hate, it creates a persecutory present object, rather than an absent one. This possesses a hallucinatory, psychotic quality which must be thwarted if the murderer is to remain sane."[12] To my mind, it is not at all obvious that psychic murder cannot lead to separation, mourning, and loss. On the contrary, psychoanalysis is built around the concept of murder, with patricide as its organizing generative concept. The point for me is that, according to psychoanalysis, psychic murder is precisely what *should* lead to separation, mourning, symbolization, and loss if we hold to the Freudian model that posits patricide as the generative gateway into becoming a subject. For Green and Mitchell, patricide creates the "Red" loss belonging to the law of castration from which thought, structure, and theory can emerge. The murder of the father does not create a persecutory present object; instead, it creates the mitigated superego allowing for the internalization of death, separation, loss, and symbolic filial genealogy. It is only the murder of the mother that results in a dangerous presence, precluding mourning and loss, and it is this specificity of matricide that needs to be explored. It is not, as Wieland suggests, that (psychic) murder cannot be mourned but more specifically that there is something sabotaging the mourning process when it comes to the psychic murder of the mother, who can only be rendered dangerously present or radically absent, representing the "anti-metaphor" or embodiments in concrete symbolism. What no theorist has interrogated through an examination of the Oresteian myth is the *cause* of this impossible break with the mother or her inability to structure a generative loss. That is to say, *the question of why the dead mother can be incorporated but not introjected* has not hitherto been addressed.

Klein, Green, and Irigaray are led to this matricidal myth via different paths, yet none of them does more than touch on it; they do not follow through a thorough examination of the myth. Neither Klein nor Irigaray, who both attempt to theorize the mother, goes as far as elaborating and explicating the constellation of phantasies in the *Oresteia* so as to posit it as a viable structural paradigm from which theorizing the mother may be possible. Additionally, Green, who proposed the creation of more than one model with more than one structural center and who has considered the theoretical problem of matricide in psychoanalysis, has not (as yet), despite his early engagement with Orestes, made use of this myth in order to develop a different theoretical constellation.

Metis is the unthought element in all the readings discussed so far. Despite my "decrypting" of her as a phantom present in Klein's comments about Athena, she remains as a void or the "anti-metaphor" that prevents any real progress from being achieved in all these treatments of the Ores-teian myth. The secret of Metis is transmitted with the myth so that each successive generation that receives the *Oresteia* receives with it the gap, or nescience, and unwittingly reproduces it in each rereading. While Klein, Irigaray, and Green are all drawn to the *Oresteia* because of a preoccupa-tion with the mother or matricide, they focus on the wrong matricide, so to speak, or the wrong mother. It is not Clytemnestra whom we should mourn, resurrect, or symbolize: it is Metis. Considering myth from the perspective of Lévi-Strauss (where each myth is considered in relation to others rather than as an isolated element) allows us to go beyond the (psychoanalytic) readings of the *Oresteia* that I have discussed and dis-cover the radically excluded matricide that the manifest matricide in the myth conceals.

Irigaray, Green, and Klein all come *close* to the real dead mother of the myth, either through reproducing the phantom effect, as in the case of Klein, or, in the cases of Irigaray, Green, and Wieland, in their contention that the mother is somehow or other not properly dead. The "undead" quality of the murdered mother that ensues from pathological mourn-ing, referred to in the readings I have discussed, can understood read as a different way of describing the phantom effect theorized by Torok and Abraham. Where these readings fail is in their inability to go beyond re-producing or describing the phantom rather than contributing to its suc-cessful burial. In order to go further with the analysis of the *Oresteia*, so that it can be effectively used in the creation of a theory of matricide, we must shift our emphasis from the manifest to the latent content of the myth and finally decrypt Metis, disinterring her from her entombment in the myth and the Western imaginary. In this way, we move from repeating the primal incorporation of the maternal object (Metis) to the capacity to introject the void/loss: "Like a commemorative monument, the incorpo-rated object betokens the place, the date, and the circumstances in which desires were banished from introjection: they stand like tombs in the life of the ego."[13]

If, as Irigaray suggests, "what the Oresteia describes still takes place," then we are in a situation where the cultural imaginary continues to oper-ate on the (primitive) psychic level of incorporation—where the mother is concerned. The *Oresteia* points to the impossible relation between ma-tricide and reparation proper. Reading the two myths together puts us in a stronger position to understand *why* reparation cannot be achieved. It is because we have been unwittingly complicit in sustaining the incorpo-rated trauma of Metis (the original crime against the mother that underlies the creation myth of patriarchy), whose phantom has been successfully transmitted for generations, "standing like a tomb" in the life of the symbolic order as we know it. Nicholas Abraham comments: "Extending the idea of the phantom, it is reasonable to maintain that the 'phantom effect' progressively fades during its transmission from one generation to the next and that, finally, it disappears. Yet this is not at all the case when shared or complementary phantoms find a way of being established as social practices along the lines of staged words."[14]

The phantom of Metis has indeed been established as a social practice, and her effect has in no way faded. The shared or complementary phantoms (of Metis) pervade our discourses, our dreams, our theories, and our social practices, so that we are inevitably caught up in a repetitive, even obsessive ritual of reprojecting or evacuating phantasmatic images and descriptions of the mother that mark her status as a phobic object, synonymous with danger, abjection, and monstrosity and whose return must be perpetually (a)voided. It is no wonder Athena was born fully armed in a position of vigilant defense.

9

Who's Afraid of Clytemnestra?

Projection is the missing link between melancholia and phantom possession.

—LAWRENCE RICKELS

And once the man-god-father kills the mother so as to take her power, he is assailed by ghosts and anxieties. He will always feel a panic fear of she who is the substitute for what he has killed. And the things they threaten us with! We are going to swallow them up, devour them, castrate them. . . . That's no more than an age-old gesture that has not been analysed or interpreted returning to haunt them.

—LUCE IRIGARAY, "WOMEN-MOTHERS, THE SILENT SUBSTRATUM OF THE SOCIAL ORDER"

PHANTASIES OF THE monstrous all-powerful mother who is the ultimate threat to identity are frequently reproduced in our cultural imaginary and our discourses. The Oresteian myth provides us with a description of these typical phantasies that are absent from the Oedipus myth. This section will go some way toward demonstrating in detail how the Oresteian myth can be used to analyze the archaic projections onto the mother that result from the incorporation of a generative matricide and the pathological mourning that ensues. By analyzing the manifest projection of Clytemnestra as a symptom that points to the incorporation of matricide as a structuring concept, our relation to the material concerning phantasies of the all-powerful mother changes. It is no coincidence that it is the Oresteian matricidal myth that posits the mother as a threat to identity. Now that we have arrived at the definition of matricide as incorporation, reading Clytemnestra is always in the context of the manifest effects of matricide as incorporation. In this way, we examine the ubiquitous phantasy of dangerous maternal power as a symptomatic projection ensuing from incorporation. The psychic threat that the mother poses, rather than being institutionalized and confirmed as a psychoanalytic truth, instead needs to be read as a symptom of an order that continues to function on the level of incorporation, where the mother is concerned. Incorporation, as we have seen, forecloses mourning. Aberrant mourning results in the endless projection of the "bad present object." The mother, in our cultural imaginary, in our discourses, and in psychoanalytic theory, is identical with this projection of the "bad present object." She does not exist outside this projection. The psychoanalytic theories (persistently) tell us that being subject to the mother's desire is to confront death and psychosis. In my view, such a position is not theoretical; rather, it is projective, that is to say, symptomatic.

Clytemnestra is a figure that forms a nodal point in our mythical imaginary, located at the point of intersection of numerous unconscious meanings and phantasies. In this way, her image is highly cathected and is preserved in the cultural imaginary as a condensation that continues to be found in diverse cultural representations, discourses, dreams, and phantasies. As I have argued, Clytemnestra functions both to screen and disclose our knowledge of Metis. A complex and powerful condensation, the figure of Clytemnestra, when analyzed and interpreted beyond the manifest content, can lead us to the navel phantasy of the myth. Clytemnestra is the nodal image that represents the point of connection and disconnection with the unknown (Metis). In this way, I interpret Clytemnestra from a new perspective by considering her as a sign pointing to another scene, the erased scenography that underpins the Oresteian myth.

Commenting on Freud's representation of women, Monique Schneider claims: "In Freud, the representation of women should not be accepted at face value, but has to be decoded, interpreted, seen in reverse. When he says that women are characterized by lack, that she doesn't have a penis, there is something there which for Freud is frightening. It is the opening. Therefore, characterizing the woman as lack represents for Freud a kind of escape from the temptation of falling into an abyss, of being sucked in by the woman, and we have to see what the phantasmatic negative of Freud's theorization is and transform some negative into positive images."[1] For Schneider, where Freud theorizes lack, there is excess: a terrifying power that Freud escapes confronting through insisting on the equation between femininity and castration. Oedipus as a model works successfully to exclude the representation of femininity as monstrous excess whereas the *Oresteia* represents the "phantasmatic negative of Freud's theorisation": the monstrous mother who threatens the subject with annihilation. Once we have discovered and analyzed the representations of woman as both excess and lack, we may go beyond this rigid and entrenched phantasy structure and clear the way for representations that are not trapped in this phantasmic binary: "It should be possible to come back to what Freud perceived as the interior of the female body, to take out the stitches to make the opening appear again, an opening which is not a wound but could be fantasized in a very different way as the entrance to an interior world creating life."[2]

Clytemnestra is located at the intersection where phantasies of feminine excess meet phantasies of feminine lack. In this way, her image/representation is cathected with a large sum of energies functioning to maintain the "phantasmatic negative" that prevents us from representing the "opening" in a very different way. We need to analyze what Irigaray calls the "age old gesture" that represents women as either lack (castrated) or an insatiable devouring void.[3] As we have seen, the void is an empty hole/space but empty only by virtue of having been emptied. The phantasy of the female body as void or abyss inevitably conjures up its opposite: the expelled (voided) excess. An analysis of the excess/lack binary that structures the representation of Clytemnestra can lead to the diminishing of its power and disclose the concealed pathogenic factor of which this entrenched phantasy is a result.

I want to examine closely two scenes in the Oresteia in which the phantasies/projections of maternal excess are most explicitly disclosed. The first is Clytemnestra's murder of Agamemnon, and the second is the scene of Orestes' confrontation with her exposed breast in the matricide scene. These two scenes, as I read them, are structurally linked. They rework the same phantasies, referring to one another and repeating (while mutating) the same setting/structure of desire. The first scene depicts a version of the primal scene, while the second depicts seduction and castration; together, these two scenes studied synchronically reproduce the constellation of all three (overlapping and interrelated) so-called primal phantasies that Freud identified.[4] But whereas Freud's description of the primal phantasies was dominated largely by the figure of the all-powerful father, the *Oresteia* structures the primal phantasies in a very different way, in relation to the all-powerful dreaded mother, instead. In this way, we are left with two omnipotent parental figures, the phantasies of whom function to produce the precarious differentiation underlying so-called oedipal subjectivity. Chasseguet-Smirgel argued that the unconscious phantasy of the omnipotent mother underlies phallic power,[5] yet in so doing she did not break out of the entrenched excess/lack binary projection that forecloses phantasizing "the opening in a different way."[6] Instead, she produces a theory that keeps the mother in her inalienable place and renders the male imaginary as theoretical truth rather than descriptive projection. In the following interpretation of Clytemnestra, I will be analyzing the phantasies she represents as symptomatic projections resulting from the voided incorporation of Metis. In this way, unlike Chasseguet-Smirgel, I challenge the status of this projection rather than reinforcing and securing its power in theoretical discourse.

"My Lord Is Home at Last"

Agamemnon arrives home, victorious from sacking Troy and is greeted by his people and his wife. Clytemnestra's initial praise and glorification of him marks the beginning of her cunning strategy that leads to his murder. Playing the role of the devoted and faithful wife (ironically echoing Penelope), she orders her women to lay down red carpets to lead him from the chariot to her embracing arms. Agamemnon is reluctant to accept this pompous ceremony for fear of hubris. To step on red rugs would offend the gods in its excessive display of an arrogance deemed inappropriate for mortals. But his wife urges him on, reminding him of his greatness and his victory, taunting his fear of the gods, and indulging his evident love of power. He gives in and agrees to step onto the red rugs:

> And now,
> since you have brought me down with your insistence,
> just this once I enter my father's house,
> trampling royal crimson as I go.[7]

His agreement to follow her ceremony marks the first stage of Clytemnestra's successful attempt to establish power. She turns to her women and says:

> Let the red stream flow and bear him home
> to the home he never hoped to see.
> (LINES 901–903, P. 137)

The symbolic significance of the red rugs is manifold. While it is usual to interpret the ceremony of the red rugs as signifying the impending doom that awaits Agamemnon and his unlimited capacity for hubris (marking his tragic flaw or omnipotent narcissism), Clytemnestra's language gives the rugs a visceral, primitive, and sexual significance: a red stream whose flow leads him to a dreaded home. The rugs lead him from the "car of war" to the threshold of the house where Clytemnestra waits to greet him. The home she refers to is not the safe place to which he has for so long desired to return but a home of danger: her own body. The red stream denotes a path of blood whose currents pull him toward the maternal body, "the first home." Before he can enter his father's house, he must cross the threshold where Clytemnestra stands. In referring to his father's house, Agamemnon, in this scene, is placed in the position of the son. This becomes reinforced by his progressive infantilization throughout the protracted homecoming scene.

Before he steps down onto the red rugs, Agamemnon asks for help removing his boots. Barefoot, he begins his regression, his descent into the infant that his wife reduces him to. Without his shoes, he begins his journey to the threshold of his "home." Clytemnestra at once turns Agamemnon into a foolish and helpless infant at the moment when he intends to celebrate his victory as a man. Shoeless and swordless (deprived of his phallic power), he is drawn along the red rug as if it were an umbilical cord leading him back to the devouring mother whose embrace of death will deliver him to Mother Earth. "Done is done," Clytemnestra exclaims, addressing the horrified chorus/audience as she presents her husband's corpse. She stands triumphant over his dead body and exclaims:

> So he goes down, and the life is bursting out of him—
> Great sprays of blood, and the murderous shower
> wounds me, dyes me black and I, I revel
> Like the Earth when the spring rain comes down,
> The blessed gifts of god, the new green spear
> Splits the sheath and rips to birth in glory!
>
> (LINES 1410–1415, P. 161)

This is the only moment in the Oresteian myth where the parental couple are witnessed together. The particular power of the scene, its cathartic effect, derives from the staging of a version of the phantasy of the primal scene. The spectator is invited to take the position of the third person/child witnessing the origins of his/her becoming. The descent down the path of the red stream (umbilical cord) leads the spectator, like the infantilized Agamemnon, back to the primitive space of the maternal body/home, the site of both conception and death. The sexual connotations are explicit: "So he goes down, and the life is bursting out of him." Here is a representation of the phantasy of sadistic and violent coitus, the parental couple joined in a union of sexual violence. But this representation of sadistic coitus places the mother as the stronger participant, inflicting damage (castration/death) on the man/father. The "life bursting out of him" is not virile sperm but "great sprays" of black blood. Clytemnestra is sprayed with a "murderous shower" of blood and likens herself to the earth that "revels" in swallowing up/incorporating the dead as nourishment. "My Lord," she declares "is home at last" (line 1423, p. 161). The maternal womb/body is conflated in this phantasy with the tomb or the grave:

> The hand that bore and cut him down
> will hand him down to Mother Earth
>
> (LINES 1579–1580, P. 167)

The climax of this interaction between Agamemnon and Clytemnestra taps into and plays with the primitive sexual theories of childhood described by Freud.[8] If, according to Freud, the child interprets coitus as a sadistic violent act where the mother is damaged by the father's phallus, the *Oresteia* stages the reverse of that "universal" primal phantasy. The mother, with intense pleasure, receives the father with activity rather than passivity, and this active sexuality is phantasized as devouring, causing the murderous spray of blood, castration, and death.[9] At the moment of death, Agamemnon cries:

> Aaagh, again . . .
> Second blow—struck home.
>
> (LINES 1370–1371, P. 159)

All that is left is a mutilated dead man and a triumphant woman reveling in erotic satisfaction. The last words Clytemnestra speaks at the close of this scene are addressed to the horrified chorus of old men: "Let them howl—they're impotent" (lines 1707, p. 172).

The point about the structural primal phantasies is that they provide the setting from which the structuration of desire is achieved.[10] In this way, the spectator is invited to identify with the setting/structure giving him/her access to cross-identifications: identification with the positions of the watching child, the mother, and the father. The Oresteian myth presents a variation of the primal scene, using the triangular setting of a couple and the spectator/chorus, that represents a primitive phantasy of sadistic coitus resulting in the father's radical impotence (death). Clytemnestra is a projection of the castrating mother who displays an excess of violence and an excess of erotic pleasure. The *Oresteia* reproduces the structure of the primal scene with the mother as the ultimate threat to identity. Rather than being swallowed, she swallows; rather than being damaged, she damages; rather than being castrated, she castrates: in other words, she stands on the side of monstrous (sexual) excess rather than lack.

The Exposure of the Maternal Breast: The Bad Present Sexual Object

O wretched sinner, who saw
Her breast burst from her gold-embroidered
gown,
And seeing, struck and slew his mother.

—EURIPIDES, ORESTES

If one gives the mother only one breast the way the Cyclops had only one eye,
she is made phallic and powerful. From this stems the theme of rejection of the
mother.

—MONIQUE SCHNEIDER

The Libation Bearers, the middle play of Aeschylus's Oresteian trilogy, dramatizes Orestes' return home from exile and his subsequent murder of his mother. Long scenes in which we witness Orestes and his sister Electra working themselves into a state of hate and violence toward their mother and repetitively declaring their moral responsibility to avenge their father's death lead to the climactic point of the play: Orestes confrontation with his mother. Orestes stands face to face with his mother, about to draw his sword, when Clytemnestra distracts him by exposing her breast, exclaiming:

Wait my son—no respect for this, my child?
The breast you held, drowsing away the hours,
Soft gums tugging the milk that made you grow?[11]

The exposure of his mother's breast causes Orestes to waver and lower his sword. Before this moment, he had displayed no ambivalence about what he had to do and accepted his role of avenging his father by committing matricide. But the sight of his mother's breast, that which once kept him alive, renders him impotent to carry out the murder. He calls to the friend who has accompanied him and cries: "What will I do Pylades?—I dread to kill my mother!"[12] The sight of his mother's breast diverts him from his mission, causing the delay of the climactic murder and resulting in further scenes of procrastination and conflict. While manifestly simple, this moment condenses or structures different chains of meanings, leading us back into the realm of the typical primal phantasies. The scene invokes and reworks the phantasies of castration, seduction, and the primal scene, organized around the maternal breast.

Clytemnestra's gesture of revealing her breast serves at once to infantilize Orestes at the very moment at which he is expected to embody his autonomous agency as a man (acting in the name of his father). Acknowledgment of the absolute dependency on the maternal body is forced on Orestes. Made to stare at his mother's breast and asked to remember his essential and primitive attachment to it, Orestes wavers and lowers his sword. He cannot act; it is as if he is turned to stone. The myth of Medusa comes immediately to mind. Like Medusa, the monstrous all-powerful archaic mother figure, Clytemnestra's breast is an image that freezes action. Perseus can only murder Medusa if he does not look at her directly. Orestes, however, is trapped in direct confrontation with the breast, which stares back at him like Medusa's omnipotent eye. Not as fortunate as Perseus, he has no prop to help him avert his look. Instead of keeping a steady eye on the path ahead of him, Orestes must look back to the primitive past and in doing so begins to regress. While Agamemnon was led back to the primitive maternal body by Clytemnestra's red rugs (symbolic of the umbilical cord), Orestes' regressive trajectory is precipitated by the sight of her breast. He is forced to look back at himself, once a helpless dependent child, passive and lacking in the face of the powerful and seductive mother of early infancy.

The exposure of the breast is a complicated moment that serves both to seduce Orestes and to threaten him with impotence/castration. The scene is a reference back to Agamemnon's confrontation with Clytemnestra in the homecoming scene. The primal scene is reworked here with Orestes placed in the position of his father. In returning "home," Orestes, like Agamemnon, confronts Clytemnestra in a scene that is explicitly sexualized. Orestes is about to penetrate his mother with his sword, but the breast that Clytemnestra exposes becomes a weapon that signifies to Orestes the danger of entering the mother's body. The danger of being castrated/annihilated by the monstrous archaic mother is invoked by the exposure of the maternal breast/Medusa's single eye.

Here we see the primitive phantasy of the breast characterized by its excess and plenitude, the powerful object containing all the riches that give and sustain life as well as denoting the mother's self-sufficient sexual pleasure and her capacity to take away the breast. In its singularity and its associative link to Medusa, the breast here is both a site of maternal phallic pleasure/excess and a devouring incorporating mouth/vagina. The displacement of the vagina to breast serves to condense the mother's reproductive and erotogenic zones into one highly cathected image, denoting both phallic and devouring qualities: the dreaded qualities of the primitive and omnipotent mother from which all originates and to which all returns.

The primitive maternal breast, then, functions actively to undercut the infant's phantasy of omnipotence and mastery; the breast is not in the infant's control. As Schneider comments: "I think that the primitive mother brings death to the extent that she denies or renders useless visions of mastery, of conquest, with which men want to identify. That is, she breaks, she destroys the image, she doesn't kill man; she kills an image he wants to have of himself.[13] Clytemnestra's breast, then, is seductive and castrating, denoting both pleasure and power and reducing the male protagonist to a state of fear and stasis. In this moment of confrontation with his mother's breast, Orestes' sword is revealed as a vulnerable instrument that can neither satisfy nor kill/defend against the primitive mother of his early infancy. It is as if the breast is laughing at him, mocking his grandiose charade with his wavering sword, inducing the most intense sense of shame and inadequacy (leading to impotence) and invoking the profound inequality between baby and mother that underlies the phantasy of phallic power/domination. If Cixous reconstructed a "laughing Medusa," Clytemnestra's breast can just as much signify a maternal jouissance whose enigmatic pleasure activates the most primitive envy and fear in Orestes: envy of the mother's breast, her creativity and generative power; fear of being castrated and swallowed up into the dreaded first home.

Orestes finally kills his mother (by stabbing her through the revealed breast), and in this way the myth reverses the positions in the phantasy by turning the initial passivity and powerlessness in the face of the mother's sexual breast into an active mastery and domination that underlies the process of defensive differentiation. Maternal excess is transformed into lack. Where there was once an omnipotent and seductive breast, there is now a wound. After being murdered, Clytemnestra returns as a ghost, but a ghost with a visceral presence:

I was slaughtered by his matricidal hand.
See these gashes—
Carve them in your heart.[14]

This image of the disclosure of her "gashes" repeats her earlier gesture of exposing her breast. Even as a ghost, Clytemnestra continues to exhibit her body as a means to induce a powerful reaction. We "carve" in our minds both her breast and then her "gash." The breast has been transformed into a wound. She moves from denoting maternal excess to maternal lack.

This lack is not so straightforward, however. The breast as excess has been transformed into a wound as lack, but this wound/lack is still monstrously present. That is, the destruction of the breast/mother does not deliver a loss. She is still there, present and audible, a phantom presence exposing her mutilated breast (wound) and carving its image in the hearts of her audience. It is highly significant in relation to the present focus on the meaning of matricide that in her ghostly (phantom) return, Clytemnestra, the "undead mother," repeats her earlier gesture of exposing her breast. Breast or gash, excess or lack, she remains the monstrous present mother who cannot be rendered gone/lost but continues to "carve" her threatening presence in our imaginary world.

We can see that the manifest phantasies condensed in the motif of Clytemnestra's breast in the *Oresteia* bring into focus the question of the location of matricide with regard to Green's "Red" and "Black/White" paradigms.[15] Here, the breast seems to belong to both models simultaneously. In undercutting the infant's phantasy of omnipotence, the breast belongs to the retrospectively constructed metaphorical breast that functions in the castration structure to establish the relation between pleasure and reality (the prohibition of incest) and in this way is subsumed under the castration model. Yet, if Clytemnestra's breast functions as a "Red" breast, then it has a double aspect. It leaves a remainder; its presence is not replaced by the loss related to the castration complex. The breast continues to function in the binary of excess/lack that pertains to the absence/presence binary characteristic of Green's "Black/White" paradigm. Within the terms of Green's proposed models, there is no place for theorizing matricide in the *Oresteia*. Clytemnestra as the manifest mother in the myth functions as both "Red" and "Black and White," but in both capacities she cannot produce a generative structuring loss; she can only give rise to the production of endless projections resulting from the encrypted phantasy of incorporation that neither of Green's models addresses. We need another model that pertains to the prohibition associated to matricide that is neither "Red" nor "Black and White." Clytemnestra and the "Red"/"Black-White" paradigms can only reinforce the mother's nonstructural status in theoretical discourse. The color of the model pertaining to Metis would be neither red nor black and white.

Abject Projections

These female fiends with bloody faces
wreathed in snakes
They have dog jaws and gorgon's eyes

—EURIPIDES, ORESTES

But black they are, and so repulsive.
Their heavy, rasping breathing makes me cringe.
And their eyes ooze a discharge, sickening,
And what they wear—to flaunt that at the gods,
The idols, sacrilege! Even in the homes of men.

—AESCHYLUS, THE EUMENIDES

Clytemnestra's ghost together with the Furies (the mother's curse) are described in horrifying visceral terms. Rather than being spectral or ghostly,
they have a bodily presence (for those who can see them) that belongs to
the realm of the abject.[16] These concrete hallucinations provoke repulsion
and disgust precisely because they contain or embody pollution, defile-
ment, and bodily waste and are defined as feminine. Bloody faces wreathed
in snakes, eyes that ooze discharge, rasping breath: this is the phobic hallucination ensuing from the fear of the archaic maternal body. "Sickening"
and "repulsive," the Furies are vampiristic, threatening to suck the subject
dry; they are representations of what Kristeva calls "powers of horror" and
are linked to the primitive phantasy of the monstrous devouring mother.
Klein calls the Furies "part objects belonging to the anal sadistic stage,"
Green calls them "psychotic hallucinations," and Irigaray describes them as
"a troop of enraged women . . . women in revolt, rising up like revolutionary
hysterics."[17] I interpret the Furies together with Clytemnestra differently, by
considering them as phobic hallucinations that are the result of a reaction
formation. Freud described reaction formation as a specific psychic mechanism that functions as a defense against a particularly distressing idea by
replacing that idea with a "counter-symptom" that is the direct opposite
of that against which the subject defends himself.[18] In this way, we can see
how Clytemnestra and the Furies behave as a countersymptom to Metis
(the distressing idea that is being defended against). The dangerous and
unrelenting presence of Clytemnestra's ghost and the Furies (in the form of
phobic hallucinations) masks the radical absence and negation of Metis.

In her book *Powers of Horror: An Essay on Abjection* (1982), Julia Kristeva
describes the phobic hallucination as a "heterogeneous agglomeration"

that belongs to the levels of both the metaphor and the drive: "It [the phobic hallucination] is . . . a metaphor. And yet more than that. For to the activity of condensation and displacement that oversees its formation, there is added a drive dimension (heralded by fear) that has an anaphoric, indexing value, pointing to something else, to some non-thing, to something unknowable. The phobic object is in that sense the hallucination of nothing: a metaphor that is the anaphora of nothing."[19] We have seen how Clytemnestra is a condensation that combines manifold meanings in relation to the phantasized primitive mother. We have also seen how the mechanism of displacement operates in this condensation through the inversion of the passive/active binary and the displacement of the phantasized devouring vagina upward to the seductive breast. In this way, Clytemnestra functions on the level of metaphor (belonging to the castration/"Red" structure), but she also has a drive dimension in terms of the fear/affect she provokes, reinforced by the Furies. It is precisely her dangerous presence (which cannot be modified or rendered lost) that belongs to Green's "Black/White" paradigm, adding to the condensation or metaphor a quality of terror (affect). It is this fear or affect attached to Clytemnestra as a metaphor that points to the "non-thing" that Kristeva refers to, the "something else" that is unknowable. The "non-thing" cannot be theorized according to any existing psychoanalytic models; it can only be indexed as that which is radically resistant to theory.

The phobic hallucinations of Clytemnestra and the Furies together function to conceal the "non-thing" (the voided Metis) by conjuring up a monstrous presence. Yet the phobic hallucination, while concealing the non-thing by turning absence into presence, simultaneously points to it in the manifestation of phobia. In this way, the phobic hallucination of Clytemnestra and the Furies results from the attempt to avoid the introjection of the object and to sustain the phantasy of incorporation. Instead of the void, we have excess; instead of the incorporated mother, we have the devouring (incorporating) mother. Clytemnestra, in Kristeva's terms, is a phobic projection that points to the "something else," an unknown scene; she is a hallucination that is the "anaphora of nothing." That is to say, her excess is simply another way of saying or indicating the presence of the non-thing. Clytemnestra indexes the remainder that has been excluded from the dominant structuring mechanism of the myth and points to the non-thing or nescience that can only make itself known via reaction formation in the form of a threatening presence. Representation of excess in the form of a phobic hallucination functions in the myth as the "countersymptom" that, if analyzed, leads us to the pathogenic factor, the original distressing idea. The phantom effect of Metis creates the phobic hallucination of Clytemnestra, who is nothing more that a veil or adornment covering the unknowable non-thing: the raped and incorporated mother, encrypted in myth and theoretical discourse.

The phobic hallucination is a complex symptom that allows us to witness both the attempt to introject the incorporated object and the failure of this process. This means, in Kristeva's words, that "an object that is a hallucination is being made."[20] The *Oresteia* demonstrates this process in that the hallucination of Clytemnestra contains within it the incorporated object (Metis) that is trying to be introjected or metaphorized. In Clytemnestra, we see "logical and linguistic workings that are attempts at drive introjection outlining the failure to introject that which is incorporated."[21] Clytemnestra and the Furies as the monstrous hallucinatory maternal presence in the myth pertain to the attempt both to introject the incorporated object (Metis) and its failure. Read this way, we are able to use Clytemnestra as an index pointing to Metis and thus can finally bring to light and analyze the real phobic (incorporated) matricide that the myth encrypts. The *Oresteia* then can be read as a description of the creation of a maternal hallucinatory object resulting from an encrypted phantasy of incorporation. Clytemnestra is significant only inasmuch as she functions as a lever to decrypt the incorporated object (Metis). We can only use the *Oresteia* in the creation of a structural theory of matricide if Clytemnestra as the symptomatic hallucinatory object is finally transformed into an object that can be used for thinking about the mother rather than for the endless projection of her phobic image. This becomes a possibility in the light of the discoveries made through analyzing the defensive function of the (manifest) myth.

In one of Orestes' fits of phobic hallucinations, he describes to Menelaus the nature of his visions:

MENELAUS: And in your fits what kind of sights appear to you?
ORESTES: I seemed to see three women; they were black as night.
MENELAUS: I will not name them; but I know what Powers you mean.
ORESTES: They are to be feared; you're wise to shrink from naming them.[22]

Now that we have named Metis as the power behind the phobic hallucination or projection of Clytemnestra, we have begun to move toward the possibility of reconstructing the concealed matricide that can allow for its introjection. That is to say, now we have something to mourn, to lose, and to symbolize. Instead of repeating the phantom effect, we can now give Metis her proper burial, so to speak. To disclose Metis means to acknowledge her loss as pertaining to an underlying law whose articulation can lead to the theorization of a potential generative matricide, a new structuring possibility.

10 ☙

Metis's Law

*The normal infantile fantasies of parthenogenesis need the differentiating pro-
hibition from the mother: you cannot be a mother now, but you, a girl, can
grow up to be one, and you, a boy cannot. . . .*

    *Men must also submit to a prohibition on their parthenogenetic fanta-
sies—they have to become 'those who cannot give birth'. Castration introduces
only one mode of symbolization. . . .*

    *This prohibition we might call 'The Law of the Mother', on a par in principle
with 'The Law of the Father' in the castration complex.*

—JULIET MITCHELL

W HILE IRIGARAY HAS powerfully described how the murder
of the mother underlies Western discourses and produces
particular pathologies and symptoms at the level of the cultural as well as the individual psyche, she has not addressed the question
of a cultural law related to matricide that is distinct from the cultural
laws and prohibitions underlying patricide. In my argument, matricide
is an nonconcept whose incorporation within the patriarchal discourses
functions to suppress the underlying laws relating to matricide that produce unconscious structures different from those of the laws underlying
patricide. What I am suggesting is that the equation of matricide with incorporation that I have so far postulated not only produces the symptoms
of pathological mourning by rendering the mother as the projected "bad
present object" that can neither be introjected nor symbolized and theorized but, further, that incorporation functions to encrypt a matricidal law
that dictates certain prohibitions belonging to the mother that patriarchal
culture systematically transgresses.

The move of emphasis from Clytemnestra to Metis allows me to use the
Oresteian myth to construct a theory of matricide rather than a description; moving back from Clytemnestra to Metis is analogous to moving from
the manifest symptom that points to the failure of the repression of the
matricidal law to the latent underlying law itself. If there is a law of Metis

incorporated and therefore encrypted within the Oresteian myth, what, then, are the prohibitions that Metis represents that have been swallowed, obliterated, and therefore transgressed by Zeus and his order? What phantasy is allowed to persist to the extent that it is given the status of natural necessity and truth in the patriarchal order by virtue of the incorporation of the underlying matricidal cultural law/prohibition? These are crucial questions for the following reason: we have discovered that the rape, incorporation, and appropriation of Metis is the concealed or encrypted crime that cannot be introjected/known/represented, but we have not found out exactly why this original violence against the mother that the Metis myth describes is so traumatic and in need of such vigilant censorship. Why is the myth of Metis so difficult to integrate? Why have generations persistently believed and reproduced Athena and Apollo's statement that Athena had no mother? What force or resistance has prevented the connection between the Metis myth and the Oresteian myth from being read? In sum, what is at stake in discovering Metis as Athena's raped and swallowed mother and rereading the *Oresteia* with Metis in mind?

I suggest that it is not only a matter of culture's refusal to acknowledge the debt to and the dependency on the mother and a refusal to make reparation to the mother who has been killed; it is, as I shall argue, culture's refusal to acknowledge her law and her prohibition. In my argument, the implications of discovering Metis as the incorporated matricide in the *Oresteia* are concerned with the identification of a prohibitive law belonging to the mother that patriarchal culture refuses to obey and so incorporates, since obedience to her law would mean giving up a phantasy that would radically undermine the father's symbolic sovereignty. In suppressing her law (via incorporation), the unconscious structures produced by her law are inevitably struck dumb, rendered unrepresentable, and radically excluded. This can all be found in the Oresteian myth as dramatized by Aeschylus in the final play of the trilogy, *The Eumenides*, when the logic underlying Athena's acquittal of Orestes is declared:

APOLLO: The father can father forth without a mother.
Here she stands, out living witness. Look—
Exhibiting Athena
Child sprung full-blown from Olympian Zeus,
Never bred in the darkness of the womb . . .[1]
ATHENA: My work is here, to render the final judgement
Orestes, I will cast my lot for you.
No mother gave me birth.[2]

The justification/condoning of matricide in Athena's court is based on the male phantasy of parthenogenesis. The belief that the father can create a baby alone lies at the basis of the logic underlying Orestes' acquittal and results in or leads to the institution of a law that declares the father as the prime author of identity. The respect for the dead father, Agamemnon, whose rule Orestes will continue, is built on Zeus's example of having created Athena by himself. The phantasy of parthenogenesis (which underlies the male imaginary) becomes transformed into law (the symbolic) in that the law of Orestes' dead father achieves its sovereign status precisely because of its roots in the phantasy of Zeus's parthenogenetic creation. Indeed, in the courtroom scene in the *Oresteia*, Orestes' advocates present no other arguments to promote his case; the so-called evidence that the father can create a baby without a mother is the basis of their case. The murder of Clytemnestra, then, will not be mourned or punished, and neither will it generate a guilty debt, since to recognize the underlying law/prohibition related to matricide—thou shall not kill thy mother—is at the same time to recognize that the father cannot father forth alone. To recognize matricide is to recognize the mother's law that prohibits the phantasy that the child and the father can give birth and subjects the child and the father to a limit, a distinction, a loss.

In relation to my argument here, I am indebted to Juliet Mitchell's recent theorization of the parthenogenetic phantasy and her hypothesis of the "Law of the Mother" that functions to prohibit this phantasy. While Mitchell's book is primarily concerned with retheorizing hysteria and sibling relations, her theory of the parthenogenetic phantasy and the mother's law proves highly relevant to my argument; indeed, it made the completion of my argument concerning Metis possible. I am using Mitchell's innovative theory in a different context from hers in order to argue and develop a different (but related) point. Her hypothesis of the "Law of the Mother" gave me a model that I could effectively use in my attempt to theorize matricide in relation to its underlying prohibitions. Her new theory enabled me to articulate in structural terms the law that I was previously only able to describe through the analysis of the Metis myth in relation to the *Oresteia*. It should also be emphasized here that I am talking specifically about the *male* phantasy of parthenogenesis. What I am attempting to do with Mitchell's theory of the maternal prohibition on the parthenogenetic phantasy is to connect it to my theory of matricide as incorporation. Indeed, having linked the concepts of matricide, incorporation, and male parthenogenesis in the myth, Mitchell's "Law of the Mother" provides a powerful structural paradigm distinct from and not reducible to castration, which I can now use to consolidate my emergent theory of matricide.

Matricide, then, must be incorporated and foreclosed insofar as it is a structure whose underlying cultural law functions to force the child/father to give up the omnipotent phantasy of taking the mother's place. The father's law depends on parthenogenetic phantasies operating intact, which is why Zeus's rape and incorporation of Metis must not be known. If Athena had had a mother, then Orestes could not have won his case.

Zeus's rape and subsequent incorporation of the pregnant Metis is censored and replaced by the parthenogenetic phantasy within which matricide has become incorporated. In the Oresteian myth, matricide and parthenogenesis are, in complex ways, inextricably linked and cannot be considered apart; they implicate each other. The phantasy of parthenogenesis is contingent on matricide (the eradication of the mother's role), yet at the same time, in order for the phantasy to remain intact, matricide must be disavowed. This is effected through the mechanism of incorporation: matricide is retrospectively voided via the process of incorporation. What results is the phantasy of parthenogenesis reigning unchecked precisely because of the process by which it has been severed from its roots in matricide. We are beginning to reach a specific definition of matricide in its location within a phantasy structure comprised of three interrelated elements: parthenogenesis (the phantasy) + incorporation of the mother (the mechanism by which the phantasy is sustained) = matricide severed from its underlying law/prohibition (the erased "non-concept"). Contrary to the Kleinian and Lacanian interpretation that (via different models) read the Oresteian myth as expressing the structure: matricide = severance = deliverance, our formulation is instead: matricide = incorporation = parthenogenesis.

The incorporation of matricide is concealed within the parthenogenetic phantasy that provides the crux of Athena and Apollo's defense of Orestes. The underlying phantasy of the *Oresteia* is that of parthenogenesis, and it is within this phantasy that we can find the meaning of matricide. Matricide as incorporation means that there will be no dead mother who will provide generative guilt resulting from the cultural memory of transgressing her law. The raped and subsequently pregnant mother represents the prohibition against the male phantasy expressing the wish to make a baby alone. To know Metis is to internalize the guilt resulting from transgressing her law. The mother's function to introduce/enforce a limit on her children that prohibits their parthenogenetic phantasy is swallowed and incorporated rather than internalized/introjected.

The significance of the incorporation of the pregnant Metis and the vigilance with which she is censored from the Oresteian myth and all its variants and readings/interpretations become increasingly clear. The pregnant mother is the navel of the myth, the point at which knowledge falls back on itself and becomes blind. Incorporated within the manifest matricide (the murder of Clytemnestra) is the eradication of the pregnant woman.[3] The pregnant woman, I suggest, does provoke the phantasy of female omnipotence (the phallic mother), and neither can she be equated with the preoedipal mother; the pregnant woman forces the knowledge of the maternal generative function and by definition prohibits the phantasy that the father can father forth alone. The image of the pregnant Metis represents the mother's dictum stating "I have got what you cannot ever have." To look at/know the pregnant mother and her law, like looking at Clytemnestra's breast or Medusa's eye, threatens the male subject by undercutting his omnipotent phantasy or infantile belief, namely, his "parthenogenetic complex."[4] The resistance to giving up this complex/phantasy mobilizes murderous and violent impulses in the male child/father leading to the mother's incorporation and subsequent erasure. In one gesture, the law of matricide is transgressed and eradicated.

The transgression of Metis's law and its subsequent incorporation means that the mother loses her function of asserting that the male child cannot give birth, and consequently the male phantasy of parthenogenesis is not held in check, that is to say, the phantasy is not given up and continues to operate on the symbolic level achieving the status of (the father's) law. Matricide is denied its function of asserting the prohibition against the parthenogenetic phantasy so that the structural generative loss/limit that it should deliver is finally foreclosed.

The implications of the incorporation of the mother's law are profound. Not only does it result in the foreclosure of an unconscious structure or set of desires from being symbolized, theorized, and represented (sublimated), but the acting-out of the parthenogenetic phantasy has immediate and dangerous effects in our contemporary society. Irigaray states that what the *Oresteia* describes still takes place; I would change that slightly by suggesting that what it *conceals* is operative today: the lack of prohibition on the male parthenogenetic phantasy means that the phantasy is systematically acted out. The lack of the mother's prohibition on the parthenogenetic phantasy, owing to the incorporation of the matricidal law, means that the phantasy is elevated to status of a belief. The belief underlying patriarchy (the father can father forth alone) is motivated by a wish fulfillment and in this way it is an illusory belief,[5] which functions to disregard reality and so creates a psychic unreality around which our symbolic order is organized. What this means is that the refusal to or inability to mourn the mother, or, put another way, the pathological mourning relating to matricide that the *Oresteia* describes, is in fact a refusal to mourn or relinquish an infantile belief. In a recent book addressing the concept of belief in psychoanalysis, Ronald Britton maintains that "when a belief fails the test of reality it has to be relinquished, in the same sense that an object has to be relinquished when it ceases to exist. As a lost object has to be mourned by the repeated discovery of its disappearance, so too a lost belief has to be mourned by the repeated discovery of its invalidity."[6] He continues, "By relinquishing objects I do not mean simply accepting the fact of their loss but, rather, accepting all the necessary changes in beliefs about the world that follow from that loss."[7]

The incorporation of the matricidal law means that there will be no introduction of the reality principle to force the relinquishing and mourning of the illusory infantile belief. The belief or phantasy rather than being relinquished/lost and thus represented in the future is mistaken for knowledge or fact and so creates a relation to the world that is based on the rationalization of that illusory belief: "Rationalization is the artifact of a constructed logical justification for a strongly held conviction that is really based on an unconscious belief."[8] By incorporating Metis and her law, Athena and her culture can secure the rationalization of the parthenogenetic belief and in so doing can *avoid* accepting the necessary changes in beliefs about the world that would follow from the acceptance of Metis's law. I will show, in part 3, that the effects of such a situation are particularly dangerous for the mother and the daughter.

PART III

11 ~

Clytemnestra's Three Daughters

K LEIN, IRIGARAY, AND GREEN use the *Oresteia* to think about masculine desire and destiny; the trajectory of Orestes, the matricidal son, is the focus of all their readings. Irigaray, like Green, identifies in Orestes the unconscious of Oedipus, finding in him a pathological masculine structure of desire with matricide at its core. In contrast, Klein announces Orestes as representing the most integrated and mature stage of human psychic development in that matricide and its so-called resolution have allowed him to overcome the depressive position successfully. In the *Oresteia*, Klein, Green, and Irigaray all read the son's relation to the mother. But Clytemnestra has three daughters: Iphigenia, Chrysothemis, and Electra, all of whom, in varying degrees, are included in and determine the manifest structure of the myth. In Euripides' play *Orestes*, Electra declares:

> Agamemnon's infamous bride
> Was Clytemnestra, whose name every Hellene knows.
> By her he had three daughters, Chrysothemis, Iphigenia,
> And me, Electra; and one son, Orestes—all
> Calling that execrable fiend mother.[1]

Euripides and Sophocles developed the characters of the daughters of
Atreus, Sophocles in his *Electra* and Euripides in his *Electra, Iphigenia
in Aulis, Iphigenia in Tauris,* and *Orestes.* In all these plays, the middle
sister, Chrysothemis, is introduced, briefly but, as I shall later show, significantly. The five tragedies that develop and elaborate the Oresteian myth,
as dramatized by Aeschylus, leave us a wealth of material that gives us
the opportunity to make a synchronic analysis of the *daughters'* relation
to matricide. These plays add to Aeschylus's trilogy additional stories,
expanding the Oresteian myth to include the daughters. Sophocles and
Euripides addressed the position of the daughters within the Oresteian
myth, yet interpretations of the myth invariably concentrate on Orestes
alone. Euripides' plays *Iphigenia in Tauris* and *Orestes* are concerned with
the children of Atreus after the death of *both* their parents. These plays are
of particular interest in relation to the present project because they chart
the fate of the siblings, who, after the death of their parents, are confronted
with the necessity of generative reorganization. They have to negotiate
their inheritance and their new positions in the family constellation, a
process that, as I shall show, is (at best) precarious as long as matricide
and its underlying laws remain incorporated. Klein, Irigaray, and Green do
not refer to any of these related tragedies in their readings of the *Oresteia.*
Yet the myths of Electra, Iphigenia, and Chrysothemis, when read in conjunction with the myth of Orestes, complicate and expand the structure of
the myth considerably and allow us to consider the problem of matricide
across a plurality of kinship relations.

The analysis of the manifest mother-daughter relations in the Oresteian
myth has several related functions for the present project. First, analyzing
the trajectories of Clytemnestra's three daughters in the context of the
argument so far means examining the ways in which the male imaginary
situates the daughters' positions in relation to the (incorporated) matricide that cannot deliver a generative loss. In this way, the consideration
of Electra, Iphigenia, and Chrysothemis is a continuation of my analysis
of the male imaginary. Further, that there are *three* daughters in the myth
offers copious material to use to analyze the symptoms belonging to the
mother-daughter relation (as it is represented in the male imaginary) as
long as it is denied symbolic mediation.[2]

Second, reading the sisters back into interpretations of the Oresteian
myth that focus solely on the trajectory of Orestes allows us to identify the
complex ways in which the structure of masculinity, with matricide at its
core, is dependent on the position of the sisters/daughters. In my rereading of the *Oresteia,* the daughters, as I shall argue, function to act out or

contain the split-off and expelled "madness" of the son as he negotiates his relation to the mother. In other words, thinking Orestes in relation to his sisters allows us to analyze the ways in which the dominant symbolic organization (or the male imaginary) constructs the masculine subject position through using the sister/daughter as the repository for the unwanted parts of the "masculine" defensively organized subject. Once we read Orestes' position as dependent on the respective positions of his sisters, we can begin to give back to Orestes his disowned projections and be in a stronger position with regard to constructing the not-yet-known mother-daughter and sister-sister relations, outside the field of the imaginary projections of the male imaginary.

Third, in analyzing the manifest mother-daughter relations in the Oresteian myth, I am primarily reading the myth as a description, rather than a prescription, of the positions available to the daughter under the patriarchal symbolic organization. That is to say, I am *not* pointing to the mother-daughter relations in the *Oresteia* for the purpose of fostering positive identifications, since these manifest mother-daughter relations are projections of the male imaginary and are, incidentally, far from positive. Nor am I using the mother-daughter narratives available in the myth as descriptions that confirm the psychoanalytic consensus concerning the intrinsically pathological and irresolvable nature of the mother-daughter relation. Rather, I am using the three daughters of the Oresteian myth to show how the patriarchal symbolic is organized in such a way that it precludes any structural mediation of the mother-daughter relation and thus leaves it susceptible to extreme pathology. My argument uses Electra, Chrysothemis, and Iphigenia to construct accounts or models that describe the symptoms of the daughter in a symbolic order that functions according to the male imaginary.

In this way, I follow Irigaray in her view that the mother-daughter relation is rendered pathological under the present symbolic order since the latter forecloses the possibility of the symbolic mediation of that relation. In my argument, as long as matricide remains an incorporated nonconcept that cannot deliver a generative introjective loss, there can be no structural genealogy, symbolic transmission, or inheritance between women. As a result, the mother-daughter relation remains the untheorized prototypical site of intense disturbance that is reproduced across both lateral between-women relations and successive vertical generations of mothers and daughters. The observed pathologies belonging to the mother-daughter relation, rather than being considered as inevitable, universal, and therefore impervious to change, can, with reference to the proposed model, be thought about critically, politically, and contextually, that is, in relation to the sociosymbolic order that produces them.

Having a model through which to think about the symptoms belonging to the daughters will, I contend, significantly change our relation to the material expressed in the myths. The framework through which I analyze the daughters is based on the hypothesis of an *absent law*. Thinking through the daughters in the myth in relation to the possible effects of the absent law of Metis prevents the methodology from resulting in the creation of a narrative that merely reproduces or reflects the observed symptoms and instead contributes to the construction of a theory of the mother-daughter relation that avoids merely describing and/or confirming what we find in the myths.

In the light of the argument presented in part 2 (in which the phantom of Metis was decrypted from the Oresteian myth and from the receptions and readings of the myth), it is necessary now to follow through the implications of the disclosure of the Metis myth as the underlying encrypted phantasy concealed/incorporated within the *Oresteia*. If matricide functions on the level of incorporation, wherein the introjection of a law leading to a generative (structural) loss is foreclosed, how do the effects of this situation manifest themselves in the daughters? Can reading the Metis myth in conjunction with the *Oresteia* bring to light a more specific understanding of the symptoms belonging to the mother-daughter relation as it is determined by the male imaginary? Having discovered the way matricide in the *Oresteia* is severed from its underlying law, we have a context in which to think about the symptoms belonging to the daughter. In this way, it is possible to attempt to trace the manifest symptoms expressed in the mother-daughter trajectories in the myth back to the hypothesized incorporated/erased law of Metis.

I am therefore adopting a different approach from that of the Freudian/Lacanian tradition that attempts to understand the vicissitudes of the mother-daughter relation with reference to the castration complex. I am also using a different model from that of Klein, who reads the mother-daughter relation primarily with reference to her concept of primitive envy.[3] Finally, I am taking Irigaray's approach to the mother-daughter relation one step further by suggesting that it is the failure of matricide to deliver an introjective loss that results in the daughter's "dereliction." Irigaray argues that the daughter suffers the particular effects of the matricide underlying the sociosymbolic order. These sever her from her origins, leaving her abandoned to an order that denies her a specific sexed subjectivity. I argue that it is the foreclosure of the laws underlying matricide, owing to its incorporation, that renders the daughter "derelict," because there is no law or prohibition that leads to the symbolization of her difference from her mother. In this way, where my argument departs from Irigaray's is in my suggestion that it is not matricide (the psychic murder of the mother) that is the problem; it is that matricide cannot function generatively if its underlying laws are erased. While Irigaray says we should not kill the mother, I am suggesting that we should not *incorporate* the mother. I am using the Oresteian myth, in this chapter, to read the symptoms belonging to the mother-daughter relation as the *effects* of the absence of the cultural laws underlying matricide. For me, it is not, as it is for Irigaray, that we should resurrect the mother; it is that we should make her death function symbolically so that we can introject, theorize, and symbolize her law.[4]

In my argument, the effects of the incorporation of Metis's law have two distinct (negative) consequences for daughters. First, the absence of the matricidal law of Metis leads to the lack of mediation or differentiation between mother and daughter. As a result, the set of unconscious phantasies and desires belonging to this area become unrepresentable/rendered mute and therefore susceptible to being acted out. Second, the incorporation of Metis's law results in a male parthenogenetic phantasy functioning intact, which has extremely dangerous consequences for the daughter. Without the law of Metis to provide a check on the omnipotent phantasies of the son/father, the daughter becomes subject to the son's/father's projections of his own disowned lack. Without the prohibitions associated with the matricidal law, the male subject recognizes no limit or boundary that would force him to give up his omnipotent phantasy of generative sovereignty; he needs the daughter/sister to function as his negative so that he will never have to know or symbolize her difference from him, her specificity; he will never have to know his own limitations/boundaries. In other words, without the law of Metis, the transgression of which forms the unacknowledged basis of Orestes' order/rule, the daughter is rendered unprotected from the effects of a male parthenogenetic phantasy that is not held in check but operates as the concealed foundational logic of the dominant symbolic order.

What I will argue in the following chapters is that the manifest mother-daughter narratives identifiable in the Oresteian myth all conceal within them traces of the rape, incorporation, and exclusion of Metis and her law. Encrypted within the daughters' trajectories (as dramatized by Aeschylus, Sophocles, and Euripides) are the traces of the voided/incorporated matricidal Metis myth whose exclusion produces the "phantom effect" or symptoms that are embodied in Clytemnestra's daughters. Clytemnestra's three daughters—in complex and distorted ways—express the symptoms that indicate the failure of the law that Athena (and her culture) incorporates, namely, the cultural laws underlying matricide. What we can learn from the daughters of the *Oresteia* are the complex and powerful consequences for women living under a sociosymbolic organization that forecloses the structural function of the mother. Additionally, an analysis of the symptoms of the daughters of the *Oresteia* can, as I will show, tell us something about the incorporated prohibitions belonging to Metis. To transform the manifest symptoms expressed in the mythical daughters back to the latent thoughts that they conceal means, in my reading of the myth, to decrypt both the traumatic memory of the crime against Metis and the transgression of her law.

In part 2, I uncovered the "phantom effect" of Metis in the Oresteian myth and in the psychoanalytic readings of the myth; I revealed the concealed matricide that formed the silent basis of Zeus's parthenogenetic creation that underlies the logic of Athena's endorsement of Orestes' freedom and rule. Now, I can take my exploration of the myth further by using it to discover what it is about the myth of Metis that requires constant censorship. In other words, the story does not end with the discovery of Metis. The significance of Metis and her incorporation, and the profound resistances to acknowledging her in interpretations/receptions of the *Oresteia,* can be understood when we postulate that it is not just the mother who cannot be introjected; it is her law. In this way, the effects of the incorporated matricide that render the mother as the "bad present object" who can only be endlessly projected rather than symbolized will now be considered as the result of the suppression of a cultural law belonging to matricide. To acknowledge Metis's law would undercut or subvert the omnipotent phantasy of generative sovereignty that upholds and sustains the underlying law of the patriarchal organization whose establishment is described in the Oresteian myth. Finding traces of Metis and her law distorted in the daughters of the *Oresteia* is the first step that could contribute to lifting the censorship that bans the unconscious structures, phantasies, and desires generated from Metis's law from enjoying theoretical and symbolic expression.

Irigaray and the Restorative Mother-Daughter Relation

Before proceeding with a close analysis of the symptomatic manifest narratives of the mother-daughter relation in the Oresteian myth with reference to the incorporated law of Metis, I want to articulate exactly how my approach to the mother-daughter relation and myth has both similarities to and differences from that of Irigaray's.

Irigaray's powerful conviction as to the restorative impact that the symbolization of the mother-daughter relation could effect has functioned both as a profound inspiration and as a problem in my own work. The problem, as I understand it, is that Irigaray is attempting to symbolize the mother-daughter relation but without a law with which to differentiate the mother from daughter. Whenever she prescribes to her feminist audiences practices that would contribute to the symbolization of the mother-daughter relation, she resorts to utopian images that are, in my view, part of the male imaginary's idealization of this relation, the reverse of which is its denigration. There is an impasse in Irigaray's work that I locate in her prescriptive attempts to restore the mother-daughter relation via Greek myth; this aspect of her work becomes difficult to use and rather risks drawing the feminist scholar back into the imaginary that she is attempting to subvert.

The problem, as I see it, is that you cannot symbolize the mother-daughter relation before you have theorized it, and you cannot theorize in the absence of a cultural law. The appeal to myth, in Irigaray's work, when it concerns the cultural restoration of the mother-daughter relation, can only reproduce the situation she is trying to rectify: the collapse of the mother and daughter into a merged identity that sustains the foreclosure of their structural differentiation. There is a missing link in Irigaray's work between her powerful deconstruction of the male imaginary and the prescriptive imperative that encourages intervention and transformation. This missing link is the identification of a law through which the realization of her project could come into being. It is not otherwise possible to escape the hold of the constructed feminine entrenched in the unconscious; positive utopian representations of the "feminine" cannot counter the effects of this entrenchment. Rather, we need to identify a different law in the unconscious that can structure the potential female imaginaries. In my argument, the law of Metis can be discovered via myth; the more complex problem is that of enabling the introjection of her law rather than its incorporation.

The following quotation from Irigaray's work condenses what I consider to be the most problematic aspect of her views on the relation between symbolizing the mother-daughter relation and Greek myth and foregrounds the problem of attempting to symbolize potential female imaginaries without a structure. I think it is important to make a close analysis of this quotation in order to make clear what can be successfully used in Irigaray's ideas about the mother-daughter relation and myth and what, in contrast, prevents an effective following-through of her ideas:

> Very few students of myth have laid bare the origins, the qualities and functions, the events that led up to the disappearance of the great mother-daughter couples of mythology: Demeter-Kore, Clytemnestra-Iphigenia, Jocasta-Antigone, to mention only a few famous Greek figures that have managed to leave some traces in patriarchal times.
>
> I suggest that those of you who care about social justice should put up posters in public places showing beautiful images of that natural and spiritual couple, the mother-daughter, the couple that testifies to a very special relationship to nature and culture. Our churches, our town halls are bare of such images. This indicates a cultural injustice that we can easily remedy. No wars, no dead, no wounded will result. We can do this before we undertake the reform in language, since that will take much longer. This cultural restoration will begin to heal a loss of individual and collective identity for women. It will heal many of women's ills—not just distress but competitiveness and destructive aggressiveness. It will help women move out of the private into the public sphere, out of the family and into the society where they live.[5]

First, if, as Irigaray suggests elsewhere in her work, myth must be read as the foundation of the male imaginary that has become law, then how is it that the mythical mother-daughter couples that she mentions above seem to achieve the status of "traces" of a prepatriarchal order? Irigaray appeals to the restoration of these mythical mother-daughter relations as if they are not productions of the patriarchal imaginary but hark back to an uncontaminated "before." Perhaps, for Irigaray, it is a matter of deconstructing the male imaginary to disclose its underlying phantasies and then to appropriate and rework the images for use in the construction of female imaginaries. Such a practice has been undertaken by feminist writers such as Hélène Cixous, in her appropriation of the myth of the Amazon Penthesilea and the figure of Cleopatra, and by Christa Woolf, in her novels *Cassandra* and *Medea*.[6] For Drucilla Cornell, the "reinterpretation or recreation" of mythical figures is a powerful feminist strategy with which to "help us give body to a dream of an elsewhere beyond patriarchy and the tragedy imposed by gender hierarchy."[7]

To "give body to a dream of an elsewhere beyond patriarchy" is another way of saying that we need to find images and symbols that can support a potential female imaginary—a project to which I am committed. In my argument, however, the embodiment of another dream or imaginary cannot occur until there is a structure through which that dream can emerge. Throughout her work, Irigaray frequently refers to Greek myth as the place where "traces" of a powerful and benign mother-daughter relation can be found, reclaimed, and used to rectify what she terms women's "dereliction." Irigaray privileges the Demeter-Persephone myth as a potential model of a mother-daughter relation that represents the relation as benign and necessary for the flourishing of and respect for fertility and life.[8] Irigaray is not alone in appropriating the Demeter-Persephone myth for a feminist project that attempts to give body to potential female imaginaries. The myth of Demeter and Persephone, who are happily reunited despite the dominant order's attempt to obliterate their relation, has frequently been utilized in psychoanalytic feminist appeals to myth, for the purpose of articulating and symbolizing a benign relation outside the castration structure.[9] There are, in my view, major problems (and dangers) in using myth for such ends.

Demeter and Persephone are, in my argument, part of the vast simulacrum of manifest mother-daughter relations that are produced by the male imaginary and cannot be effectively used for feminism unless they are decoded and restructured according to an approach that is concerned with moving out of the realm of description and/or projection and into that of theory. It is not enough to go back to myth and describe and promote the apparently once-harmonious mother-daughter relation before the patriarchal order effected its violent obliteration. In my argument, myth is not being used for the purpose of looking back to an imaginary and utopian "before" but instead is being used as a way of creating a future that does not yet exist.[10] In this way, Demeter, in my argument, is read in relation to other manifest mythical mother figures like Clytemnestra and Jocasta who cannot be considered as symbolic products proper but instead are screens concealing the radical exclusion of the mother and her law from representation and theory. The mother-daughter relation, in my argument, *does not yet exist,* since its symbolic status remains precluded as long as matricide remains on the level of incorporation rather than introjection. Appealing to the Demeter-Persephone myth as a positive representation risks sustaining the situation wherein the mother is denied a structural function and in so doing reproduces the terms of the male imaginary.

Irigaray moves from identifying the mother-daughter couples in myth to prescribing the distribution of "beautiful images of that natural and spiritual couple." Not only are the words "beautiful," "natural," and "spiritual" somewhat vague and opaque, but their cumulative effect in Irigaray's work functions to foreclose any possibility of articulating the hate and negativity belonging to the mother-daughter relation.[11] It is as if Irigaray prohibits herself from examining the positive uses of identifying the negativity belonging to the mother-daughter relation for fear of falling back into the castration model that characterizes the relation as one based on rejection and hate. The unrelenting positive language she uses to describe and promote the mother-daughter relation, however, belongs, in my view, to a reaction formation; it does not rescue the mother-daughter relation from the binary castration model and therefore remains caught in the structure that can only reproduce either its idealization or its denigration.

Demeter-Kore, Clytemnestra-Iphigenia, and Jocasta-Antigone are not mother-daughter couples that could be used to represent the differentiation between mother and daughter. Instead, these manifest mother-daughter couples in our cultural imaginary function precisely to merge the positions of mother and daughter. When analyzed in the context of the myths and tragedies in which they appear, what we find is that Clytemnestra and Iphigenia are in fact one and the same projection; they are distorted replicas of one another, as are Jocasta and Antigone and Demeter and Kore. These mother-daughter couples, rather than offering women a representation of a mediated relation, in fact work in the service of the male imaginary (to which they belong) that systematically forecloses the relation between women and instead, as I shall later show, constructs these simulacra of mother-daughter couples with the aim of collapsing the mother and daughter into one position in order then to exclude it from the dominant structure.

While I can understand the motivation or desire to find myths that appear to hold "traces" of a so-called benign mother-daughter relation that can in turn be used to enrich a potential female imaginary, my own approach to myth with regard to rethinking the mother-daughter relation differs considerably from such projects. Rather than attempting to recover or refind something lost and essentially harmonious and benign and thus perpetuating a nostalgic utopian fantasy, I am more concerned with working within myth to undo the projections of the male imaginary with a view to reorganizing the very foundations of its structures. Myth must be used to effect the emergence of *new* structures that can bring to representation and theory unconscious phantasies that have hitherto been rendered mute.

The particular force of feminism's use of psychoanalysis is that it makes it a necessity for feminism to analyze its own unconscious, its own fantasies and projections. The desire to find a benign positive prototypical mother-daughter relation belongs to a powerful fantasy or wish that, if left unanalyzed, counteracts a psychoanalytic feminism that aims to effect sociosymbolic change. Idealization of the mother-daughter relation is just as dangerous as its systematic denigration; it remains within the same paradigm that functions in accordance with the male imaginary that appropriates the maternal as the mute grounding of the very possibility of its discourse. The point at which myth is used to find "traces" of what I consider to be a nostalgic and unanalyzed phantasy is the point at which the use of myth becomes detrimental to feminism. The powerful goddesses, Amazon daughters, and transgressive "strong" mythical mothers devoted to their "beautiful" daughters that populate our myths are manifestly seductive, yet feminists working with myth must, like Odysseus, vigilantly protect themselves from being seduced by these so-called positive representations. To be seduced by the manifest in myth is to submit to the siren call, that is, to be lured into a dead end where there shall be neither social transformation nor theory.

The mother-daughter relations in Greek mythology that Irigaray suggests we retain and develop are, in my argument, precisely what need to be broken down; they represent the equivalent of the "dream work" that functions to conceal/censor the latent/incorporated matricidal law and its transgression. In order to use Irigaray's powerful work and develop her call for radical intervention, we should avoid joining in her celebration and perpetuation of the manifest benign aspect of mythical mother-daughter images. Instead, we must concentrate on the mother-daughter relation in myth with a view to examining its potential cultural and symbolic value within the laws of the symbolic order.

The Other Side of Utopia: Melanie Klein and the Mother-Daughter Relation

It is Klein and Irigaray who, in their different ways, have brought to light most powerfully the psychic problems within the mother-daughter relation. Reading Irigaray's work on the mother-daughter relation in parallel with that of Melanie Klein can massively enrich our uses of both these theorists. Klein brings to Irigaray's work a necessary dose of pessimism and negativity that checks the splitting-off, in Irigaray's work, of the destructive aspects of the mother-daughter relation. Irigaray brings to Klein's work a theory of the symbolic that puts Klein's observations into a sociopolitical ideological context and so introduces the possibility of change into Klein's otherwise normative schema.

Reading Klein undercuts any utopian desires the feminist scholar may harbor with regard to the mother-daughter relation. Demeter and Persephone read with Klein's theory in mind can be interpreted very differently from the benign interpretation offered to us by Irigaray. We could just as well interpret Demeter's rage with regard to the loss of her daughter, and the resulting famine and human catastrophe (as well as the violent treatment of a baby in her care), as belonging to the phantasy of the omnipotent mother from whom the daughter cannot escape.[12] While I do not hold to this interpretation, the point I am raising is that once we have considered Klein's disturbing accounts of infantile phantasy and primitive envy, it becomes impossible to sustain an approach to the relation to the mother that short-circuits its destructive aspects. We need Klein to undercut our phantasy of an early maternal Eden before Hades came along and destroyed it all. What we need, however, in order to use both Klein and Irigaray's powerful work on the mother and the mother-daughter relation, is a theory of a matricide whose underlying laws can function to bring a structure to what both Klein and Irigaray have in their different ways brought to light.

Klein's concentration on the primitive infantile phantasies directed at the mother's breast led her to create a theory of envy that has radically illuminated psychoanalytic insight into early psychic mechanisms and phantasies that remain alive, in varying degrees, in the adult mind. Klein allowed us to gain a different perspective on the mother-daughter relation through her concept of primitive envy. Rather than focusing on the daughter's hatred for her mother in the castration complex, as in Freudian theory, Klein discovered earlier phantasies whereby the mother is phantasized as all-powerful and retaliatory, causing the daughter to develop profound anxieties about the destruction of her internal organs by the phantasized archaic mother. Rather than perceiving the mother-daughter relation as a potential to establish a generative link, transmitting a healthy identification, wherein the daughter can receive confirmation of her reproductive potential and her adult sexed subjectivity, Klein brought to light how this process is sabotaged by early sadistic and persecutory phantasies rooted in envy that tenaciously color the mother-daughter relation well into adult life. The aspect of Klein's work that clarifies the profound difficulty of negotiating the depressive position or achieving the resolution that she saw in Orestes comes to light most explicitly in her thoughts about the daughter, that is, in her contention that the daughter's capacity to overcome the vicissitudes of envy in relation to the mother is minimal.

Thinking about Klein and Irigaray's different approaches to the mother-daughter relation leads us straight into the heart of a radical split, that is, the split between denigration and idealization. Klein leaves us with a terrifying and irresolvable pathological model of the mother and daughter, while Irigaray gives us an often idealized model in which the mother and daughter are declared a benign loving couple with the potential for the creation of a field of desire specific to women, thus crafting a new sexual/social space wherein female subjectivity can emerge outside the dictates of male phantasy. Klein tells us about interminable hate, violence, and stagnation, while Irigaray tells us of the profound love, passion, and fecundity existing between mother and daughter. Klein tells us of the mother as object of the daughter's primitive envious phantasy, while Irigaray works to posit the mother as a subject of desire, thus perceiving the relation in terms of two subjects.

We can begin to appreciate the extent of the entrenchment in the unconscious of the male imaginary's archaic projection onto the mother. Attempts to theorize the mother seem invariably to reproduce the structure of the male projections so that the idealization/denigration split cannot be overcome. Irigaray is aware of this problem and often comments on the extreme difficulties involved if women are to be able to refuse the projections of the male imaginary; she acknowledges that the task of finding a way of existing that involves something other embodying the projections or reacting to them via aggressive enactment is almost impossible as long as there is no representational support through which to counter the projective operations underlying the male imaginary.[13] Irigaray implicitly argues that the phantasized "devouring monster" mother of Kleinian and post-Kleinian theory is, itself, a description of the male imaginary's archaic projection onto the mother that psychoanalytic theory reflects and reproduces rather than analyzes: "The mother has become a devouring monster as an inverted effect of the blind consumption of the mother."[14]

Irigaray sees the fantasy of the devouring mother as part of a "defensive network projected by the man-father or his sons on to the abyss of a silent and threatening belly." The mother, then, provokes anxiety, phobia, disgust, and a haunting fear of castration, and women are invariably, for Irigaray, "placed in the sites of these projections." She identifies these infantile phantasies directed at the mother, which belong to the paranoid position that Klein describes, as remaining operative on the cultural level, where they become established and fixed rather than modified and worked through. Implicitly, Irigaray suggests that as long as there are no valid representations of female sexuality, no words, images, or symbols except "filthy, mutilating" words, then there can be no descriptions of the relation to the mother other than those that speak of the "devouring mouth," the "phallic threat" of the mother, "a cloaca or anal and urethral outfall."[15] There can be no depressive position, according to Irigaray, in a culture that is based on the unacknowledged "consumption of the mother" and forecloses the theorization and symbolization of the mother as a sexed subject of desire. But the problem of how to find a place outside the field of projections from which the creation of valid representations could emerge is where Irigaray's work becomes most problematic.

Irigaray, too, cannot seem to avoid reacting to and reproducing the projection onto the maternal that she so forcefully wants to undercut by offering up its opposite: the utopian benign mother who can give her daughter protection from the operations of the father's law that otherwise render her derelict. Yet the mother that Irigaray visualizes (Demeter, for example) cannot possibly protect her daughter from the projections of the male imaginary since that mother is herself an aspect of the projection. Together, Klein and Irigaray's work gives us vivid descriptive accounts of the archaic projections onto the mother that are not modified but continue to function to varying degrees, for Klein, in the adult mind and, for Irigaray, on the cultural symbolic level. Reading the two theorists together brings into sharp relief how completely locked into the terms of the male imaginary we inevitably are. Even when, as a feminist theorist, like Irigaray, one attempts to theorize the mother and her status within the cultural order, one cannot help falling back into the practice of repeating the projective operation that sustains the order one is trying to undermine and change.

What we will find, however, is that despite the antithetical trends in Klein and Irigaray's treatment of the mother-daughter relation, we do not have to collaborate with the splitting that either definitively pathologizes the relation (Klein and Lacan) or overidealizes it (Irigaray). Reading these two theories together brings to light the fundamental problem that underlies both Klein and Irigaray's contrasting treatments of the mother and the mother-daughter relation: neither is concerned with the cultural laws belonging to the mother that would allow for the symbolization of difference between mother and daughter, and in this way neither approach can lead to bringing the mother-daughter relation into theory. As Juliet Mitchell writes in her updated introduction (2000) to *Psychoanalysis and Feminism:* "We have a great deal of rich work on mothering, but no place for the mother within the laws of the human order."[16] While Klein's interest was the phantasized mother of early infancy and Irigaray's work on the mother concerns precisely what Mitchell refers to, that is, the mother's nonstatus within the laws of the human order, what neither theorist addresses is the cultural significance of matricide with regard to the unconscious laws it may generate.

In order to move out of the realm of description, projection, and repetition and finally break the circular process that prevents psychoanalytic feminism go beyond concentrating on the mother as theorized within the entrenched castration (binary) structure, it is necessary to shift attention away from the manifest (projections) and toward the theorization of a latent matricidal law. There can be no mother to protect her daughter from the projections of the male imaginary and give her access to a sexed symbolic genealogy that is specific to her structure as long as there is no law belonging to the mother. Bringing Metis and her law into the picture means that we can use both Klein and Irigaray's work on the mother-daughter relation together with the Oresteian myth in a way that moves beyond the dichotomy of idealization or denigration of the maternal.

Klein, Irigaray and Electra: Reading the Manifest

In their readings of the Oresteian myth, Klein and Irigaray, while concentrating predominantly on Orestes' trajectory, do mention one of the daughters: Electra is given brief consideration. For Irigaray, she takes on the burden of the madness in relation to the mother that belongs to a whole culture, and, for Klein, Electra's "hate" is a result of "early disturbances in the girl's relation to her mother" that are characterized by her oedipal conflicts. For Klein, Electra's condition derives from the "frustration of her longing to be loved by her mother" and "her rivalry with her mother for her father's love."[17]

While Klein chose a myth other than Oedipus in order to talk about a different structure of desire relating to the son, the case of the daughter is left to hover on the margins of her text, abandoned to the periphery of a model that addresses the daughter briefly and only in relation to her disturbed oedipal complex and the consequential liability to fixation and regression. In Klein's reading, Electra, in dramatic contrast to Orestes, is marked by her inability to achieve psychic change. She resists development, taking on the position of being interminably unfinished or stuck in a constant state of regression, never too far away from the madness that underlies the process of becoming a subject. Klein does not delve more deeply into Electra's situation; the daughter's psychic stasis, her addiction to hate and destructiveness are, in Klein's reading, written off as inevitable and seemingly not worthy of further analysis. In this way, Klein's essay on the *Oresteia*, which celebrates the myth's depiction of the mature resolution of the depressive position, does so at the expense of the daughter, whose psychic disturbances are far from resolved.

Irigaray's observation of Electra, the daughter who remains "mad" and unable to be helped by the goddess who cures Orestes of his "madness," leads her to identify a process wherein these two situations are inextricably linked, that is to say, the daughter's madness and the son's cure have an inextricable relationship: "All desire is connected to madness. But apparently one desire has chosen to see itself as wisdom, moderation, truth, and has left the other to bear the burden of the madness it did not want to attribute to itself, recognize in itself. This relationship between desire and madness comes into its own, for both man and woman, in the relationship with the mother. But all too often, man washes his hands of it and leaves it to woman—women."[18]

Irigaray seems to be implying that the daughter's madness is not even her own, not a madness specific to her desire but a madness expelled from the oedipalized masculine subject. Later in the same essay, she illustrates this idea by applying it specifically to the Oresteian siblings: "Electra, the daughter will remain mad. The matricidal son must be saved from madness to establish the patriarchal order. . . . The murder of the mother results, then, in the non-punishment of the son, the burial of the madness of women—and the burial of women in madness."[19] Container of his projections, his madness, Electra becomes or lives Orestes' split-off self. He will not look back in the direction of his mother wherein his madness lies since she, the daughter, does it for him; she will remain (too) close to this madness, this relation to the mother. While Athena helps the son to look away or forward, the daughter Electra is willfully attached or morbidly addicted to the regressive gaze. Consequently, she is arrested in an interminable madness in relation to the mother. Electra is not required to come before the law to answer for her part in the matricide. While her role is determining in the middle/structural center of the myth (she fuels Orestes' will to commit the matricide and is actively involved in concocting its design), she is written out of the resolving play of the trilogy where she is invisible in the eyes of Zeus and Athena's law and is killed off into silence/stasis. We leave her in the frenzy of hate and violence, caught up in a destructive primitive reverie, repeatedly and obsessively going over the old ground of her disturbed relation to her mother. There is no law, no cure, to give her a position from which to think about what she has done/felt, and instead she is abandoned and stuck (derelict). One may say she has got away with it, so to speak. That is, the law overlooks her crime and she avoids judgment, slipping through the net of the legal order. *She has not got away with anything, however, since she has not got away.* She remains (psychically) too close to the murdered mother who, in her mind, will never die since Electra cannot get away, move on, or experience a loss that may be generative: she is forever looking back to the mother whom she cannot properly kill.[20]

Irigaray's analysis of the relation between Electra and Orestes draws (implicitly) on Kleinian theory. She produces a reading of Electra's madness that depends on the Kleinian concept of projective identification:[21] Orestes expels his unwanted madness in relation to the mother into Electra and simultaneously needs her to remain as/contain his unwanted primitive self. He needs her to remain in the retrograde position so that he can look triumphantly forward, free from the shackles of his early relation to the mother. The madness of the relation to the mother does not go away; it cannot be magically removed by Athena's denial. What is needed is for someone else to live the madness so that Orestes and Athena (the "motherless daughter") can wash their hands of it. The madness that ensues from matricide is disowned by the son and projected into the daughter whom we do not hear about again; she will remain famous for her unrelenting hatred of her mother and her "unceasing" tears. Once Orestes has been set free, neither he, nor Athena, nor Klein will look back to consider Electra's fate. In considering Electra's madness in relation to Orestes, however, Irigaray manages to think about Electra through a model different from the oedipal. What is more she does this by using a Kleinian concept so that Irigaray's reading curiously turns out to be more Kleinian than Klein's own reading of Electra.

Klein's reading of the *Oresteia* mimics the structure of the myth, where Electra is abandoned at the point in the *Oresteia* where looking backward (to the mother) gives way to looking forward. Klein can see resolution in Orestes because she overlooks the structural connection that links the positions of Electra and Orestes. Klein overlooks Electra's role as container for the split-off underlying psychotic structure of Orestes' achieved masculine subject position. She merely acknowledges Electra's situation as being typical of the mother-daughter relation, which, in her eyes, is invariably sabotaged with an excess of primitive envy and oedipal rivalry. Irigaray's reading of Electra that implicitly uses Kleinian theory brings into sharp relief how Klein fails to link or think Electra in relation to Orestes and so misses the opportunity to analyze a manifestation of projective identification, a mechanism she was the first to theorize and that is fundamental to her description of the paranoid schizoid position.

Electra, the daughter, is the retrograde, and in looking back (to her mother) she is, in effect, turned into a pillar of salt, immobilized, stuck in the salt of tears, the salt that forever stings and activates the pain of her wounds, preventing those wounds from ever healing:

> Abandoned to despair. I worship Niobe,
> The inconsolable, entombed in stone,
> Weeping eternally
> With tears unceasing[22]

If Klein managed to see in Orestes the capacity to resolve and avoid regression, it is because the daughter is left to carry the burden/madness of regression or looking back. Klein abandons Electra in her reading, leaving her to remain untheorized/analyzed and mad, while Orestes walks into so-called freedom and health. Klein, in her reading of the Oresteian myth, mimics this process of projection. The son is given access to possibility of progress, saved from the madness of the regressive gaze at the expense of the daughter/sister who must always act out the regressive degenerative pull backward (for him). She is condemned to memory while he is given access to desire. The conflict between memory and desire is split between Electra and Orestes. He can forget while she can only remember. The daughter has become the pillar of salt (stasis/despair/tears) that he will not accept as belonging partially to him. She acts out for him what is universally irresolvable with regard to the bodily encounter with the mother.

Too see all positions depicted in the myth as structurally linked allows us to examine and untangle projective mechanisms, giving us the possibility to think about where and to whom each phantasy structure belongs. If Orestes achieves the depressive position, then Electra keeps alive his paranoid schizoid self, which is never superseded. Disentangling the daughter from her function as container of the son's madness may allow us to rethink or restructure a different constellation or organization of phantasy. It may be possible to disrupt the ubiquitous placing of the daughter/sister as retrograde, as a pillar of salt, forever looking back to a dead sea in which nothing moves or grows.

The male imaginary (that has become law) situates the son as the one who can resolve and move forward, rendering him equal to the challenge of consolidating patriarchal power, with femininity as the indispensable container for all that he needs to disavow in himself. The mother-daughter relation becomes the out-of-focus substratum underlying paternal law where the madness belonging to the bodily encounter with the mother is contained outside the symbolic walls of the polis and given solely to the daughter to suffer. Electra wails while Orestes rules, and Orestes *can* rule precisely *because* Electra wails. Someone has to wail since the violence does not go away: it will always surface somewhere, irrespective of its rightful owner or place. The question of whose madness one is given/forced to live is at stake here. Instead of perpetuating the ubiquitous belief that the mother-daughter relation is necessarily and universally mad and necessitates the father to come and put an end to its horrors, we first need to be more discerning about whose madness is whose.

Electra's "madness" is represented in the myth as manifesting itself in relation to her mother. I have noted how Irigaray has argued that this madness is not specific to the daughter but is a projection from the son, Orestes. In this way, for Irigaray, there is no mother-daughter relation represented in the myth; there are only symptoms pointing to the absence of a symbolically mediated relation existing outside the projections of the male imaginary. In my reading of the daughters in the *Oresteia*, I, like Irigaray, read their positions as symptomatic of an order that has no place for a feminine specificity. In order to go further than describing the daughter's dereliction, however, we need to move from the manifest to the latent. That is, we need to consider Electra and her sisters in relation to Metis. The "madness" of the daughter, in my reading, is an effect of the incorporated matricidal law.

12 ❧

The Latent Mother-Daughter

I N CONSIDERING ATHENA in relation to Metis, we reach a stronger
position from which to rethink the mother-daughter relation once
matricide can be posited as a structural center that can deliver an
introjective loss. That is to say, in bringing to light Metis's law, we can
finally introduce the missing link that could bring the mother into theory,
into representation, into the generative register of introjection, and thus
into structure; namely, into a position that determines aspects of the sociosymbolic cultural organization.

Restructuring the Oresteian myth by rectifying the exclusion of the
Metis-Athena relation radically alters the possibilities of using the myth
not only to describe and counter the workings of the male imaginary but,
further, to symbolize and theorize a structural relation based on a law that
has hitherto remained incorporated within the myth. With the analysis
of Athena in relation to Metis in place, we can then reread the relations
between Clytemnestra and her three daughters in the context of the decrypted law of the mother that functions both to provide a check on the
male parthenogenetic phantasy and to symbolize the difference between
women as well as their sameness/identification. Further, we can use the
decryption of Metis and her law to rethink Orestes' relation to his sisters
and in so doing obtain a more sophisticated understanding of the psychic

uses he makes of his sisters for the purpose of sustaining his radical disavowal of the existence of the matricidal law.

Approaching myth in relation to its structuring power, through which cultural laws are both transmitted and concealed, means using myth as a political tool with which to intervene in the current symbolic (phallic) hegemony. Discovering the incorporated law of Metis in the Oresteian myth allows us to move toward the symbolization and theorization of more than one sociosymbolic bond and underlying unconscious structure that are not reducible to the phantasy constellation belonging to the phallic/castration model.

Part 2 described how the law of Metis, which I have argued remains incorporated in the Oresteian myth, refers to the prohibition of the parthenogenetic phantasy that Juliet Mitchell has recently theorized.[1] I have argued that in Zeus's gesture of swallowing the pregnant Metis, he not only murders the mother but incorporates her law. What results is the erasure of any evidence of her law so that Zeus's parthenogenetic phantasy remains intact, hence Athena's so-called motherless status. Matricide, as sanctioned by Athena, becomes the foundation of the patriarchal law-of-the-father, yet the specific laws underlying matricide are erased because of the incorporation of Metis. What this means is that Zeus's order is based on the transgression of Metis's prohibition (the father *cannot* father forth alone) yet avoids the guilt and acknowledgment of this transgression by virtue of the incorporation of Metis, which erases the fact of the existence of any law. In other words, you cannot be accused of transgression if there is no law to transgress. It is indeed an ingenious operation that Zeus effects: his swallowing of Metis efficiently removes the evidence of the mother's law so that his parthenogenetic creation of Athena is transformed from an act of transgression (the parthenogenetic phantasy that has not been prohibited) into the founding "truth" that underlies the sovereignty of the father:

> APOLLO: A father can father forth without a mother.
> Here she stands, our living witness. Look—
> *Exhibiting Athena.*
> Child sprung full blown from Olympian Zeus,
> Never bred in the darkness of the womb.[2]

What is more, it is Metis's daughter, Athena, whom Zeus delegates to keep intact the parthenogenetic phantasy through her role in condoning/

sanctioning Clytemnestra's death and prohibiting the mother's death from being mourned. In so doing, the underlying law belonging to matricide that prohibits the parthenogenetic phantasy is radically disavowed by Zeus and Athena. Matricide in the *Oresteia* is severed from its underlying law and is subsumed under the law-of-the-father; Athena effects a process wherein matricide loses its generative prohibitive function and instead functions to keep intact the parthenogenetic phantasy/complex that it is supposed to limit and smash:

> ATHENA: My work is here, to render the final judgement.
> Orestes,
> I will cast my lot for you.
> No mother gave me birth, . . .
>
> (LINES 748–751, P. 264)

> The man goes free,
> Cleared of the charge of blood.
>
> (LINES 767–768, P. 265)

The use of Clytemnestra to screen Metis in the Oresteian myth functions to sever matricide from its underlying prohibition and thus appropriates matricide as the foundation of the paternal law, blinding its subjects to the parthenogenetic phantasy on which that law is based. The incorporation of Metis is fundamental to Orestes' acquittal; it is only Athena who could function as Orestes' faithful advocate by virtue of her being the embodiment/proof of the parthenogenetic phantasy that her very existence keeps intact. If evidence of Metis were brought into Athena's courtroom, then Athena's logic could not convince the jury; the parthenogenetic phantasy on which her logic depends would have collapsed.

The Furies, who represent the prosecution of Orestes, do not bring the existence of Metis into the court case; they fail to produce the one piece of evidence that would disclose Athena's defense of Orestes to be fundamentally flawed. In this way, we can see that even the Furies (who supposedly represent the "ancient law," line 793, p. 266) have no knowledge or memory of Metis, so they are unequal to the challenge of articulating the specificity of the transgression underlying the new rule of the Olympian gods. The Furies can only lament and protest against Orestes' acquittal through ranting shrieks; they have no language to express the incorporated law of Metis, and so their protest can only take the form of expressing the *affects* resulting from the absence of something voided/excluded. They protest,

yet they are unaware of what they are protesting about; they have no law
with which to counter Zeus's and thus finally they inevitably submit to
Athena and join her culture in the forgetting of their cause. In their protest
at Orestes' acquittal, the Furies, throughout the court case scene, repeat
the following chant:

> You, you younger gods!—you have ridden down
> The ancient laws, wrenched them from my grasp—
> And I, robbed of my birthright, suffering, great with wrath,
> I loose my poison over the soil, aieee!—
> Poison to match my grief comes pouring out my heart,—
> Cursing the land to burn it sterile and now
> Rising up from its roots a cancer blasting leaf and child,
> Now for Justice, Justice!—cross the face of the earth
> The bloody tide comes hurling, all mankind destroyed.
> . . . Moaning, only moaning? What will I do?
> The mockery of it, Oh unbearable,
> Mortified by Athens
> We the daughters of the Night,
> Our power stripped, cast down.
>
> (LINES 792–805, P. 266)

The "only" currency available to the Furies is "moaning." And this moaning fails to produce a case against the Olympian gods that would alter the
results of the so-called legal proceedings. It is as if the Furies are denied
legal representation; they have no one to translate their "moaning" into
the terms of the law, no representative who remembers the other/incor-
porated law that, if identified, would provide a framework through which
to argue their case.[3] Instead, the Furies can only moan, aware of their inevitable defeat and resigned to the rhetorical language of despair: "What
will I do?" The only other form of expression in their repertoire is that of
threatening violent revenge; moaning or violent enactment are their only
options.

The Furies, in my reading, are the embodiment of the oral rage and
aggression that results from the reaction to being subject to an order that
denies the matricidal law. In her essay "Women's Time," Julia Kristeva articulates the reactions of the "too brutally excluded subject": "When a subject is too brutally excluded from this socio-symbolic stratum; when for
example, a woman feels her affective life as a woman or her condition as
social being too brutally ignored by existing discourse or power (from her

family to social institutions); she may, by counter-investing the violence she has endured, make of herself a 'possessed' agent of this violence in order to combat what was experienced as frustration—with arms which may seem disproportional, but which are not so in comparison with the subjective or more precisely narcissistic suffering from which they originate."[4] Irigaray, too, has shown us that an inevitable reaction among women to the masculine imaginary's projective mechanisms, other than embodying them, is fury, rage, and violence—violence that can be directed against men, against other women or their children, or against themselves: "The world of women seems very like that of certain primitive societies that have no official sacrifice, no recognized rites, no indigenous jurisprudence. Revenge is taken outside of law or rights, in the form of private attacks, whether concerted or not."[5]

The Furies can only react; they can only rage and threaten violence since they have no law through which to counter Athena's judgment. But if the rage of the Furies is a reaction, then this reaction can easily be transformed into its opposite. The Furies will become kind; their rage will flip over into a sinister compliance. Athena persuades them to turn into the "Kindly Ones," she cunningly effects a reaction formation in the Furies:

> Let me persuade you.
> The lethal spell of your voice, never cast it
> Down on the land and blight its harvest home
> Lull asleep that salt black wave of anger—
>
> (LINES 839–842, P. 268)

The Furies, after much persuasion, finally submit. They reply:

> Your magic is working . . . I can feel the hate,
> The fury slip away.
>
> (LINES 908–909, P. 271)

Athena's dealing with the Furies constitutes the last and in some senses most crucial aspect of the work she is obliged to undertake in resolving the matricidal case. What she is actually dealing with when she confronts the Furies is, in my reading, the "phantom effects" of the incorporation of Metis, her own mother. Athena effects a (precarious) temporary containment of the Furies' hate through coercive persuasion that induces a reaction formation. The Furies, without a law, without representational support that is based on the inclusion of the matricidal law within the sociosymbolic order, are turned unknowingly into the agents of their own annihilation. Yet the fury and the hate that they feel to have slipped away inevitably returns; it returns in Clytemnestra's daughters. The Furies' raging outbursts are displaced on to Clytemnestra's daughters but undergo a transformation. The fury, as it is manifested in the daughters, becomes internalized or directed inward and, as I will show later, produces a chronic morbid depression. Athena's transformation of the Furies into the Kindly Ones is an operation that leaves a remainder; Athena cannot tame the fury that returns in Orestes' sisters.

Athena's dealing with the Furies, who are also referred to as the "*daughters* of the Night," is the only time in the Oresteian myth in which she comes into direct contact with other female characters. Athena neither confronts nor mentions Orestes' sisters, despite Electra's fundamental role in the matricide and despite Agamemnon's murder of Iphigenia, which was the salient motive for Clytemnestra's revenge. The daughters' names will not be mentioned in the court case; for Athena, they do not exist. Athena's banishing of the "daughters of the Night" results in the banishing of all the other daughters in the myth so that the resolution Athena supposedly effects involves not only Orestes' so-called liberation but also the removal of *all* the daughters in the myth from further consideration. This is reflected in readings of the myth that focus on Orestes' acquittal and the taming of the Furies; the daughters become invisible once the "magic" of Athena's persuasion blots out the existence of the remainders that cannot be subsumed within or represented by her supposedly integrative "democratic" law.

The Furies are supposed to be defending Clytemnestra against the charge of killing Agamemnon. We remember that Clytemnestra killed Agamemnon in order to avenge her daughter, Iphigenia, whom Agamemnon sacrificed before sailing to Troy:

> He thought no more of it than killing a beast
> And his flocks were rich, teeming in their fleece,
> But he sacrificed his own child, our daughter,
> The agony I laboured into love
> To charm away the savage winds of Thrace.[6]

In defending Clytemnestra in Athena's court, the Furies are at the same time fighting for the punishment of the father who killed the daughter as well as for the punishment of the son who killed the mother. The Furies in this way protest against an order that does not prohibit the murder by the father/son of the mother/daughter. In their failure to counter Athena's judgment owing to the absence of the matricidal law, the Furies point to the situation wherein the crime against the mother is inevitably repeated against the daughter. The refusal/inability to mourn the mother and recognize her law results in the lack of protection of the daughter in the face of the omnipotent desires of the father/son. This is a crucial point because it clearly demonstrates the way in which the male imaginary collapses the positions of mother and daughter, rendering them undifferentiated. The *two* crimes that the law will not punish or prohibit in the Oresteian myth are against both daughter and mother.

Athena's silence on the subject of Iphigenia merits attention. Rather than presenting a rationalization of her dismissal of Agamemnon's crime, she merely ignores Iphigenia's murder as if it never happened or else as if it were not relevant to the case over which she presides. The failure to recognize Agamemnon's crime means that Athena underwrites it, rendering the incestuously violated daughter a sanctioned sacrificial victim of a culturally permitted kinship violence; because it is unacknowledged and legally unpunished, father-daughter violence and incest is implicitly authorized. Athena will set no store by the daughter's death; she will not punish the father who kills his daughter in order to secure his power and will not support the mother who defends her daughter. Owing to her belief in the story of her miraculous origin, she will "honour the male in all things," one of these "things" being the sexual violence against the daughter.

Clytemnestra and the Furies represent the attempt to protest the father's murdering the daughter; they fail because the law of Zeus, embodied by Athena, will only prohibit the murder of the father. *There is no internalized prohibition that protects the daughter from the destructive omnipotence of the father.* The Furies, in fighting for the punishment for the crime against the mother by the son, simultaneously point to the absence of an institutionalized/internalized prohibition against father-daughter incest and infanticide. I will be elaborating this point in a moment, but I want to suggest here that, in the absence of Metis's law, the crime against Iphigenia by her father, which in my reading is motivated by the unchecked infantile parthenogenetic phantasy, is neither acknowledged nor condemned.

The incorporation of the law underlying matricide means the suppression of a prohibition that would protect the daughter from the dangerous effects of the acting-out of the male phantasy of parthenogenesis. Without the support of Metis's law—the father *cannot* father forth alone[7]—the Furies fail to make Athena's culture acknowledge the sacrifice of Iphigenia as a transgression. While the myth depicts Agamemnon's crime against his daughter as manifested in a literal murder/sacrifice, we can interpret the literal violence in the myth as pointing to the violence of a parent/child relation in which there are no internalized boundaries. The father/daughter relation in the myth points to the situation wherein the daughter is exposed to or radically unprotected from the destructive intrusive projections of the father, who still functions in accordance with the parthenogenetic phantasy, a situation that is inevitable in the absence of the hypothesized matricidal law/prohibition.

The destructive omnipotence of the father that we have seen in Zeus's rape, incorporation, and murder of Metis and in Agamemnon's murder of his daughter is split off or disavowed by Athena, who reveres both Zeus and Agamemnon as idealized objects. Athena's refusal to acknowledge Agamemnon's crime against Iphigenia is read here as a continuation of her inability to acknowledge Zeus's crime against Metis, and in this way we can understand why Athena disregards the fate of Iphigenia in her judicial decision. Iphigenia's murder, I shall demonstrate, is a distortion of the rape and incorporation of Metis. If we consider Iphigenia as part of the manifest, the dream work that conceals the latent trauma/thought, then we can use the myth of Iphigenia to lead us back to Metis and her law. Athena's disavowal of the fate of Iphigenia and her inability to acknowledge the Oresteian daughters in the terms of her court of law are due to the fact that the daughters, in distorted forms, reenact or reproduce aspects of the incorporation and transgression of the matricidal law. To acknowledge this law would threaten to undermine the very foundations of Athena's brave new world. To know the daughters would mean that Athena would have to confront the destructive omnipotence of the father; further, to discover her mother and her prohibitions would demolish the parthenogenetic omnipotent phantasy that Athena sustains, promotes, and institutionalizes.

Instead of analyzing Iphigenia and the Furies in relation to Clytemnestra, the manifest mother of the myth, here we read the daughter in relation to the voided/latent mother, Metis. In this way, we can begin to develop a new mother-daughter structure/model via the Oresteian myth that has not hitherto been constructed.

I want to show that the myth depicting the crime against Iphigenia that is mentioned in Aeschylus's *Oresteia* and dramatized by Euripides expresses the same underlying structure as the Metis myth. Thus, in my reading, Iphigenia brings into the *Oresteia*, albeit in a distorted form, the

concealed structure of masculine desire on which the Oresteian matricidal myth is based: namely, the phantasy of male parthenogenesis and its
concomitant mechanism of violent incorporation. Through reading the
Metis-Iphigenia mother-daughter relation rather than the Clytemnestra-
Iphigenia relation in the *Oresteia*, we move toward using the myth for the
theorization of the hitherto incorporated matricidal law.

13 ❧

Iphigenia Becomes Metis

Every attempt that has hitherto been made to solve the problem of dreams has dealt directly with their manifest content as it is presented in our memory. . . . We are alone in taking something else into account. We have introduced a new class of psychical material between the manifest content of dreams and the conclusions of our enquiry; namely their latent content, or (as we say) the "dream thoughts" arrived at by means of our procedure. It is from these dream thoughts and not from a dream's manifest content that we disentangle its meaning. We are thus presented with a new task, that is, of investigating the relations between the manifest content of dreams and the latent dream thoughts, and of tracing out the processes by which the latter have been changed into the former.

—SIGMUND FREUD, "THE DREAM WORK"

IN THIS CHAPTER, I will show how the myth of Iphigenia uses a series of oppositions, reversals, displacements, and condensations in order to conceal/disguise the crime against Metis for which it is a substitute. In other words, the Iphigenia myth, in my reading, is the result of the processes belonging to what Freud termed the "dream work" that functions to disguise, distort, and censor the latent thoughts (the incorporation of Metis) from consciousness. The "dream work" distorts the material belonging to the latent thoughts to such an extent that at first glance we may not observe the precise replication of structure in these two myths. The *Oresteia* allows the traces of Metis to enter into its structure only in a highly disguised form.

Iphigenia replaces Metis in the Oresteian myth like a secondary reconstruction that censors the unbearable latent thought and prevents it from reaching consciousness. According to Lévi-Strauss's methodology of structural analysis, myth needs to be analyzed according to variation and theme; duplication, triplication, or quadruplication of the same sequence occurs, such that myth exhibits a "slated structure, which comes to the surface, so to speak, through the process of repetition." Yet the slates will not be identical: "a theoretically infinite number of slates will be generated, each one slightly different from the others."[1] Undertaking a structural analysis of myth means considering a number of mythical

variants/slates together and analyzing the differences among the variations, through attention to the inversion of terms and relations wherein
one term is replaced by its opposite, as well as inversions between the
function value and the term value of two elements.[2] The following reading of Iphigenia in relation to Metis, then, is informed by Freud's theory
of the "dream work" and Lévi-Strauss's method of the structural analysis
of myth. What I want to show through this kind of reading is that in the
myth the Oresteian daughters express aspects of the (voided) structure of
the Metis myth: matricide-incorporation-parthenogenesis. First, however,
I will summarize the myth of Iphigenia.

Agamemnon leads the Greek army to sack the city of Troy. The ships,
however, become stuck at the bay of Aulis owing to the stagnation of the
winds brought about by Artemis. Artemis declares that she will not bring
back the winds until Agamemnon sacrifices his eldest daughter. Artemis
is punishing Agamemnon for a crime of hubris directed against her in the
past when he arrogantly boasted of being a better hunter than she, despite
her being a goddess and his being a mere mortal. Agamemnon consents
to Artemis's demand and calls for his daughter to be brought to the naval
camp on the pretext that she is to be married. Instead of the promised
groom, the virgin bride is met by her father on the wedding altar and is
penetrated through the throat by his sword. Iphigenia vanishes at the point
the sword meets her throat, and the body of a deer mysteriously appears
in her place.[3] Her disappearance is interpreted by the chorus and by her
father as a great relief: the vanishing is used as evidence that she has been
"wafted to the gods,"[4] and thus the replacement of her body with the deer's
allows her murderer to avoid experiencing any guilt associated with his
crime. Artemis sends back the winds, and the fleet sails to Troy where the
Greeks achieve victory, fame, and sovereign rule.

Remember the structure underlying the myth of Zeus and Metis: rape-
incorporation-appropriation = paternal generative omnipotence + denial
of the matricidal law. Let me demonstrate how this same structure underlies the Iphigenia myth. Through Iphigenia, the voided crime against
Metis is (in a distorted form) woven into the manifest structure of the
Oresteian myth.

The pregnant mother (Metis), the obstacle to the parthenogenetic
phantasy that must be voided, is replaced by her opposite: the virgin
daughter. This is the first fundamental reversal undertaken by the dream
work/male imaginary identifiable in the Oresteian myth. The marriage-
death equation expressed in the Iphigenia myth can be read in terms of an
incestuous rape; the father takes the place of the groom and penetrates the
daughter's throat with his sword in the context of marriage. The manifest

image of father's sword and daughter's throat through symbolism and displacement masks the phantasy of father-daughter incest; sword/phallus, throat/vagina.[5]

Agamemnon's shedding of his daughter's blood functions like a key to unlock the gateway of his heroic trajectory. The sexual violence that produces the spilling of virgin (hymen) blood allows him to go forth as a man and fight wars, conquer cities, and sustain his sovereign rule. In this way, Agamemnon's act can be read as a violent appropriation of the virgin daughter's potential fertility (her blood that signifies generativity). Through an incestuous rape of, theft from, and murder of the daughter, the father secures his political power and military victory.

The dead deer that appears in the place of Iphigenia's body is a crucial element in my reading of the myth; it provides the link that brings into view the close relationship between the Iphigenia myth and the Metis myth. I suggest that the motif of the deer condenses within it phantasies of incorporation that result in the foreclosure of mourning and the concomitant refusal/inability to give up infantile phantasies or beliefs.

The deer allows the men to believe that there has been no injustice, no murder, no crime. The effect of Iphigenia's vanishing is that there shall be no body to bury, no daughter to mourn, no evidence of the brutal rape and murder to which she was subjected; in other words, there shall be no guilt and no loss. But Clytemnestra immediately sees through the function of this "story" of her daughter's disappearance: "My child, which of the gods has stolen you? Surely I must think that this is a false story which has been told to comfort me, so that I should cease from my bitter mourning for you?"[6] The disappearance of Iphigenia functions in the same way as the swallowing/incorporation of Metis: death is denied/disavowed, and mourning and guilt are foreclosed. The deer that replaces Iphigenia is read here as a "concrete" object that creates a presence where there should have been a loss. The disappearance of the murdered girl produces a (hallucinatory) presence rather than a loss that can be mourned. Iphigenia is absent (but not considered dead), and the deer is present, so there is no gap or goneness through which a loss can be represented. The presence of the deer eradicates the evidence of the murder by standing in for the mutilated body of the daughter but at the same time does not *represent* the dead virgin daughter. The deer, according to Hanna Segal's theory of symbolism, can be read as a "concrete representation" working in the service of symbolic equivalence rather than symbolism proper.[7] The deer does not function to help the men overcome or work through a loss but rather works to deny loss. The deer precludes the mourning of the girl by retroactively changing the meaning of the events. It is as if the deer's presence says to the audience that has just witnessed the murder of a girl, "the girl was not killed; what you thought you just saw did not actually happen." The men have no longer seen a daughter killed; they have seen a deer killed. The deer erases the crime so that Agamemnon and his men can disavow any part in the enactment of the incestuous rape and murder that has been committed and can proceed as if they have done no wrong.

In my reading, the disappearance of Iphigenia at the moment the father commits his violence against her, together with the instantaneous appearance of the deer, signifies exactly the same mechanism of incorporation that Zeus uses in his violent act against Metis. Like Metis, Iphigenia disappears after being raped and murdered, and, as with Metis, the crime against her will be erased, and she will not be mourned. In both situations, what results is the presence of concrete objects that cannot be used to think or represent but can only be repetitively projected. The deer does not lead the men to think about Iphigenia and what has been done to her; instead, it screens this memory precisely to avoid thinking about the object and the violence done to it. The deer wipes out the crime at the moment it is committed. Iphigenia disappears but is not lost; she is absent but not dead enough to generate guilt. The deer, in my reading, points to the pathological mourning resulting from incorporation/erasure of the murdered object rather than an introjection of its loss and in this way forms the bridge or link between the myth of Iphigenia and the myth of Metis.[8]

The structure of the Iphigenia myth precisely mirrors the structure of the Metis myth; it is a matter of undoing the mechanisms that conceal the shared underlying "slated" structure. The chart below illustrates the parallel structures of the two myths and the way the latent (Metis) is transformed to the manifest (Iphigenia):

Latent	Manifest
Metis-mother	Iphigenia-daughter (*reversal*)
Taken by force	Daughter's compliance/consent (*reversal*)
Literal rape by Zeus	Father penetrates daughter's throat (*distortion*)
Pregnant mother	Virgin daughter (*reversal*)
Swallowed by Zeus	Daughter's body vanishes (*distortion*)
results in:	*results in:*
Incorporation of mother	Appearance of deer (*displacement*)
Appropriation of generative capacity	Appropriation of virgin blood

Matricide	Infanticide (*reversal*)
Erasure of Metis—no evidence	Erasure of evidence—deer appears
No guilt or knowledge of transgression	No guilt
Metis cannot be mourned	Iphigenia will not be mourned
Parthenogenetic phantasy intact	Father robs daughter of fertility
Paternal omnipotent sovereignty secured	Father can now win war/secure power

If we are convinced by the way the Iphigenia myth reworks and distorts the structure of the Metis myth, then we gain a new understanding of the logic underlying Athena's refusal to acknowledge the crime against Iphigenia. Athena's condemnation of Clytemnestra is at the same time her refusal to hear/know Iphigenia; if Athena remembered the crime of Iphigenia and saw fit to punish the perpetrator of this crime, then the traces of Zeus's crime against her mother might threaten to return. There will be no guilt resulting from the sacrifice of Iphigenia; all evidence of the crime will be obliterated. Agamemnon repeats Zeus's prototypical crime, and there is no law to prohibit his destructive omnipotence. In sanctioning the murder of Clytemnestra by absolving Orestes, Athena implicitly announces to her court that *the rape and murder of the daughter by the father will not be legally punished.* Iphigenia is not mentioned once during the whole court case scene; the story of Iphigenia disappears from the Oresteian myth as soon as Athena comes on to the stage. Athena's presence means the absence of Iphigenia, who is read here as the phantom or distorted reproduction of Metis. The crime against the daughter conceals within it the crime against the raped and incorporated mother, and Athena, the parthenogenetic production of Zeus, erases the Iphigenia/Metis structure from the myth. In place of the raped and murdered mother/daughter stands Athena, the triumphant phantasy of paternal parthenogenesis.

The violence against Iphigenia is described as a "madness" directed at *both* the daughter and the mother:

OLD MAN: Iphigenia—her father—with his own hand—means to murder her

CLYTEMNESTRA: What? Oh, what a filthy thing to say! You must be raving mad.

OLD MAN: With his sword he'll cut through her white throat—poor miserable child!

CLYTEMNESTRA: Oh! What shall I do? Can it then be my husband who is mad?

OLD MAN: *Yes, he's mad—towards you and your daughter:*
otherwise he is sane enough
It is a pitiful crime against you both.[9]

The madness of Agamemnon is directed toward *the mother and the*
daughter: otherwise, he is "sane enough." Violence toward the daughter
is simultaneously violence toward the mother. In killing the daughter,
Agamemnon is at the same time killing the mother (again). Mother and
daughter are merged into one and the same, standing in for one another in
the male imaginary, without differentiation. The madness that is directed
toward the mother and the daughter by the fathers Zeus/Agamemnon is
derived from an unlimited hubris/omnipotence linked to the phantasy of
parthenogenesis; the other's envied generative properties are appropriated via sexual violence and incorporation. The father has internalized no
limits or boundaries but instead functions on the primitive level of oral
incorporation or primary identification wherein no boundary between self
and object is experienced.[10] The father who rapes and murders his daughter (Agamemnon) is the same father who rapes and swallows the mother
(Zeus); namely, this is the father who believes he can "father forth alone."

If Zeus's incorporation of Metis and her law was so successful in oblit-
erating the prohibitions underlying matricide and if Athena was so successful in erasing the memory of Iphigenia (who conceals Metis) and the
"moaning" of the Furies (the phantom effect of the incorporation of Iphi-
genia/Metis) from her polis, then what evidence is there left in the myth
to allow us to hypothesize the existence of the so-called missing/incorpo-
rated law? To reconstruct Metis's law in order to rectify the gap in introjection resulting from Metis's incorporation by Zeus, we need to examine the
copious material expressed in the myth that describes the manifest symptoms that are left as the only traces of the obliterated law. Clytemnestra's
daughters remain as our evidence of the traces and symptomatic effects
of the incorporation of Metis's law that were not successfully obliterated
by Athena's work or the dream work that the Oresteian myth uses to suppress Metis and her prohibitions. Analyzing the daughters will undo the
last operations of the dream work that conceals the law that we are attempting to decrypt.

I will now proceed to analyze further a constellation of symptoms belonging to the daughters of the *Oresteia* using my hypothesis that these
symptoms can be decoded to reveal the very law for which they are pathological substitutes.

14 ॐ

Virginity and Sibling Incest

IN HER SPEECH announcing Orestes' acquittal, Athena declares:

I honour the male *in all things but marriage.*
Yes, with all my heart I am my father's child.[1]

IT IS A puzzling declaration, since Athena contradicts herself explicitly. She is not her father's daughter with "all" her heart because when it comes to marriage she stands against the "male." In rejecting marriage, Athena stands against the institution that is based on the exchange of women by men. It is significant that Athena mentions the part of her heart that does not honor the father; she opposes marriage, motherhood, and the family through the fierce protection of her virginity. She announces herself as her "father's child" yet refuses his law, the law that would result in her taking up the position of object to be exchanged by men and that forms the cornerstone of the kinship structure underlying the patriarchal civilization that she (manifestly) promotes. In all versions of the Oresteian myth, all the daughters of the *Oresteia*, whether they are goddesses or mortals, without exception, remain virgins. The meaning of this observation is complex and will be unfurled as the study of the daughters progresses. The postulation of a metaphorical interpretation of the literal virginity expressed in the myth is the focus of this chapter.

I want to suggest tentatively here a connection between the state of virginity identifiable in all the daughters in the myth and the incorporation of the matricidal law. Athena, the prototypical *parthenos*, believes in her father's independent generation; her attachment to virginity, in my argument, will be linked to the transmission of this phantasy. Interpreting the meaning of the manifest virginity in the myth will lead via complicated routes back to Metis and her incorporated matricidal law.

There are not just three daughters in the Oresteian myth; there are six. Athena, Artemis, and Hermione,[2] in addition to Clytemnestra's three daughters, need to be considered as significant aspects of the daughter projection or simulacrum represented in the manifest content of the myth. While there are obvious differences between the groups of daughters—for one thing, Athena and Artemis are goddesses while the others are mortals—we can situate them together in the first instance by observing that the common denominator underlying all their situations is that they are all neither wives nor mothers; they are *virgin* daughters who remain outside the system of exchange that characterizes the (patriarchal) kinship organization. Their position in the kinship network is that of daughter/sister/virgin. In the Oresteian matricidal myth, none of these daughters ever achieves additional positions within the kinship structure; their perpetual virginity remains the significant characteristic that links them, despite their variable reactions to the matricide.

Virgin goddesses are not ubiquitous in the panorama of Greek deities; in fact, there are only three: Athena, Artemis, and Hestia. It is not without significance that it is only *virgin* goddesses who preside over the mortals in the matricidal Oresteian myth. Both Artemis and Athena choose to be virgins forever, devote themselves to hunting and war, and actively repel any sexual advances or offers of marriage that come their way. Any female in Greek myth who embraces hunting or war, whether she is Amazon or goddess, by definition rejects marriage and motherhood since hunting/war and marriage/motherhood are, as Jean-Pierre Vernant explains, "two complementary institutions." To remain in the state of virginity usually means (in Greek myth) to be involved in warfare and represents the refusal "to take the pathway that leads to the full femininity that marriage represents for every adolescent girl crossing the threshold of puberty."[3] Virginity, then, is directly associated with warfare and hunting; it is related to the positions of attack and defense; Athena, for example, is fully armed, always ready for battle, and Artemis is never without her lethal bow that strikes her victims dead in one blow. The virgin-daughter goddesses are associated with violence, aggression, and death, and in their explicit rejection of marriage and reproduction, *they stand against the family and its reproduction;* they do not promote the flourishing of successive generations. Instead, they set an example that, if revered and mimicked by mortals, would result in the extinction of family lines. The myth positions virgin-daughter goddesses in fundamental roles that determine the fate of the Atreus family line. If we hold that in myth no detail is ever gratuitous, the motif of the virgin daughter that appears on the levels of both the divine and the mortal would seem to hold a rich significance.

We have seen that all the mortal daughters of the Oresteian myth are also virgins, and there is no evidence in any of the numerous versions of the myth and the plays dramatizing different aspects of its themes that they ever marry or reproduce. The three daughters of Clytemnestra are not given away in marriage and remain childless. The mortal daughters of the *Oresteia,* however, do not choose virginity like their immortal counterparts. Rather, they constantly lament their unmarried and childless status as if this is a situation to which they are subjected rather than one they had positively embraced. Clytemnestra's three daughters are all adolescents, so marriage is constantly on their horizons, the next inevitable stage of their lives, yet for all of them it never happens.

The closest any of the daughters gets to motherhood is Electra in her fabricated pregnancy; she lies to her mother, sending her a message announcing that she has given birth to a baby boy in order to lure her mother to her so that Orestes may kill her.[4] The closest any daughter comes to marriage is Iphigenia, whose marriage turns out to be her funeral when she is sacrificed by her father on the wedding altar. As I have noted, Iphigenia, in Euripides' plays, does not die but is snatched away by Artemis at the moment the sword hits her throat, her body replaced with that of a deer. In Euripides' play *Iphigenia in Tauris,* which reflects on what happened to Iphigenia once she had vanished from the wedding altar, Artemis carries Iphigenia off to a "barbaric" land and orders her to preside over her sacrificial temple. Iphigenia, in this version of the myth, becomes Artemis's chosen virgin priestess; she must be virgin forever, like Artemis and Athena, and live out a life of barren exile. Chrysothemis, the middle daughter referred to only briefly in Sophocles' and Euripides' plays, also remains unmarried and a virgin. There are no records (to my knowledge) in the available documentation of Greek myth that contradict my observation that all the Oresteian daughters remain unmarried virgins. Certainly, the daughters remain unmarried in the Oresteian plays, which form my mythical corpus. Numerous speeches in all the plays represent the daughters of Atreus complaining repetitively of their virginity. The following are a few examples among many:

Now in this bleak exile beside the Inhospitable Sea
I live without husband, child, city or friend[5]

(IPHIGENIA)

I have no child, no man to love[6]

(IPHIGENIA)

I have no husband at my side
To fight for me, I have borne no children.[7]

(ELECTRA)

Husbandless, childless, I drag out my life
In misery from year to endless year[8]

(ELECTRA)

A myth in which there are so many daughters but no brides or potential marriages is most certainly unusual. The absence of marriage in the Oresteian myth, expressed through the ubiquitous virginity that characterizes all the daughters, without exception, is a striking anomaly, since marriage and the exchange of virgins between men usually express a fundamental part of the structure of myth. But if a salient feature characterizing the daughters is their status of *parthenos,* what is the meaning of the motif of virgin; what function does virginity among the siblings serve? How can virginity be understood in relation to the structure of the matricidal myth? Athena, Artemis, and Clytemnestra's three daughters are exceptions in the vast panorama of Greek myth by virtue of their virgin status. What is more, the mortal virgin daughters in the *Oresteia* stand apart from the other numerous daughters in Greek myth, not only by virtue of their virgin, unmarried status but also because they neither kill themselves nor are murdered; they remain alive *yet without becoming mother or wife.*[9] While psychoanalytic feminist critics have paid considerable attention to the meaning of the dead female virgin bride, the virgin sacrifice, or the virgin suicide in narratives of the Western tradition,[10] the meaning of the *living* virgin unmarried daughter (three of whom can be found in the *Oresteia*) has been overlooked. Iphigenia, for example, is invariably interpreted by critics from the perspective of the sacrifice, so she is subsumed under the category of dead virgin that functions structurally as a necessary element in the masculine heroic trajectory.[11] But the version of the myth that represents Iphigenia's disappearance followed by her living exile as virgin priestess is excluded from these interpretations. But the position for daughters in Greek myth is not only that of virgin sacrifice/suicide or bride. The virgin daughters who neither marry, nor reproduce, nor die appear in the Oresteian matricidal myth, a myth whose deities are two *virgin* goddesses.

The resolution of the *Oresteia* leaves three daughters alive and *unable* to give up their status of virgin. While critics tend to read the myth's resolution in terms of Orestes' acquittal, what is left over, or excessive, to the so-called resolution of Orestes' conflict, are the three virgin daughters who are forgotten at the moment Orestes is set free. With Orestes' freedom, one would expect his sisters to be given away in marriage in order to signify the flourishing of the patriarchal civilization over which Orestes reigns. Yet the brother, Orestes, in the place of his father, does not organize or mediate the marriages of his sisters. The myth closes with a mysterious remainder; the elements that are excessive to the structural resolution that critics have seen in Orestes remain uninterpreted, seemingly without function. The virgin daughters, whose virginity and death are *not* utilized as commerce to be exchanged by men, are aberrant, anomalous elements that the myth leaves unresolved and excessive to the models and interpretations through which the myth has hitherto been understood.

The anomaly of the perpetual virginity in the daughters of the *Oresteia* needs to be examined as a crucial aspect of the phantasies that the myth attempts to both negotiate and conceal. For my purposes here, there is a need to explore whether a connection exists between the symptom of the daughters' virginity and the problem of matricide, since it is within a myth that concerns itself with the negotiation of matricide that the anomalous surviving virgin daughters are found.

Perpetual virginity and its relation to the rejection of marriage function to subvert or obstruct the kinship laws ensuring that the social order can function. It is ironic that a myth that supposedly celebrates a new victorious order represented by Athena's democracy and Orestes' new rule, an order that is declared peaceful, civilized, and just, erases marriage from the equation that forms its foundation. The deliverance of a new and generative culture via the murder of the mother delivers a world wherein daughters remain daughters, virgins remain virgins, and the laws underlying the family cease to function; without marriage, there is no structure through which Athena's patriarchy can be expressed and sustained. The absence of marriage and the presence of virgins allows us to read the myth in a radically different way from those readings that interpret it as successfully negotiating contradictions and conflicts, illustrated by the "success" of Athena's apparent resolution. The existence of the virgins that are excessive to the supposed integration or resolution that theorists (like Klein) want to see in the Oresteian myth, together with the lack of marriage or promise of marriage, subverts or puts paid to the idea of a functional patriarchal democracy or the hopeful generative future that Orestes' victory over the mother is supposed to denote. At the end of Aeschylus's *Oresteia*, when Athena gives Orestes his freedom, it is noticeable that the myth transgresses the standard form wherein the hero, in his victory, is invariably given the prize of a bride. Athena hands over no brides, and Orestes (in addition to his sisters) never marries.

I suggest that we interpret the literal virginity expressed in the myth as indicating a situation of generative impossibility, a situation that has come about in the context of matricide and its incorporation.

Loving Orestes

Say "brother," sister!
These dear words can take the place of children, marriage—

—EURIPIDES, *ORESTES*

According to my reading, virginity in this myth signifies generative impossibility; the myth depicts a situation wherein the daughters and son of the *Oresteia* are unable to marry, that is, they cannot secure conjugal relations outside of the family. To take this interpretation further, it is now necessary to examine the daughters in the myth in relation to their structural positions with regard to their *lateral* relations, in order to find out what relationship stands in for or replaces their missing marriage partners. That is to say, it is time to explore the generative impossibility that virginity signifies in relation to the particular kinship situation in which it is found. If the daughters of the *Oresteia* do not look outside the family, where is it that they are looking, that is, to whom are they specifically attached or, put another way, what specific position do they inhabit within their immediate kinship constellation? In my reading, virginity or generative impossibility needs to be examined with reference to the lateral relations expressed in the myth; marriage is located across a lateral axis, and although there is no marriage in the myth, there are certainly highly significant lateral relations. In my reading, the brother replaces the husband. If sibling relations stand in for marital relations, then one can hypothesize via this structural reading that *virginity, which equals generative impossibility, is related to sibling incest.* It then becomes a matter of identifying what this constellation of symptoms points to with respect to the hypothesized incorporated matricidal law. But, first, I need to illustrate and clarify how the myth's structure expresses a connection among virginity, generative impossibility, and sibling incest.

Despite the daughters' lamentations concerning their perpetual virginity, none of them is represented as attempting to secure any amorous attachments outside the family. The only amorous lateral relation that they have is with their brother. It is Orestes who acts as or replaces the figure of the rescuing male hero who liberates the bride as in the standard structure of the "mono-myth" that Jean-Joseph Goux has identified.[12] What we have is a series of morbidly depressed daughters who cannot act, cannot love, cannot marry, and cannot move on from their infantile positions in the family. They are stuck and can only lament; it is only with the introduction of Orestes into their lives that their trajectories are able to change or shift to a different direction.

Electra is most famous for her relentless sorrow, her stubborn attachment to misery, and her interminable mourning. Her words can only spit venom at her mother, her mother's lover, her sister, and anyone who approaches her. She cannot be consoled; her father, whom she excessively idealizes — despite his murder of her sister and his long absence throughout her childhood — is dead, and her mother, with whom she is perpetually in combat, seems to be more interested in her lover than her daughter. Electra cannot move away from the mother she professes to hate; she cannot leave her childhood house nor her mother's skirts. She waits, like the princess locked in the tower, for the male hero to come and break the spell, to break the bonds of her infantile attachments and liberate her into her womanhood via marriage. *But it is Orestes for whom she waits.*

Orestes' return functions structurally as the intervening element external to the family that mobilizes Electra's desire. Orestes stands in for, or is identical with, the position of the rescuing male hero/groom, yet he is the brother, not the potential suitor who comes from outside the family to perform the function of mobilizing the daughter's trajectory. Orestes comes home to kill his mother, and Electra's hate immediately turns into a fervent love; from that point on, she remains stubbornly attached to Orestes. She changes from being virgin daughter (before the killing of their mother) to virgin sister (after the murder) and forms a happy couple with Orestes, looking nowhere else for love, as if she had found her perfect match.

In Euripides' play *Iphigenia in Tauris*, Orestes' role functions in exactly the same way. Again, it is the brother who rescues the sister from the depression and bondage she suffers, and it is Orestes to whom she expresses profound love and devotion. Again, as with Electra, it is Orestes' intervention that allows Iphigenia to move on to a different trajectory. Euripides' *Iphigenia in Tauris* has in it strong elements of romance; it has a happy ending, reunion, hyperbolic expressions of affection, escape from a strange and distant land—and the romance is expressed through the brother-sister relation. Iphigenia's situation before Orestes' arrival is bleak and barbaric. Serving Artemis as virgin priestess, she prepares young men who have trespassed on the land for human sacrifice. Close to death and violence, Iphigenia sounds very much like Electra in her morbid laments:

> I am sunk in bitter tears and deep distress.
> Music is turned to mourning, songs to a tuneless wail.[13]

Orestes arrives on the shores of Tauris, having killed his mother and still hounded by the Furies. He has been sent to this distant land (by Apollo) as the last part of his mission, which requires him to steal the statue of Artemis and take it back to Athens. Caught as a trespasser, Orestes is handed over to Iphigenia for sacrifice. Brother and sister do not recognize one another, and the scene that follows echoes the famous recognition scenes in the Electra plays. Once reunited, the siblings rejoice, and the play continues with the unfurling of the plan of escape, which is ends successfully with brother and sister running away together safely. The romantic structure of the play operates with the brother in the place of the suitor/groom.

Now that I have shown how brother-sister relations replace marital/romantic relations in the myth's structure, I want to develop my interpretation of virginity masking sibling incestuous attachments by concentrating on two proposed marriages that are mentioned in the plays but do not actually take place in any representation of the Oresteian myth. These hypothetical marriages bring to view (again) the structure wherein marital relations are replaced by sibling relations.

In Euripides' *Electra*, the deities tell Electra that she is to marry Pylades, Orestes' friend. This marriage never materializes anywhere in Greek myth, and there are no children born to Electra. Pylades, Orestes' faithful friend/brother/double, functions as an extension of Orestes in all the plays in which he appears. He has no role other than to accompany Orestes wherever he goes and to reflect Orestes' situation back to him. In my reading, Electra's proposed marriage to Pylades (which never actually takes place) can be interpreted as reinforcing the incestuous link she has with Orestes. Structurally, Orestes and Pylades occupy the same position; they are doubles, so Electra's hypothetical coupling with Pylades mimics the Electra-Orestes sibling relation. That there are no representations of the Electra-Pylades marriage in the tragedies and further that Electra is always represented as the unmarried childless virgin daughter/sister seems to support this reading.

In Euripides' play *Orestes*, which depicts Orestes at the height of his madness following the matricide, Orestes attempts to kill Helen along with Hermione, her daughter, as a continuation of his mission to murder wicked women. As he is about to cut the throat of his cousin, Hermione, Apollo arrives to resolve the violent chaos and declares that the girl, at whose throat Orestes holds his sword, shall become his wife. Orestes and Hermione's future marriage, which is not referred to in Aeschylus's *Oresteia* but is added by Euripides in his later reworking of the myth as a trope of resolution, can be interpreted again as expressing an underlying structure of sibling incest. Hermione's structural position in the Oresteian myth is that of double or counterpart to Iphigenia. Helen's daughter, Hermione, is compared to Iphigenia; she is the daughter who should have been sacrificed in place of Iphigenia, since the war with Troy was the "fault of Helen."[14] Thus Hermione/Iphigenia are structurally linked, such that Orestes' cited marriage to Hermione can be read as reproducing the brother-sister structure. The point is that the Oresteian myth, as we have received it through the tragedies, does not represent any of the Atridean siblings marrying or reproducing and instead, according to my reading, replaces marital relations with sibling couples.

Electra's incestuous passion for Orestes is, out of all the daughters, most apparent. "I will die or live with you,"[15] she declares to Orestes. Immediately after they have killed Clytemnestra, Electra pleads with Orestes for permission to embrace him before they decide what they should do next:

ELECTRA: Let me first take you in my arms!
ORESTES: Embrace me if it gives you pleasure.
        An embrace is little help to those within one step of death.
ELECTRA: My dearest! Oh my darling brother!
        How I love to call you my own brother! Our two hearts are
          one.[16]

There is no embrace written in the stage directions, but Orestes' response to Electra's amorous request may indicate the nature of the desired embrace:

ORESTES: Oh you will melt my firmness. Yes, I must hold you
          In my most loving arms—come! Why should I feel shame?
          Body to Body—thus, let us be close in love.
          Say "brother," sister! These dear words can take the place
          Of children, marriage—to console our misery.[17]

In relation to the reading I have so far pursued, this exchange between Electra and Orestes becomes significant and worth emphasizing. First, to interpret exchanges such as the one cited above as expressing sibling incestuous desire is only possible *after* we have postulated, via a structural reading of the myth, the connection among virginity, generative impossibility, and sibling incest. I am not arguing that exchanges such as this one provide evidence or proof that there is a sibling sexual relationship. Such an argument would be impossible and in any case flawed since I am not basing my interpretations of the myth on the language of the plays. What was initially meant by the ancient dramatists is not my concern; rather, what the myths express through their *structure* forms the basis of my readings. In this way, exchanges such as the one cited above between Electra and Orestes can be interpreted as illustrating my hypothesis of the virginity = sibling incest equation. In other words, it makes sense to read this exchange in this way once we have established how the brother-sister relation stands in for marital relations via structural analysis.

The incestuous sibling relation replaces and transgresses the sanctioned and institutionalized marital sexual relation that is based on the prohibition of incest. "Brother" and "sister" take the place of "husband" and "wife" and "mother" and "father." In my reading of the myth, *virginity means sibling incest.* Virginity is the evidence that points to the situation wherein the phantasy of sibling incest is not given up but remains operative.

Love of Sameness: The Footprint and the Lock of Hair

In a sense, what the Oresteian matricidal myth represents through its structure is, paradoxically, the dissolution of differences or, to put it another way, the failure of symbolization. Virginity, sibling incest, and the unmediated love of sameness that is expressed in the Oresteian children draw attention to the absence of symbolic relationships in a patriarchal order that denies the law of the mother.

In the famous recognition scene in the *Oresteia* that is reworked in both the Electra plays by Sophocles and Euripides, Electra and Orestes, who have never seen each other as young adults, are reunited as brother and sister by a curious process of identifying their "identical" features. Electra's desire is organized around establishing sameness. She will only love the stranger who has arrived once she is assured that they are "identical." The sameness is established by the lock of hair that Orestes has left on their father's tomb as an offering, which Electra finds and declares to be exactly the same texture and color as hers. Further, the footsteps left in the sand fit hers exactly, with no remainder. The lock of hair and the footprint are indicative elements in the *Oresteia* that paradoxically work to symbolize the failure of classification or the failure of creation of distinctions. More precisely, the footprints and lock of hair are elements in the *Oresteia* that serve to disclose the vulnerability of the differential kinship system, pointing to sameness as the root of generative impossibility/sterility.

The discovery of the identical lock of hair and identical footprint in the *Oresteia* produces a somewhat confusing, if not disturbing, effect. Since the brother and sister are of different ages and sexes, we expect there to be both difference and resemblance between Orestes and Electra. But their foot size and the texture and color of their hair cannot be distinguished. The literal sameness depicted in the myth can be interpreted as pertaining to a psychic undifferentiation where brother and sister are reduced to/merged into one. It is this sameness that so excites Electra. Finding the lock of hair, Electra declares, in Aeschylus's *Oresteia*:

ELECTRA: Look the texture, just like—
LEADER: Whose? I want to know
ELECTRA: Like mine, identical
             Can't you see?
ELECTRA: A new sign to tell us more.
             Footmarks . . . pairs of them, like mine.
             Two outlines, two prints, his own, and there,
             a fellow traveller's.
             Putting her foot into Orestes print
             The heel, the curve of the arch like twins.
             While Orestes emerges from behind the grave, she follows
                cautiously in his steps until they come together.
             Step by step, my step in his . . .
             we meet—
             Oh the pain, like pangs of labour—this is madness![18]

This moment anticipates the reunion and characterizes their attachment, which, I argue, stands in for marital sexual relations. They are not twins, but they are *like* twins; everything Electra sees in Orestes is *like* her. That their footprints are identical means they are interchangeable; they are one and the same, standing on the same feet, in the same position, in the same shoes, so to speak. This love of sameness works to defend against acknowledging separateness. The recognition of the specific properties/difference of the other is foreclosed so that Electra becomes or *is* Orestes; the minimal difference between the siblings is eradicated by the footprint and the lock of hair that finally close the tiny differentiating gap that allows for the kinship system to function. Virginity and sibling incest express a love of sameness that points to the failure/absence of a differentiating function that would allow for a symbolic relationship.

The *Oresteia* closes with all siblings unmarried and childless; no indication of a future generation is suggested. Athena sets Orestes free but denies him a bride, and the daughters will remain virgin daughters/sisters caught in an incestuous love for their brother. In my reading of the myth, virginity means sibling incest and discloses a love of sameness that works to dissolve distinctions, creating a radical generative symbolic impossibility.

The constellation of symptoms I have identified in the daughters of the *Oresteia* occurs in the context of the incorporation of the matricidal law. The daughters and son of the *Oresteia* cannot move out of their immediate kinship situation. The killing of the mother and the court case that endorses this act do not result in a move into new family constellations via marriage in order to reproduce a brave new generation/world. The daughters remain wedded to the position of virgin and incestuously attached to their brother. The family is, in this way, threatened with annihilation.

While the "blood for blood" chain of revenge murders initially formed the threat of the annihilation of the house of Atreus, Athena's new system of "civilized" democratic justice fails to prevent the family from extinction. The family certainly stop killing each other after the murder of Clytemnestra and Orestes' acquittal, but the children who remain alive and apparently free after the deaths of both their parents refuse to/cannot move out of their incestuous sibling attachments and consequently cannot move out of their positions as virgin daughters/sons. The family, it would seem, has no future; it destroys itself *not by kinship murder but by sibling incest*. Orestes, the only male left in the family, not only fails to marry and reproduce, but he also does not perform the function of giving his sisters away in marriage; he does not partake in the system of exchange that ensures the continuation of the patriarchal civilization. Yet in opting out of this system and remaining incestuously attached to his sisters, he, in effect, announces the death/annihilation of the order he has fought so hard to inherit. Athena can resolve the problem of the family members' killing one another, but she has no law, no method of intervention, that can break the incestuous circle or the love of sameness that will ensure that the passage from the biological family to social order/network is secured.

In my reading, the *Oresteia* describes the failure or impossibility at the heart of the patriarchal order; it provides us with a picture of sterility rather than generativity. Athena's order is an order that fails to provide its subjects with symbolically mediated relations. The law-of-the-father, in this myth, is exposed as working in the service of desymbolization and symbolic sterility. Rather than creating distinctions through which sociality is expressed, it produces a culture that suffers a radical failure of introjection, a culture operating on the level of incorporation, which results in the collapse of differences and the foreclosure of generative symbolically mediated relations. The incorporation of matricide that underlies the paternal order produces presence and sameness rather than loss and difference. The father will not recognize his difference from the mother or the difference of his children from himself, and the children will not recognize their difference from one another.

The relation among matricide, incorporation, and parthenogenesis can now be developed further. Underlying the Oresteian myth is the structure

matricide–incorporation–parthenogenesis = presence and sameness = symbolic generative impossibility

The following formula helps to clarify and unpack this structure:

"The father can father forth alone"/"Athena has no mother" (*basis of the paternal law*) = male parthenogenetic phantasy = matricide + incorporation (*expressed through the Metis myth*) → failure of introjection/mourning = matricide severed from its underlying law → lack of prohibition of male parthenogenetic phantasy →:

1. Sanctioned rape and murder of the daughter by the father (*repetition of crime against Metis*)
2. Sanctioned murder of Clytemnestra (*effect of crime against Metis*)
3. Perpetual virginity in daughters and son = sibling incest
4. Love of sameness and the denial of difference
5. Chronic morbid depression in daughters =

6. Generative impossibility/symbolic sterility =
7. Annihilation of genealogy =
8. Dereliction

Although my picture resembles Irigaray's, my conclusion moves beyond her in that she *describes* the *symptoms* of dereliction while I am exposing the *structure*. In the Oresteian myth, the incorporation of matricide creates pathological effects or symptoms that the myth represents as threatening the social order with extinction. We can now begin to see more clearly the effects of the erasure of Metis's law, the catastrophic results of its incorporation and its systematic transgression. In the Oresteian myth, fathers father forth without the mother, fathers rape and kill their daughters and are not punished by the institutionalized law, daughters remain virgins and siblings remain incestuously attached; sameness is desired rather than differentiation; virginity and incest reign unabated, and successive generations fail to be born. If the *Oresteia* has been interpreted as the description of the institution of the paternal law, in my rereading, it is as much a myth about the effects of the incorporation of the mother's law; one law is dependent on the concealment and violation of another.

Interpreting the myth this way allows us to postulate a more specific understanding of Irigaray's notion of "dereliction" in relation to a newly theorized concept of matricide. That is to say, if what the *Oresteia* describes still takes place, as Irigaray contended, then this means, in the light of my rereading of the myth, that the current sociosymbolic organization functions in accordance with the incorporation of the matricidal law. We can use this interpretation of the myth to suggest that what this means in our contemporary reality is that fathers may be literal biological fathers, mothers may be literal mothers, and marriage may take place, but these are not sociosymbolic positions; they belong to a primitive register where oral incorporation remains the predominant mode of psychic exchange.

The *Oresteia* discloses the failure at the heart of patriarchy, the failure to overcome the oral phantasy of incorporation that we have seen belongs to a male parthenogenetic phantasy that precludes introjective symbolic functioning. The so-called father's law, rather than being interpreted as the symbolic third term synonymous with psychic health, is shown to be based on an infantile phantasy of parthenogenesis that has not been prohibited. In this way, the father's law can be interpreted as the result of a transgression of another law, the destructive repercussions of which are visible in the mythical daughters. If the father's law prohibits incest with the mother and in so doing prevents psychosis, at the same time, and on another level, it effects the transgression of the matricidal law and thus permits father-daughter and sibling incest. The dominant order that cannot introject the maternal prohibition creates a culture that cannot move beyond the phantasy of omnipotence, causing an inevitable "derelict" situation of symbolically generative impossibility. While Irigaray has argued that the symbolic is in fact the imaginary that has become law, I have developed her argument by disclosing or stating the *specific* structure of the unconscious/imaginary phantasy that has become law.

The *Oresteia*, read in relation to the Metis myth, illuminates our understanding of contemporary realities by bringing into view the underlying processes that account for the situation wherein one prohibition comes to mean the incorporation and transgression of another. Coexistent modes of prohibition and symbolization cannot seem to be tolerated/theorized. If the matricidal law were to be acknowledged, then the paternal law would necessarily be forced into a reorganization. Introducing an excluded element inevitably changes the whole constellation. Different laws create different cultural organizations. To posit a culture that can accommodate more than one law means to fight for a culture that is "yet to be."

Such a vision of a postpatriarchal culture is not driven by a desire for some kind of totalizing all-inclusive nonrepressive (nostalgic) utopia. There will always be a remainder, always exclusions, residues, excesses left over from the processes of structuration. What I am concerned with in theorizing a matricidal law is the conception of a culture that could recognize and accommodate more than one mode of symbolization. As long as the entrenchment of the masculine imaginaries continues to determine social realities, women have little room to represent a specificity that is independent of their relation to male phantasies. It is not a matter of trying to do away with conflict; on the contrary: it is a matter of working to develop a symbolic space in which *more than one* structure of conflict can be negotiated/mediated.

In my conclusion, I will address further the significance of the interpretation of the myth that I have undertaken in relation to the contemporary (feminist) context. I have arrived at a definition of matricide and have hypothesized a theory of a matricidal law. Rereading the *Oresteia* in relation to the myth of Metis has resulted in bringing matricide into theory as a potential structural concept. The question now concerns how far Metis can be used to facilitate the "yet to be" or potential female imaginaries. How can Metis as a structuring model produce a "change in discourse" leading to the "creation of new forms"?[19] With this question in mind, I want to pose another: What about Chrysothemis, Clytemnestra's middle daughter, to whom no tragedian gave more than a few words?

Conclusion: The Question of Chrysothemis

Instead of daughter to the noblest father,
Call yourself mother's daughter,
Then everyone will know you for what you are
Disloyal to your dead father and your friends.

—SOPHOCLES, *ELECTRA*

I N THE EARLY stages of my research for this work, I, like most feminists working with myth, could not get away from the manifest level. Following Irigaray, I struggled with Demeter and Persephone, with Antigone, Phaedra, and Clytemnestra's daughters, in hope that I could make use of these representations in order to respond to Irigaray in her imperative to create the "yet-to-be" female imaginaries. Running concomitant with my theoretical work that sought to use myth to address the problem of matricide in psychoanalysis, I was also seeking a way to rewrite certain aspects of the mythological corpus to discover whether mythical appropriation could work to counter the effects of the alienating dominant imaginary. With this question in mind, I became interested in the shadowy figure of Chrysothemis, the middle daughter of Clytemnestra and Agamemnon in the Oresteian myth. Chrysothemis, unlike Iphigenia and Electra, is not a mythical daughter whose name is the title of any tragedy, though she appears briefly in Sophocles' *Electra* and is mentioned in Euripides' plays *Orestes* and *Iphigenia in Aulis.* Chrysothemis performs a function similar to that of Ismene in Sophocles' tragedy *Antigone.* Like Ismene, Chrysothemis is the sensible daughter who draws attention to the extremity of her wild sister's actions and desires. In Sophocles' *Electra,* she tries (in vain) to persuade Electra to give up her stubborn hatred of her mother and her desire to avenge her father's death and urges her sister to find a satisfactory way of living under the circumstances to which they are subjected. Chrysothemis, as represented by Sophocles, lives in a seeming equilibrium with her mother and finds Electra's constant lamentations both unproductive and bewildering. On the face of it, Chrysothemis occupies a marginal and unmemorable position in the Oresteian family constellation. Her name has been committed to our mythical corpus, yet with a seeming insignificance. It was for this reason that I wanted to explore the potential of using the unwritten position of this third daughter of the *Oresteia* in order to think through a different position for the daughter/sister in the light of my theoretical work on matricide. The fact that there was a third daughter in the Oresteian myth whose significance had not been developed led me to think about her as a potential space in the myth that I could use for the development of my theoretical work.

It was Chrysothemis's very insignificance in the manifest versions of the Oresteian myth that caught my imagination, and I began to fantasize about a hypothetical lost play of Euripides. I wondered what Euripides might have done with Chrysothemis if he had turned his mind to her role in the Oresteian conflict, as he did with Electra and Iphigenia. I then realized that I was not actually unduly concerned with what Euripides might have written; really, I was thinking about what *I* might write, what I would do with Chrysothemis if I turned my mind to writing her position into the Oresteian situation. At this point, a different method of working became an exciting possibility for my research. Chrysothemis seemed to me to hold enormous potential: a different way into the myth that could allow me to play and experiment with my theoretical ideas concerning the role of myth in its restructuring capacity. Here was this daughter who had little to say but was nevertheless there, like an empty space inside a matricidal myth; she seemed to be waiting to come into being. Starting from the premise that however seemingly insignificant a mythical element may appear, no element in myth is ever gratuitous or without meaning, I embarked on a different way of working. At this early stage in my research, I wrote a play entitled *Chrysothemis*.

Writing this play was another route through which I was attempting to explore the theoretical problems of matricide; it was part of my research process or an aspect of the feminist praxis with which I was involved. The play was only successful in that it catalyzed a change in my theoretical approach to myth. The difficulties that I encountered in writing it helped me understand that approaching myth on the manifest level could not lead to theoretical innovation allowing for a change in discourse.

In writing *Chrysothemis*, I began by thinking about the implications of Electra's accusation that Chrysothemis is the "mother's daughter," "disloyal to her dead father and [her] friends."[1] What could it mean to be the mother's daughter in the context of the Oresteian family conflict and in my psychoanalytic feminist context? My play was centered on this problematic. Dramatically, it was organized around the relationship between Chrysothemis and Clytemnestra in the face of Iphigenia's sacrifice. I wrote Chrysothemis's position in relation to that of her murdered sister and her murderous mother. In this way, I tried to explore both the vertical and lateral between-women relations in the context of the destructive effects of the paternal law. What emerged was a play that was driven by a conscious desire to find a different way of situating mother-daughter, daughter-mother, and sister-sister relations that did not reproduce the dynamics of the fusion-rejection either/or binary that determines the mother-daughter relationship under the present sociosymbolic organization. Through Chrysothemis, I wanted to think about the mother-daughter relation as a possible site of ethical, creative, constructive, and potentially subversive exchange. I was too constricted by Clytemnestra, however; I could not use her to further my ends because she was so laden with associations and so entrenched in the position of all-powerful so-called phallic mother. I ended up reproducing the same symptoms or phantasies of the male imaginary that I had diagnosed in my rereading of the *Oresteia* in contemporary terms. I could not make Chrysothemis live theoretically or aesthetically as long as I was working with manifest projections such as Clytemnestra. More precisely, I could not change the structure of the mother-daughter relation through writing this play while mother still occupied a position that lacked an underlying structuring law. The problem was that at the time of writing *Chrysothemis* I had not yet discovered Metis, so I was still lacking a theoretical definition of matricide and had not yet identified the matricidal law. Inevitably, I ended up with a merged mother-daughter relation whose voices were hard to distinguish. This was a crucial turning point for my theoretical work because it forced me to find a way of approaching myth different from that of Irigaray and allowed me to understand that working with the manifest level of myth could not be an effective feminist strategy.

It was at this point that I had to abandon Irigaray's approach to myth. I was not convinced by a strategy that sought to appropriate positive images for the purpose of intervening in the symbolic hegemony that Irigaray had so powerfully diagnosed. I had tried to follow Irigaray's prescription with *Chrysothemis,* but I was not satisfied with the result. There seemed to be a slippage, or a contradiction, between Irigaray's deconstructive work and her prescriptive work, which became most apparent to me in her approach to myth. Using myth to interpret the male imaginary was certainly constructive and allowed me to develop Irigaray's analysis of the ways in which mythical structures determine our contemporary discourses. But using it for the purpose of creating a mode of symbolization that did not yet exist could not, in my thinking, be achieved through appropriating existing positive representations. If Irigaray's project was to transform the very structures underlying symbolic life and if one of her strategies to do this involved a return to myth, then surely such a massive undertaking would necessitate more than the gesture of appropriation of already existing representations.

In writing my play *Chrysothemis*, I was still working with myth on the manifest level. It was an exemplary instance of a feminist return to myth that inevitably reproduced the terms of the imaginary order that it was supposed to be contesting. To work with myth on the level of the manifest is to recycle unanalyzed symptoms, and it is also to remain inside the parameters of the structures underlying the male imaginary that by definition foreclose the possibility of a change in discourse. I had to do something else with myth in order to find a way of working toward the theorization of a mode of symbolization that did not render women "derelict." It was only when I gave up on Clytemnestra as the murdered mother through whom I could theorize matricide that I was able to think about matricide in relation to its underlying law. Rereading the *Oresteia* through the myth of Metis led me to conclude that if we move beyond concentrating on the manifest in myth and tragedy, then using myth in conjunction with psychoanalysis to create a change in discourse leading to new forms could be more easily realized. Finding Metis concealed within the Orestean myth and receptions and interpretations of the myth allowed me finally to understand how myth can be reworked to effect the transmission of an alternative social bond. It was on this point that I consolidated a position that was different from that of Irigaray and led my research along a different trajectory, which saw my thinking ending up in a very different place from where it started.

Discovering Metis meant that I could move from using the *Oresteia* to *describe* the manifest symptoms of an order based on matricide to *theorizing* matricide and its underlying law. In the light of this theoretical position, returning to Chrysothemis, whom I have not yet given up on, despite the first failed attempt in writing her play, would be an altogether different undertaking. Now that I have found Metis and theorized a matricidal law, *I would be writing from the perspective of a different structural center.* With the theorization of Metis and her law in place, together with the unwritten position of the middle Oresteian daughter, we may now be in a position to visualize or create a mother-daughter structure through which a different dream/discourse could emerge. There is no way of telling, as yet, how this different perspective will influence the rewriting of *Chrysothemis* and the writing of future plays and theoretical works. But the important point, for me, is that the discovery of Metis and the theorization of her law will certainly lead to more attempts to develop a different mode of symbolizing, of theorizing, creating, teaching, and living.

Notes

Preface

1. I will henceforward use the "ph" spelling for "phantasy" in order to avoid the whimsical/escapist connotations attached to the term "fantasy" and to emphasize that what concerned me is the primary content of unconscious mental processes rather than conscious fantasies or daydreams. I am using this distinction as outlined by Susan Isaacs in "The Nature and Function of Phantasy," first published in 1952 by the Hogarth Press and reprinted in *Developments in Psychoanalysis,* ed. Joan Riviere (London: Karnac, 1989). Isaacs's definition of "phantasy" and the distinction she makes between the "ph" and "f" spellings are however quite different from Freud's formulation. Freud's definition of *"Phantasie"* is more complex and does not distinguish so clearly between conscious and unconscious phantasies, as Isaacs does. See Jean Laplanche and J. B. Pontalis, *The Language of Psychoanalysis* (London: Karnac, 1988), p. 314, for a discussion of Freud's definitions of *"Phantasie"* and the different ways that psychoanalytic theorists have used the concept and the different spellings. For the sake of pragmatic clarity, I will use the "ph" spelling henceforward to refer to imaginary unconscious mental content.
2. Claude Lévi-Strauss, *The Raw and the Cooked: Introduction to a Science of Mythology* (1964), trans. John Weightman and Doreen Weightman (London: Penguin, 1986), p. 12.
3. I am referring here to the Lacanian model that theorizes the name-of-the-father as serving this purpose, thus creating a position from which to think about one's relation to others and allowing for the possibility of symbolic functioning.

1. Postpatriarchal Futures

1. "Under erasure" refers to Derrida's method of crossing through a phrase or word in order to alienate it. This is intended to draw attention to the metaphysical

underpinnings that the concept implies. By putting concepts "under erasure," the ideological implications are acknowledged, and the author demonstrates a critical distance despite having no choice but to continue to use the word/concept.

2. Discussing feminist poststructuralist discourses, Jane Flax comments, "Soon it seems nothing exists outside of a text; everything is a comment on or a displacement of another text. . . . Attention shifts away from the many and varied sources of women's oppression to whether or not we can in fact escape from the structuring imposed by language" (*Thinking Fragments: Psychoanalysis, Feminism, and Postmodernism in the Contemporary West* [Berkeley: University of California Press, 1990], p. 178).

3. Kate Soper, "Feminism, Humanism and Postmodernism," in *The Woman Question*, ed. Mary Evans, 2d ed. (London: Sage, 1994) pp. 10–21.

4. Joel Whitebrook, *Perversion and Utopia: A Study in Psychoanalysis and Critical Theory* (Cambridge, Mass.: MIT Press, 1996), p. 11.

5. Ibid., p. 14.

6. Theorists such as Judith Butler would disagree with my contention that Irigaray's approach embraces a nonobjectionable synthesis. The antisynthesis argument that Whitebrook discusses is most apparent in feminist theory in Judith Butler's work; for her critique of Irigaray's "totalising gesture," see *Gender Trouble: Feminism and the Subversion of Identity* (London: Routledge, 1990), p. 13.

7. Luce Irigaray, *I Love to You: Sketch of a Possible Felicity in History*, trans. Alison Martin (London: Routledge, 1996), p. 5.

8. Ibid., p. 10.

9. Juliet Mitchell, quoted in *Women Analyze Women: In France, England and the United States*, ed. Elaine Hoffman Baruch and Lucienne J. Serrano (New York: New York University Press, 1988), p. 220.

10. For a detailed discussion of the development of Mitchell's thought and the consequences of her Lacanian position for her feminism, see Jane Gallop, "Moving Backwards or Forwards," in *Between Feminism and Psychoanalysis*, ed. Teresa Brennan (London: Routledge, 1989), pp. 27–39.

11. The following comment from Elizabeth Wilson is more or less representative of the general thrust of the critical responses to the feminist defense of Lacan: "There remains something both odd and profoundly troubling about a theoretical position that emphatically rejects biology yet recreates symbolic universals whose imperatives appear equally inescapable. . . . The last thing feminists need is a theory that teaches them only to marvel anew about the subjective reality of subordination and which reasserts male domination more securely than ever within theoretical discourse. . . . We need more than an endless contemplation of how we came to be chained." (Elizabeth Wilson with Angela Weir, *Hidden Agendas: Theory, Politics and Experience in the Women's Movement* [London: Tavistock, 1986], p. 150).

12. Jessica Benjamin, *Shadow of the Other: Intersubjectivity and Gender in Psychoanalysis* (New York: Routledge, 1998), p. 48.

13. François Roustang, *Dire Mastery: Discipleship from Freud to Lacan*, trans. Ned Lukacher (Washington, D.C.: American Psychiatric Press, 1986)*t*.

14. It was Freud himself who (in 1915) warned against conceptual rigidity in relation to the development of psychoanalysis: "The advance of knowledge, however, does not tolerate any rigidity even in definitions. Physics furnishes an excellent illustration of the way in which even 'basic concepts' that have been established in the form of definitions are constantly being altered in their content" ("Instincts and their Vicis-

situdes" (1915), in *The Standard Edition of the Complete Psychological Works of Sigmund Freud*, trans. and ed. James Strachey, 24 vols. (London: Hogarth, 1951–1973), 14:117. I will henceforth refer to *The Standard Edition* with the abbreviation *SE*.

15. Roustang, *Dire Mastery*, p. 74.

16. From a philosophical perspective, Lacan seems astonishingly monolithic. It is commonplace in philosophy to have a situation of competing conceptual systems, yet in Lacanian theory, there is a distinct intolerance of different coexisting conceptual systems. There is a striking univocal tendency within academic uses of psychoanalysis, most explicit in the attachment to Lacan. The need to systematize or integrate theory into a monolithic totalizing whole becomes paramount. In my view, such rigidity goes against the very essence of the psychoanalytic inquiry.

17. Judith Butler, "Against Proper Objects," in *Feminism Meets Queer Theory*, ed. Elizabeth Weed and Naomi Schor (Bloomington: Indiana University Press, 1997), p. 22.

18. Silvia Vegetti Finzi, *Mothering: Toward a New Psychoanalytic Construction*, trans. Katherine Jason (New York: Guilford, 1996) p. 65.

19. See Joan Riviere, "Womanliness as a Masquerade," *International Journal of Psychoanalysis* 10 (1929), reprinted in *Formations of Fantasy*, ed. Victor Burgin, James Donald, and Cora Kaplan (London: Methuen, 1986), pp. 35–44. Riviere's article led to a vast amount of feminist literature that sought to appropriate the "masquerade" for an antihumanist feminist position. For a further discussion of the feminist appropriation of the "masquerade," see Mary Ann Doane, *The Desire to Desire: The Woman's Film of the 1940s* (Bloomington: Indiana University Press, 1987).

20. With "hysteric," I am referring to psychoanalytic feminist interpretations of hysteria as a protest against the status of femininity in the patriarchal order. See Hélène Cixous and Catherine Clément, *The Newly Born Woman* (1975), trans. Betsy Wing (London: Tauris, 1996) for one of the earliest feminist appropriations of the hysteric.

21. Rosi Braidotti, "Cyberfeminism with a Difference," in *Feminisms*, ed. Sandra Kemp and Judith Squires (Oxford: Oxford University Press, 1997), p. 529.

22. Ibid., p. 528.

23. Euripides, *The Bacchae and Other Plays*, trans. Philip Vellacott (London: Penguin Classics, 1973), lines 1233–1342, p. 237.

24. Butler, *Gender Trouble*, p. 56.

25. Jacqueline Rose, "Femininity and its Discontents," in *Sexuality in the Field of Vision* (London: Verso, 1986), p. 91.

2. Myth, Phantasy, and Culture

1. The concept of the symbolic I am referring to here is not absolutely allied with Lacan's theory of the Symbolic inasmuch as my intention is to question theories of the symbolic rather than to accept existing definitions. Lacan's theory of the Symbolic inevitably informs my research. When I refer to the symbolic, however, I do so without the capital letter; that is to say, as distinct from Lacan, I am proposing a *nonmonolithic* symbolic.

2. In order to keep the concepts of the imaginary and symbolic apart, my own initial extremely broad working definitions of the two concepts can be described as follows: the *symbolic* refers to *form* and the *imaginary* refers to *content*; thus the symbolic functions to structure the imaginary content. In relation to this model,

phantasy is the subjective imaginary content that is always already structured by the symbolic.

3. Claude Lévi-Strauss, *Myth and Meaning: The Massey Lectures* (1977) (London: Routledge, 1978), p. 4; idem, *The Raw and the Cooked: Introduction to a Science of Mythology*, trans. John Weightman and Doreen Weightman (London: Penguin, 1986), p. 12 (first published by Plon in 1964).

4. Lévi-Strauss, *The Raw and the Cooked*, p. 12.

5. Ibid., p. 28.

6. Lévi-Strauss, *Myth and Meaning*, p. 44.

7. While I follow Lévi-Strauss in his assumption about the unconscious structures operating in myth together with his methodology of differential myth analysis, I do not hold to his universalizing of these structures across disparate cultures. I am concerned solely with Western culture and mythologies and make no claims whatsoever about non-Western symbolic organizations.

8. The definition of the term "imaginary" is the subject of an ongoing debate. There is no definitive conclusion as to what it actually is. In its broadest and most minimal definition, we can say that the imaginary refers to unconscious phantasy. The imaginary can be thought of as the subjective contents of unconscious phantasy that are always already structured by the symbolic order. In her book *Imaginary Bodies: Ethics, Power and Corporeality* (London: Routledge, 1996), Moira Gatens makes an important intervention into the conception of the imaginary by referring to *imaginaries*, that is to say, moving away from a notion of a univocal imaginary to a more diverse, dynamic, complex notion of multiple imaginaries. If there are multiple imaginaries, multiple residues, multiple structures, we end up with a dynamic system constantly open to transformation and refiguration. While Irigaray refers to the imaginary in the singular, I follow Gatens in using the plural so as not "to reduce the complexity and variety of social imaginaries to a univocal sexual imaginary" (p. 147). What I am concerned with in this feminist analysis of social imaginaries is the manner in which dominant sexual imaginaries become fundamental to social imaginaries—or, in other words, how, in Irigaray's terms, the masculine imaginaries dominate and determine symbolic, social, political, and legal life.

9. Luce Irigaray, "The Poverty of Psychoanalysis," in *The Irigaray Reader*, ed. Margaret Whitford (Oxford: Blackwell, 1991), p. 94.

10. The causal relation is bound to be complex and not definitive; once set up, the process would become two-way. See Margaret Whitford, *Luce Irigaray: Philosophy in the Feminine* (London: Routledge, 1991), pp. 89–92, for a lucid explication of the complex relation between the imaginary and the symbolic in Irigaray's work.

11. Luce Irigaray, quoted in Elaine Hoffman Baruch and Lucienne J. Serrano, eds., *Women Analyze Women: In France, England and the United States* (New York: New York University Press, 1988), p. 159.

12. Irigaray, "The Bodily Encounter with the Mother," in *The Irigaray Reader*, p. 36.

13. I take up this point later, in part 2 and in the conclusion.

14. Luce Irigaray, quoted in *Women Analyze Women*, p. 159.

15. See Jean-Michel Quinodoz, "Dreams that Turn Over a Page: Integration Dreams with Paradoxical Regressive Content," *International Journal of Psychoanalysis* 80, part 2, (April 1999): 225 –239. What Quinodoz suggests is that, however primitive the content of a dream, it is never regression proper because something is being symbolized. The dream, however regressive in content, is still functioning to enable

the dreamer to think about and integrate those primitive phantasies. I suggest that, like dreams, myth is always symbolic despite the regressive primitive content.

16. André Green, *On Private Madness* (London: Rebus, 1996), p. 147.
17. While "acting out" and "working through" are clinical terms pertaining to the analytic encounter, I use them in the context of the cultural sphere. In this (nonclinical) context, there is not, to my mind, a clear or unproblematic theoretical distinction between acting out and working through; invariably, they inhabit one another, making the distinction between each mode of functioning sometimes obscure. In this way, not all of the sociosymbolic order could be interpreted as the result of a pathological acting-out; there must be something that could not be pathological about the imaginary and its transformation into the symbolic. What "working through" could mean in this context is a complex question. What would a symbolic that has worked through its imaginary phantasies look like? In my context, one can say that working through the imaginary phantasies that organize the present dominant sociosymbolic order would prevent these phantasies from being projected onto the feminine and mistaken as rational and universal truths. Perhaps one can describe the process whereby the imaginary is structured by the symbolic as somewhere between acting out and working through; it is a matter of degree (i.e., not everything can be conscious). Additionally, what is considered "acting out" (in the cultural sphere) is a political question. For a definition of "acting out" and "working through," see Freud, "An Outline of Psychoanalysis" (1940), in *SE*, 23:176; and idem, "Remembering, Repeating and Working Through" (1914), *SE*, 12:151. See also Laplanche and Pontalis, *The Language of Psychoanalysis*, pp. 4–6, 488–489.
18. Carol Kohn, "Sex and Death in the Rational World of Defence Intellectuals," in *The Woman Question*, ed. Mary Evans (London: Sage, 1994), pp. 118–137.
19. Ibid., pp. 126–127.
20. Margaret Whitford, "Rereading Irigaray," in *Between Feminism and Psychoanalysis*, ed. Teresa Brennan (London: Routledge, 1989), p. 117.
21. Perhaps the rage and anger of the early years of the women's movement could be seen as a collective return of the repressed. The project of creating potential female imaginaries could be viewed as allowing for another mode of "acting out." Rather than making a hierarchical, clear-cut distinction between "acting out" and "working through" (where the former is always allied with pathology and the latter is always allied with health), perhaps we need to think of the creation of female imaginaries as accommodating different modes of "acting out" leading to different modes of "working through," which may allow for different modes of symbolization. The creation of female imaginaries that would inform a potential female symbolic could mean, initially, the "acting-out" of a different type of dream, a different set of unconscious phantasies, a different type of madness. Or, put in another way, the creation of female imaginaries could allow women the right to their own madness rather than the madness projected into them as a result of the workings of the male imaginary. Irigaray contends that deconstructing the phantasies informing the male imaginary is a way of "escaping a world of madness which is not ours" and that "we would do better to take back our own madness and return men theirs" (*The Irigaray Reader*, p. 42). The creation of female imaginaries could be a way of allowing women access to their own specific madness, a madness that is not a projection.
22. Sigmund Freud, "The Method of Interpreting Dreams: An Analysis of a Specimen Dream" (1900), *SE*, 4:111.

23. Green, "Conceptions of Affect," in *On Private Madness,* p. 205.
24. See, for example, Nancy Chodorow, *The Reproduction of Mothering: Psychoanalysis and the Sociology of Gender* (Berkeley: University of California Press, 1978); Susie Orbach and Luise Eichenbaum, "Feminine Subjectivity, Countertransference and the Mother-Daughter Relationship," in *Daughtering and Mothering: Female Subjectivity Reanalysed,* ed. Janneke van Mens-Verhulst, Karlein Schreurs, and Liesbeth Woertman (London: Routledge, 1993), pp. 70–83; Jane Flax, "Mother-Daughter Relationships: Psycho-dynamics, Politics and Philosophy," in *The Future of Difference,* ed. Hester Eisenstein and Alice Jardine (Jersey City, N.J.: Rutgers University Press, 1987), pp. 20–40; and Marianne Hirsch, *The Mother-Daughter Plot: Narrative, Psychoanalysis, Feminism* (Bloomington: Indiana University Press, 1989).
25. This discussion of what constitutes structural theory as opposed to description is further elaborated in the subsequent chapter, "Matricide in Theory."
26. For an account of "dereliction" see Luce Irigaray, *An Ethics of Sexual Difference,* trans. Carolyn Burke and Gillian C. Gill (London: Athlone, 1993), p. 126. See also Margaret Whitford's discussion of "dereliction" in *Luce Irigaray,* pp. 77–78.
27. See especially Janice Doane and Devon Hodges, *From Klein to Kristeva: Psychoanalytic Feminism and the Search for the "Good Enough" Mother* (Ann Arbor: University of Michigan Press, 1992); Jessica Benjamin, *The Bonds of Love: Psychoanalysis, Feminism, and the Problem of Domination* (New York: Pantheon, 1988); idem, *Shadow of the Other: Intersubjectivity and Gender in Psychoanalysis* (New York: Routledge, 1998); and Jacqueline Rose, "Of Knowledge and Mothers: On the Work of Christopher Bollas," *Gender and Psychoanalysis* 1, no. 4 (1996): 411–427.
28. I think there is more potential in object-relations theory for a structural psychoanalytic feminism than Doane and Hodges suggest in *From Klein to Kristeva.* Rozsika Parker, in her important book *Torn in Two: The Experience of Maternal Ambivalence* (London: Virago, 1995), has shown how Winnicott's work can be effectively used to develop a theory of maternal subjectivity. Parker's concentration on Winnicott's paper "Hate in the Counter-transference" (1947) led her to use his theorization of maternal hate to provide a crucial differentiating function between mother and infant. Parker theorizes maternal ambivalence as both a crucial and a creative basis for the differentiating function belonging to the mother. Although Parker does not take up the question of sexual difference, her work on Winnicott has significant implications that could be fruitfully developed. I would also like to add here that Doane and Hodges do not consider the work of post-Kleinians such as W. R. Bion (whose work is extremely influential in contemporary British clinical psychoanalysis). Indeed, to my knowledge, feminist theorists have not yet considered Bion's work. I think there could be much potential in a feminist use of his theory of thinking. Bion conceptualizes the maternal "alpha function," which is, as I understand it, predominantly a structuring function. According to him, the infant projects its raw unprocessed anxiety ("beta elements") into the mother, who, through her "containing" and structuring "alpha function," returns the projections to the child in a more digestible (bound) form, giving the infant the capacity to think (see W. R. Bion, *Learning from Experience* [London: Maresfield, 1962]; and idem, *Second Thoughts* [London: Maresfield, 1967]). Bion's theory may be useful for a structural psychoanalytic feminist position; developing his concept of the "alpha function" with a view to exploring its implications concerning the mother's structuring power as underlying the capacity for thought and symbolization may lead to interesting developments. While I cannot develop these speculations here, a

feminist exploration of Bion's work could be a worthwhile part of a future research project.

29. Benjamin, *Shadow of the Other,* p. 57.

30. See André Green's comments on the distinction between phenomenology and structural theory in relation to the differences between the British and French psychoanalytic traditions in *The Dead Mother: The Work of André Green,* ed. Gregorio Kohon (London: Routledge, 1999), p. 28.

31. Janine Chasseguet-Smirgel, "Feminine Guilt and the Oedipus Complex," in *Female Sexuality: New Psychoanalytic Views,* ed. Janine Chasseguet-Smirgel (London: Karnac, 1985), p. 117.

32. Green, "Conceptions of Affect," in *On Private Madness,* p. 205.

33. Irigaray, *An Ethics of Sexual Difference,* p. 124.

34. While the notion of integration, to my knowledge, belongs predominantly to Kleinian and post-Kleinian psychoanalysis, I am addressing it here in the context of the question of symbolic structuring rather than that of the object, as in Kleinian thought.

35. It is important to stress that the model of the kaleidoscope is only an analogy functioning to clarify the differences between monolithic and diverse structuring. I am not suggesting that social change or diverse structuring can be achieved through the (Butlerian) voluntarism characteristic of the easy gesture of turning a kaleidoscope. Rather, I want to give a visual image of the differences between a monolithic Symbolic and a symbolic that can accommodate more than one structuring operation.

   The idea of substructures or subsymbolic (not presymbolic) networks coexisting alongside the phallus but inside the symbolic is developed in a fascinating way by the artist, practicing analyst, and innovative psychoanalytic theorist Bracha Lichtenberg-Ettinger. Her theory of the "matrixial psychical dimension" refers to "a feminine sub-symbolic network of borderlinks and interactions" that create "fields of desire and meaning" that provide an "alternative expedient alongside the phallus so that non phallic passages to the symbolic are possible" (interview, *Women's Art Magazine,* no. 56 [1994]: 2). André Green is not alone in suggesting the possibility of other symbolic processes, that is to say, symbolic without the capital "S." See Bracha Lichtenberg-Ettinger, *The Matrixial Gaze* (Leeds: University of Leeds Feminist and Art Histories Network Press, 1994).

36. See Jacques Derrida, "Structure, Sign and Play in the Discourses of the Human Sciences," in *Writing and Difference,* trans. Alan Bass (London: Routledge, 1978), pp. 278–295.

37. Green, "Conceptions of Affect," in *On Private Madness,* p. 205.

38. Judith Butler, "Against Proper Objects," in *Feminism Meets Queer Theory,* ed. Elizabeth Weed and Naomi Schor (Bloomington: Indiana University Press, 1997), p. 23.

39. Ibid., p. 23.

3. Matricide in Theory

1. I discussed the model of symbolic castration in chapter 1. It is necessary here, however, to add a brief outline of the castration complex in its relation to the terms of the cultural order. The castration complex is closely linked to the oedipal complex. The threat of castration functions as a prohibition emanating from the father that

sets the seal on the prohibition of incest with the mother and is the embodiment of the Law that founds the human order.

2. André Green, "The Dead Mother," in *On Private Madness* (London: Rebus, 1996), p. 144.

3. Luce Irigaray, "The Bodily Encounter with the Mother," in *The Irigaray Reader*, ed. Margaret Whitford (Oxford: Blackwell, 1991), p. 36.

4. Green, "The Dead Mother," p. 145.

5. Ibid.

6. Ibid.

7. André Green, "Conceptions of Affect," in *On Private Madness* (London: Rebus, 1996), p. 205.

8. Green, "The Dead Mother," p. 145.

9. Ibid.

10. One cannot help speculating on the ways in which this castration theory may appropriate or at least resonate with the ambivalent phantasies associated with the real blood of menstruation and the broken hymen. Yet the phantasized blood of castration gives rise to the possibility of symbolic inheritance whereas the blood of menstruation and of the breaking of the hymen remains as excess or abject blood—that which does not figure in any symbolic economy. It is almost as though the theory of castration, which describes the fear of this bloody context of generative loss, is built on the fear or envy of the real nonphantasized experience of the bloody contexts of female sexuality and generative reproduction. The threat of loss in castration anxiety has been linked by Freud to the male horror and dread of blood that is provoked by both the blood shed by the broken hymen and the blood of menstruation; see Sigmund Freud, "The Taboo of Virginity" (1918), *SE*, 11:191–208. The association between femininity and blood fuels the ambivalence concerning the destructive and generative properties of blood. Women experience this shedding of blood, which has the meaning of both loss and gain, whereas men can only fear it and envy it simultaneously. What is feared is loss (castration) and what is envied is its generative reproductive capacity. Thus castration theory seems to appropriate the real of female blood shed by phantasizing the act of a bloody mutilation in a symbolic frame that gives blood a structural meaning that signifies the transmission of paternal power. For an original and thought-provoking discussion of ideas related to these speculations, see Eva Feder Kittay, "Mastering Envy: From Freud's Narcissistic Wounds to Bettelheim's Symbolic Wounds to A Vision of Healing," in *Gender and Envy*, ed. Nancy Burke (London: Routledge, 1998), pp.171–198.

11. The ritual of circumcision is the obvious ceremonial act that (concretely) stages the moment where the son, through his shedding of blood, is accepted into the social symbolic structure of (Judaic) paternal transmission. The circumcision of the boy concretely stages the phantasy of castration in a context that is symbolic and generative. It is a ceremony performed between men, the paternal castrater makes the cut, causing a real flow of blood and a real scream of pain in the infant that signifies his entrance into a social order of paternal genealogy. See Bruno Bettelheim's interpretation of circumcision as an attempt to turn male envy of women's procreative capacities into mastery, *Symbolic Wounds: Puberty Rites and the Envious Male* (New York: Collier, 1962).

12. Irigaray, "The Bodily Encounter with the Mother," p. 36.

13. The question of a "matricidal law" is the subject of part 2.

14. Green, "The Dead Mother," p. 147.

15. Ibid.
16. Ibid., p. 148.
17. Ibid., p. 147.
18. While I acknowledge that the ambiguities I have referred to in Green's essay may be a result of my own particular limitations, I think it is fair to suggest that the essay leaves open the question of the potential of the "Black and White" model as a matricidal structural paradigm.
19. Held in November 1998 at the Brunei Gallery in London.
20. From my notes taken during the conference "A Celebration of the Work of André Green."
21. Gregorio Kohon, ed., *The Dead Mother: The Work of André Green* (London: Routledge, 1999), p. xiii.
22. Ibid., p. 52.
23. Luce Irigaray, *Thinking the Difference: For a Peaceful Revolution,* trans. Karin Montin (London: Athlone, 1994), p. 101.
24. Jean-Joseph Goux, *Oedipus, Philosopher,* trans. Catherine Porter (Stanford, Calif.: Stanford University Press, 1993), p. 101.

4. Oedipus and Monotheism

1. I am referring to particular contemporary (French) psychoanalytic theorists, namely, André Green and Jean Laplanche, who have followed through Freudian and Lacanian theory but have found different ways of thinking about the unconscious. See Jean Laplanche, *New Foundations for Psychoanalysis,* trans. David Macey (Oxford: Blackwell, 1989). My point here is that feminism is not alone in making these interventions. While feminism's critique of psychoanalysis was the first powerful intervention, leading to the attempt to expand psychoanalytic theory, it is also true that psychoanalytic theorists from outside feminism have also begun to move in this direction. These theoretical innovations come mainly from France, but the "Intersubjective" theory developed in the United States by Daniel Stern has certainly influenced the British psychoanalytic scene and been utilized by feminist psychoanalysts such as Jessica Benjamin for the purpose of developing psychoanalytic theory outside the castration model. With regard to other psychoanalytic feminist theorists who are trying to conceive of models of symbolization and unconscious processes outside the castration structure (other than Irigaray), see Teresa De Lauretis, *The Practice of Love: Lesbian Sexuality and Perverse Desire* (Bloomington: Indiana University Press, 1994); Elizabeth Grosz, *Space, Time and Perversion* (London: Routledge, 1995); Elisabeth Bronfen, *The Knotted Subject: Hysteria and Its Discontents* (Princeton, N.J.: Princeton University Press, 1998); Jan Campbell, *Arguing with the Phallus: Feminist, Queer and Postcolonial Theory. A Psychoanalytic Contribution* (London: Zed, 2000); Silvia Vegetti Finzi, *Mothering: Toward a New Psychoanalytic Construction,* trans. Katherine Jason (New York: Guilford, 1996);Jessica Benjamin, *Shadow of the Other: Intersubjectivity and Gender in Psychoanalysis* (London: Routledge, 1998); Juliet Mitchell, *Mad Men and Medusas: Reclaiming Hysteria and the Effects of Sibling Relations on the Human Condition* (London: Allen Lane / Penguin, 2000); Judith Butler, *Antigone's Claim: Kinship Between Life and Death* (New York: Columbia University Press, 2000); Carol Gilligan, *The Birth of Pleasure: A New Map of Love* (New York: Vintage, 2002); and Juliet Mitchell, *Siblings: Sex and Violence* (London: Polity, 2003).

2. See Nancy Chodorow, *The Reproduction of Mothering: Psychoanalysis and the So-ciology of Gender* (Berkeley: University of California Press, 1978); see also Carol Gilligan, *In a Different Voice: Psychological Theory and Women's Development* (Cambridge: Harvard University Press, 1982).

3. That Carl Jung engaged with myths other than Oedipus does not mean his work is relevant here. Jung did not use myths in the way I am discussing, that is, from a structural approach. He departed from Freud's structural model of the psyche in his use of archetypes, and his work on myth has not, in my opinion, led to the kinds of interventions into psychoanalysis with which I am concerned. Jung's work with myth belongs to a prestructural anthropology, and thus I do not consider his work relevant to this debate.

4. Claude Lévi-Strauss, *Myth and Meaning: The Massey Lectures* (London: Routledge, 1978), p. 44.

5. Jean-Pierre Vernant, Jean-Joseph Goux, and René Girard have criticized Freud's use of the Oedipus myth (in different ways), but they have not done this by using Lévi-Strauss's specific model of myth as an orchestral score. Their critiques do not focus on Freud's unilateral approach to myth. Also, Vernant, Goux, and Girard, despite working from different hypotheses and perspectives, all critique Freud's use of the Oedipus myth from a position that seeks to undermine the validity of psy-choanalysis. This is not my intention. My question concerning Freud's use of myth is different in that I am concerned with Freud's monolithic approach to myth and seek to introduce Lévi-Strauss's theory of myth in order to *expand* psychoanalysis rather than to undermine it. For critiques of Freud's use of the Oedipus myth, see Jean-Pierre Vernant and Pierre Vidal-Naquet, "Oedipus Without A Complex," in *Myth and Tragedy in Ancient Greece*, trans. Janet Lloyd (New York: Zone, 1988), pp. 85–112; Jean-Joseph Goux, *Oedipus, Philosopher*, trans. Catherine Porter. (Stanford, Calif.: Stanford University Press, 1993); and René Girard, *Violence and the Sacred*, trans. Patrick Gregory (London: Athlone, 1988), chap. 7.

6. Claude Lévi-Strauss, "The Structural Study of Myth," in *Structural Anthropology*, trans. Claire Jacobson and Brooke Grundfest Schoepf (London: Penguin, 1968), 1:211. The French original was published in Paris by Plon in 1958.

7. Ibid., p. 213.

8. Juliet Mitchell, *Psychoanalysis and Feminism: A Radical Reassessment of Freudian Psychoanalysis* (London: Allen Lane, 1974).

9. Juliet Mitchell, "Sexuality, Psychoanalysis and Social Changes," in *The Institute of Psychoanalysis News* (London: Institute of Psychoanalysis, 1998), p. 3.

10. A large area within psychoanalysis remains uncritically within the monolithic oedi-pal model and does not seek to expand its references. This was particularly apparent at a recent conference in London called "The Oedipus Complex Today," held at the French Institute in London in October 1998. The question the conference aimed to address concerned how relevant the oedipal model was to contemporary reality. The speakers all claimed that the oedipal model was still central and that any at-tempt to deny it or marginalize it theoretically was a pathological move that inevi-tably embraced chaos and disorder. This line of thought was most strongly espoused by Janine Chasseguet-Smirgel, who mounted an attack on what she termed the "French postmodernists," claiming that they were representative of an "antithought" position, preferring "soup" to "differentiation." She managed to pathologize dispa-rate theorists such as Deleuze and Guattari, Jacques Derrida, Jean Laplanche, and the American intersubjective tradition in exactly the same way, thus homogeniz-

ing every theory that departed from her own as representing a similar tendency to deny differentiation. It did appear that she herself had difficulty in making distinctions between the radically different theories she attacked. This is an example of the entrenched equation between Oedipus and sanity that psychoanalysis heralds as one of its truths and results in any attempt to think through a different model being viewed as pathological. See the book edited by Janine Chasseguet-Smirgel, *Creativity and Perversion* (London: Free Association Books, 1985), esp. pp.10–14, for a written account of her position.

11. For an example of these new psychosexual substructures, see, for example, Juliet Mitchell's discussion of the clinical phenomenon of male heterosexuality without castration in relation to Adam Limentani's paper "To the Limits of Male Heterosexuality: The Vagina Man," in her article "Sexuality, Psychoanalysis and Social Changes."

12. I am referring to Chasseguet-Smirgel's comments at the conference "The Oedipus Complex Today," mentioned in n. 10 above.

13. Sigmund Freud, "On Dreams" (1901), in *SE*, 5:666.

14. Lévi-Strauss's use of the analogy of the orchestral score in his discussion on reading myth is complicated because, while he speaks of finding the meaning of myths, an orchestral score does not produce meaning in itself but rather allows for the possibility of the articulation of meanings. That is to say, structure is not a meaning but rather allows for the possibility of the emergence of meaning. In this way, the consideration of other myths alongside Oedipus will, in my argument, allow for the possibility of the creation of potential meanings by opening up or expanding the structural constellation.

15. Hélène Cixous, "Sorties: Out and Out: Attacks/Ways Out/Forays," in Hélène Cixous and Catherine Clément, *The Newly Born Woman,* trans. Betsy Wing (London: Tauris, 1996), pp. 63–132.

16. The idea of a stage with many doors brings to mind Ionesco's play *The Chairs* (1958). The stage is round, and its circumference is set with lots of doors. The stage itself is filled with empty chairs for the imagined guests that the two characters in the play are supposedly receiving. The audience has to fill these empty chairs with the imagined guests, who invisibly enter the stage from all the different doors. I explore here the idea of a psychic stage with many doors leading to a dramatic symbolic space in which there are various empty, yet-to-be-filled, yet-to-be-imagined places/spaces/positions accessible through a multitude of doors/ways in.

17. François Roustang, *Dire Mastery: Discipleship from Freud to Lacan,* trans. Ned Lukacher (Washington, D.C.: American Psychiatric Press, 1986), p. 72.

5. Oresteian Secrets

1. The following tragedies are concerned with the Oresteian myth: *Agamemnon, The Libation Bearers,* and *The Eumenides* (Aeschylus); *Electra* (Sophocles); and *Iphigenia in Aulis, Iphigenia in Tauris, Electra, Orestes, Helen,* and *Hecuba* (Euripedes).

2. The four children are Iphigenia, Chrysothemis, Electra, and Orestes. At the point at which Aeschylus begins his treatment of the myth, however, there are only two children living in Argos: Chrysothemis and Electra. Iphigenia has been killed ten years earlier, and Clytemnestra has sent Orestes into exile, for fear that he may avenge his father's death.

3. Clytemnestra also murders Cassandra, Agamemnon's Trojan mistress.

4. Christina Wieland, *The Undead Mother: Psychoanalytic Explorations of Masculinity, Femininity and Matricide* (London: Rebus, 2000), p. 50.

5. Elizabeth Bronfen's reading of Sophocles' tragedy of *Oedipus* leads her to suggest that a matricidal phantasy underlies the Oedipus myth. See *The Knotted Subject: Hysteria and Its Discontents* (Princeton, N.J.: Princeton University Press, 1998), p. 13.

6. Jean-Joseph Goux argues that the myth of Oedipus is an anomaly because reason is substituted for combat. See *Oedipus, Philosopher,* trans. Catherine Porter (Stanford, Calif.: Stanford University Press, 1993), pp. 5–24. Goux does not, however, discuss the process by which each myth is a re-working of another. In my argument, contrary to Goux, Oedipus can be read as a matricidal myth especially when considered in relation to the Oresteian myth.

7. For further comments on Freud's conflicted and troubled relation to blood and wounds, see Monique Schneider, quoted in Elaine Hoffman Baruch and Lucienne J. Serrano, eds., *Women Analyze Women: In France, England and the United States* (New York: New York University Press, 1988), p. 176; and idem, quoted in Raoul Mortley, ed., *French Philosophers in Conversation: Levinas, Schneider, Serres, Irigaray, Le Doeuff, Derrida* (London: Routledge, 1991), pp. 25–43.

8. It should be noted here that there are no potential mother-daughter structures in the Oedipus myth since when Antigone appears in the myth, Jocasta is already dead.

9. I have already presented the heuristic gesture of using the dream as the paradigm or model from which to analyze myth (see part 1). I undertake a further detailed discussion of exactly how we can make use of Freud's method of dream interpretation with regard to the analysis of myth when I present my reading of the daughters in the Oresteian myth in part 3.

10. For a discussion of the psychic importance of an internal representation of a benign parental couple, see Melanie Klein, *Love, Guilt and Reparation and Other Works: 1921–1945* (London: Virago, 1988), pp. 313–316. I discuss Klein's theories later.

11. Luce Irigaray, "The Bodily Encounter with the Mother," in *The Irigaray Reader,* ed. Margaret Whitford (Oxford: Blackwell, 1991), pp. 37, 39.

12. Silvia Vegetti Finzi, *Mothering: Toward a New Psychoanalytic Construction,* trans. Katherine Jason (New York: Guilford, 1996), p. 113.

13. The myth of Zeus and Metis is documented in Hesiod's "Theogony," in *Hesiod and Theognis,* trans. Dorethea Wender (London: Penguin Classics, 1973), p. 52; Apollodorus, *The Library of Greek Mythology,* trans. Robin Hard (Oxford: World Classics, 1997), p. 31; and Robert Graves, *Greek Myths* (London: Penguin,1955), p. 1:45–46. Metis is not represented or mentioned in any of the tragedies of Aeschylus, Sophocles, and Euripides, however.

14. Hesiod, "Theogony," p. 52.

15. Ibid.

16. Nicholas Abraham and Maria Torok, *The Shell and the Kernel: Renewals of Psychoanalysis,* trans. and ed. Nicholas T. Rand (Chicago: University of Chicago Press, 1994), 1:125–138.

17. For further discussions of the ways in which the maternal functions as the negative ground of meaning, see Luce Irigaray, "The Bodily Encounter with the Mother" and "Women-Mothers, the Silent Substratum of the Social Order," in *The Irigaray Reader;* Michelle Boulous-Walker, *Philosophy and the Maternal Body: Reading Silence* (London: Routledge, 1998); and Lynne Hoffer, *Maternal Pasts, Feminist Fu-*

tures: Nostalgia, Ethics, and the Question of Difference (Stanford, Calif.: Stanford University Press, 1998).

18. Luce Irigaray, "The Bodily Encounter with the Mother," p. 41.
19. Sigmund Freud, "Case Histories: The Rat Man," in *SE*, 10:233.
20. H.D., *Tribute to Freud* (Manchester: Carcanet, 1970), pp. 68–69.
21. For excellent psychoanalytic feminist critiques of Freud's occlusion of the maternal, see Madelon Sprengnether, *The Spectral Mother: Freud, Feminism and Psychoanalysis* (Ithaca, N.Y.: Cornell University Press, 1990); Marcia Ian, *Remembering the Phallic Mother: Psychoanalysis, Modernism, and the Fetish* (Ithaca, N.Y.: Cornell University Press, 1993); and Jessica Benjamin *Shadow of the Other: Intersubjectivity and Gender in Psychoanalysis* (New York: Routledge, 1998), chap. 2.
22. Gregorio Kohon, ed., *The Dead Mother: The Work of André Green* (London: Routledge, 1999), p. 54.
23. Finzi, *Mothering*, p. 88.
24. Luce Irigaray, "The Forgotten Mystery of Female Ancestry," in *Thinking the Difference: For a Peaceful Revolution,* trans. Karin Montin (London: Athlone, 1994), p. 100.
25. Ibid.

6. The Blind Spot of Metis

1. Sigmund Freud and Josef Breuer, *Studies on Hysteria* (1893–1895), in *SE* 2:37.
2. The point to emphasize is that, while the Metis myth can be found in various documentations of Greek myth, she is excluded from the tragedies of Aeschylus, Euripides, and Sophocles. This means that in terms of the cultural reception of myth via tragedy, Metis will be relatively unknown. It is the fact that her story is left out of the plays that is significant in this context.
3. Maria Torok, Barbro Sylwan, and Adele Covello, "Melanie Mell by Herself," in *Reading Melanie Klein,* ed. John Phillips and Lyndsey Stonebridge (London: Routledge, 1999), p. 57.
4. Nicholas Abraham and Maria Torok, *The Shell and the Kernel: Renewals of Psychoanalysis,* trans. and ed. Nicholas T. Rand (Chicago: University of Chicago Press, 1994), 1:94.
5. Freud comments in "Moses and Monotheism" (1939): "Under the influence of external factors *into which we need not enter here and which are also in part insufficiently known,* it came about that the matriarchal social order was succeeded by the patriarchal one—which of course involved a revolution in the juridical conditions that had so far prevailed. An echo of this revolution seems still to be audible in the Oresteia of Aeschylus. Such a shift represents a momentous step for civilisation" (*SE* 23:114; my italics).
6. In his book *The Tragic Effect: The Oedipus Complex in Tragedy,* trans. Alan Sheridan (Cambridge: Cambridge University Press, 1979), André Green mentions Klein's paper on the *Oresteia* as an afterword to his own discussion of the myth, which I discuss later in this section. Green comments that he had come across Klein's essay on the *Oresteia* after he had written his own commentary. In an appendix, he briefly reviews her paper.
7. Melanie Klein, "Some Reflections on the *Oresteia*" (1963), in *Envy and Gratitude and Other Works: 1946–1963* (London: Virago, 1988), p. 298.
8. Ibid., p. 295.

7. Melanie Klein and the Phantom of Metis

1. Melanie Klein, "Some Reflections on the *Oresteia*" (1963), in *Envy and Gratitude and Other Works: 1946–1963* (London: Virago, 1988), p. 283.
2. Euripides, *Orestes*, in *Orestes and Other Plays*, trans. Philip Vellacott (London: Penguin Classics, 1972), p. 309.
3. Ibid., p. 313.
4. Klein, "Some Reflections," p. 286.
5. Ibid., p. 295.
6. Ibid., p. 298.
7. Aeschylus, *The Eumenides*, in *The Oresteia: Agamemnon, The Libation Bearers, The Eumenides*, trans. Robert Fagles (London: Penguin Classics, 1977; reprint, London: Penguin Classics, 1979), lines 748–753, p. 264.
8. I will discuss Klein's interpretation of Clytemnestra as representing the "bad breast" in the section "The Exposure of the Maternal Breast" in the following chapter.
9. I am intentionally using Kleinian terminology here in order to demonstrate how she could have interpreted Athena in a radically different way if she had considered the myth of Metis, Athena's mother. "Manic denial," in the Kleinian system, is a defense mechanism belonging to the paranoid schizoid position that is employed to ward off the experience of loss and sustain the phantasy of omnipotence.
10. See Pearl King's introduction to *The Freud–Klein Controversies, 1941–45*, ed. Pearl King and Ricardo Steiner (London: Routledge, 1991), pp. 1–5.
11. Ibid., p. 1.
12. Christiane Olivier contends: "If psychoanalysis had been written by a woman, no doubt there would never have been any mention of castration," quoted in Nancy Burke, ed., *Gender and Envy* (London: Routledge, 1998), p. 212.
13. It is interesting to note that Klein was writing another paper at the same time as her essay on the *Oresteia*, which was also left unfinished at her death. In this paper, "On the Sense of Loneliness" (1963), Klein examines the sense of inner alienation and the feeling of not belonging resulting from the impossible desire to achieve complete understanding and union with the other. It is, I think, significant that she was thinking about loneliness in this way while writing about the *Oresteia*, in that her theoretical alienation from Freud was becoming more obvious and perhaps more difficult to bear as she sought to make use of another myth. This is, of course, pure speculation, but it is interesting that Klein's last works before her death were concerned with the *Oresteia* and the experience of loneliness. Could this disclose a preoccupation with the fear of innovation: a fear of creating new thought and of the inevitable consequential alienation?
14. Nicolas Abraham, "Notes on the Phantom," in Nicholas Abraham and Maria Torok, *The Shell and the Kernel: Renewals of Psychoanalysis*, trans. and ed. Nicholas T. Rand (Chicago: University of Chicago Press, 1994), 1:175.
15. Ibid., p. 176.
16. Editor's note, in ibid., p. 169.
17. Abraham and Torok use the word "nescience" to describe the phantom effect. It refers to the gap in knowledge where the trauma resides.
18. Klein, "Some Reflections," p. 297.
19. "Aphanisis" is a term introduced by Ernest Jones that describes the disappearance of or the death of sexual desire. See Jean Laplanche and J. B. Pontalis, *The Language of Psychoanalysis* (London: Karnac, 1988), p. 40.
20. Melanie Klein, "Some Reflections," p. 297.

21. See, for example, Freud's case history of "Little Hans": "Analysis of a Phobia in a Five-Year-Old Boy" (1909), *SE* 10:3–148.
22. Maria Torok, "Story of Fear: The Symptoms of Phobia—The Return of the Repressed or the Return of the Phantom?" in *The Shell and the Kernel*, p. 181.
23. Ibid., p. 180.

8. Metis in Contemporary Psychoanalysis

1. André Green, *The Tragic Effect: The Oedipus Complex in Tragedy*, trans. Alan Sheridan, Cambridge: Cambridge University Press, 1979), p. 43.
2. See Christina Wieland, "Matricide and Destructiveness: Infantile Anxieties and Technological Culture," *British Journal of Psychotherapy* 12, no. 3 (1996): 300–313. In this article, Wieland argues in a similar vein to Green that matricide as a mechanism of separation from the mother is pathological in its disallowing of a gradual working-through of loss and results in the banishment of the early mother in the unconscious as a bad object and the elevation of the father into superego resulting in the Western psyche's inability to work through infantile anxieties with the idealized paternal superego used as a defense against them.
3. This account of masculinity is implicit in R. Stoller's work, wherein male identity is established as a secondary phenomena through the denial of or defense against the primary identification with the mother. See Robert Stoller, *Sex and Gender: On the Development of Masculinity and Femininity* (New York: Science House, 1968). Jessica Benjamin uses Stoller's theories to argue that masculinity relies on "false differentiation" that employs domination to defend against the relation to the mother, driven by the phantasy of being reabsorbed by the powerful mother. Masculinity is built on this curious method of asserting difference so that the achievement of masculinity/individuation comes to be dependent on repudiation, denigration, and domination of the maternal body, with the phallus representing the defense against and hostility toward dependency. See Jessica Benjamin, *The Bonds of Love: Psychoanalysis, Feminism and the Problem of Domination: Psychoanalysis, Feminism, and the Problem of Domination* (New York: Pantheon, 1988), chap. 2.
4. In *The Black Sun: Depression and Melancholia*, trans. Leon S. Roudiez (New York: Columbia University Press, 1989), Kristeva adheres to Lacanian logic in her contention that autonomy depends on matricide: "Matricide is our vital necessity, the sine qua non of individuation" (p. 27).
5. Luce Irigaray, "The Bodily Encounter with the Mother," in *The Irigaray Reader*, ed. Margaret Whitford (Oxford: Blackwell, 1991), p. 38.
6. Ibid., p. 37.
7. Ibid., p. 38.
8. Hanna Segal, *Dream, Phantasy and Art* (London: Routledge, 1991), p. 40.
9. Ibid.
10. Christina Wieland, *The Undead Mother: Psychoanalytic Explorations of Masculinity, Femininity and Matricide* (London: Rebus, 2000), p. 13.
11. Ibid., p. 19.
12. Ibid., p. 12.
13. Nicolas Abraham and Maria Torok, "Mourning or Melancholia: Introjection versus Incorporation," in *The Shell and the Kernel: Renewals of Psychoanalysis*, trans. and ed. Nicholas T. Rand (Chicago: University of Chicago Press, 1994), 1:129.
14. Nicholas Abraham, "Notes on the Phantom: A Complement to Freud's Metapsychology," in *The Shell and the Kernel*, 1:176.

9. Who's Afraid of Clytemnestra?

1. Monique Schneider, quoted in *Women Analyze Women: In France, England and the United States* (New York: New York University Press, 1988), ed. Elaine Hoffman Baruch and Lucienne J. Serrano, p. 174.

2. Ibid., p. 199.

3. Luce Irigaray, "The Bodily Encounter with the Mother," in *The Irigaray Reader*, ed. Margaret Whitford (Oxford: Blackwell, 1991), p. 36.

4. For Freud's theory of the primal phantasies, see "A Case of Paranoia Running Counter to the Psychoanalytic Theory of the Disease" (1915), in *SE*, 14:269; and "Introductory Lectures on Psychoanalysis" (1916–1917), *SE*, 16:371. For a detailed discussion and development of Freud's theory of the primal phantasies, see Jean Laplanche and J. B. Pontalis, "Fantasy and the Origins of Sexuality," in *Formations of Fantasy*, ed. Victor Burgin, James Donald, and Cora Kaplan (London: Methuen, 1986), pp. 5–34.

5. Janine Chasseguet-Smirgel, "Feminine Guilt and the Oedipal Complex," in *Female Sexuality: New Psychoanalytic Views*, ed. Janine Chasseguet-Smirgel (London: Karnac, 1985), pp. 94–134.

6. Schneider, quoted in *Women Analyze Women*, p. 199.

7. Aeschylus, Agamemnon, in *The Oresteia: Agamemnon, The Libation Bearers, The Eumenides*, trans. Robert Fagles (London: Penguin Classics, 1977; reprint, London: Penguin Classics, 1979). lines 954–957, p. 140.

8. Sigmund Freud, "The Sexual Theories of Children" (1908), *SE*, 9:220.

9. In Clytemnestra, there is an echo of Helen, her twin sister, whose sexual desire results in the Trojan War, bringing men and cities to destruction. These terrible twins, the femmes fatales of Western mythology, create a doubling effect that multiplies and repeats, disclosing the fierce anxiety attached to this phantasy of insatiable, desiring, castrating female sexuality. The twin motif depicts excess and repetition, powerfully signifying complex anxieties related to castration. The Helen-Clytemnestra doubling creates the phantasmatic figure of the double-headed hydra, the monstrous feminine.

10. See Laplanche and Pontalis, "Fantasy and the Origins of Sexuality," pp. 5–34.

11. Aeschylus, *The Libation Bearers*, in *The Oresteia*, lines 883–885, p. 216.

12. Ibid., line 886, p. 217.

13. Schneider, quoted in *Women Analyze Women*, p. 191.

14. Aeschylus, *The Eumenides*, in *The Oresteia*, lines 106, 107, p. 235.

15. See chapter 3.

16. I am using the term abject in the Kristevian sense.

17. Melanie Klein, *Envy and Gratitude and Other Works: 1946 –1963* (London: Virago, 1988), p. 290; André Green, *The Tragic Effect: The Oedipus Complex in Tragedy*, trans. Alan Sheridan (Cambridge: Cambridge University Press, 1979), p. 56; Irigaray, "The Bodily Encounter with the Mother," p. 37.

18. For a further definition, see Jean Laplanche and J. B. Pontalis, *The Language of Psychoanalysis* (London: Karnac, 1988), pp. 376–378.

19. Julia Kristeva, *Powers of Horror: An Essay in Abjection*, trans. Leon S. Roudiez (New York: Columbia University Press, 1982), p. 42.

20. Ibid., p. 40.

21. Ibid.

22. Euripides, *Orestes*, in *Orestes and Other Plays*, trans. Philip Vellacott (London: Penguin Classics, 1972), lines 113–120, p. 314. The three women are the Fates: the

spinner of life, she who measures, and a third, who cuts the thread. Freud's interpretation of this mythical trinity led him to conclude that the three-women motif condenses the universal relations a man has with the feminine-maternal: the mother who bore him, the beloved who is a substitute for his mother, and Mother Earth (the grave). See "The Theme of the Three Caskets" (1913), in *SE*, 12:289–302.

10. Metis's Law

1. Aeschylus, *The Eumenides*, in *The Oresteia: Agamemnon, The Libation Bearers, The Eumenides*, trans. Robert Fagles (London: Penguin Classics, 1977; reprint, London: Penguin Classics, 1979), lines 672–767, p. 261.
2. Ibid., lines 748–751, p. 264.
3. It is interesting to remember here the point in Freud's Irma dream (SE, 4:96–121) when he considers Irma as part of the dream work functioning to conceal the figure of his pregnant wife, who stands behind the manifest female figures in the dream. Shoshana Felman's rereading of the Irma dream foregrounds the pregnant woman as the navel of the dream, the point at which Freud stops analyzing the associations to the dream. See Shoshana Felman, "Competing Pregnancies: The Dream from which Psychoanalysis Proceeds," chap. 4 in *What Does a Woman Want? Reading and Sexual Difference* (Baltimore: Johns Hopkins University Press, 1993), pp. 68–120.
4. Juliet Mitchell, *Mad Men and Medusas: Reclaiming Hysteria and the Effects of Sibling Relations on the Human Condition* (London: Allen Lane / Penguin, 2000), p. xi.
5. See Freud's essay "The Future of an Illusion" (1927): "We call a belief an illusion when a wish fulfillment is a prominent factor in its motivation" (*SE*, 21:31).
6. Ronald Britton, *Belief and Imagination: Explorations in Psychoanalysis* (London: Routledge, 1998), p. 14.
7. Ibid., p. 18.
8. Ibid., p. 11.

11. Clytemnestra's Three Daughters

1. Euripides, *Orestes*, in *Orestes and Other Plays*, trans. Phillip Vellacott (London: Penguin Classics, 1972), lines 20–24, p. 301.
2. If any of the daughters of Atreus are mentioned in readings of the Oresteian myth, invariably it is Electra, albeit briefly. Klein and Irigaray both mention Electra in their readings (in marginal ways), as I discuss later in this chapter. Jung's attempt to postulate an Electra complex is not considered worthy of attention here since, following Freud, I do not agree that the little girl's structure is the symmetrical opposite of the little boy's. The approach here is to explore the daughters' relation to matricide with a view to identifying structures of desire that are not reducible to the oedipal and castration model. Rather than concentrating on Electra alone, which is often the case in readings of the myth (since she is the most vocal and visible), bringing the other two daughters onto the stage is crucial, since neither Electra nor Orestes can be sufficiently analyzed in isolation; they are part of a sibling structure that, when considered, allows us to elaborate our examination of matricide and interpret its vicissitudes across more than one axis and in more than one myth.
3. I discuss Klein's theory of primitive envy and her treatment of the mother-daughter relation later.

4. There are obvious similarities in these approaches: I, too, am attempting to resurrect the mother by making her death function symbolically, but the difference between my own approach and Irigaray's concerns our different definitions of matricide.

5. Luce Irigaray, "A Chance for Life," in *Sexes and Genealogies*, trans. Gillian C. Gill (New York: Columbia University Press, 1993), p. 189.

6. See Hélène Cixous, "Sorties," in *The Newly Born Woman* ed. Hélène Cixous and Catherine Clément, trans. Betsy Wing (London: Tauris, 1996). pp. 63–130; Christa Woolf, *Cassandra: A Novel and Four Essays*, trans. Jan Van Heurck (London: Virago, 1984); and idem, *Medea: A Novel*, trans. John Cullen (London: Virago, 1998).

7. Drucilla Cornell, *Beyond Accomodation: Ethical Feminism, Deconstruction and the Law* (London: Routledge, 1991), p. 173.

8. For Irigaray's most extensive reading of the Demeter-Persephone myth, see *Thinking the Difference: For a Peaceful Revolution*, trans. Karin Montin (London: Athlone, 1994), pp. 100–113.

9. For a discussion of the feminist appropriation of the Demeter myth, see Marilyn Arthur, "Politics and Pomegranates: An Interpretation of the Homeric Hymn to Demeter," in *The Homeric Hymn to Demeter*, ed. Helen Foley (Princeton, N.J.: Princeton University Press, 1984).

10. For an extensive discussion of the nostalgic trends in feminist theory, see Lynne Huffer, *Maternal Pasts, Feminist Futures: Nostalgia, Ethics, and the Question of Difference* (Stanford, Calif.: Stanford University Press, 1998).

11. This is not to say that Irigaray does not diagnose the negative dynamics operating between mothers and daughters, but she accounts for this by describing these destructive aspects as symptomatic of the patriarchal order. This implies that Irigaray has a postpatriarchal vision of an essentially benign mother-daughter relation, free of all negative and conflicting aspects.

12. On Demeter's "rage," see Foley, *The Homeric Hymn to Demeter*.

13. Estela V. Welldon's book *Mother, Madonna, Whore: The Idealization and Denigration of Motherhood* (New York: Guilford, 1988) addresses the ways in which motherhood can become the site wherein women act out their perversions if there is no possibility of a symbolic that can represent a maternal subject position. Welldon's clinical accounts of maternal perversions are set in the context of the impossibility of theorizing motherhood outside the idealization/denigration opposition.

14. Luce Irigaray, "The Bodily Encounter with the Mother," in *The Irigaray Reader*, ed. Margaret Whitford (Oxford: Blackwell, 1991), p. 40.

15. Ibid., p. 41.

16. Juliet Mitchell, introduction to *Psychoanalysis and Feminism: A Radical Reassessment of Freudian Psychoanalysis*, rev. ed. (London: Penguin, 1999), p. xxxvi.

17. Melanie Klein, *Envy and Gratitude and Other Works: 1946–1963* (London: Virago, 1988), p. 284.

18. Luce Irigaray, "The Bodily Encounter with the Mother," p. 35.

19. Ibid., p. 37.

20. Julia Kristeva discusses feminine depression in relation to the daughter's difficulty in achieving psychic matricide. See *The Black Sun: Depression and Melancholia*, trans. Leon S. Roudiez (New York: Columbia University Press, 1989), pp. 27–30.

21. For an extensive discussion of Klein's concept of projective identification and the development of this concept in post-Kleinian psychoanalysis, see Joseph Sandler, ed., *Projection, Identification, Projective Identification* (London: Karnac, 1989).

22. Sophocles, *Electra,* in *Electra and Other Plays,* trans. E. F. Walting (London: Penguin Classics, 1953), lines 84–87, p. 73.

12. The Latent Mother-Daughter

1. Juliet Mitchell, *Mad Men and Medusas: Reclaiming Hysteria and the Effects of Sibling Relations on the Human Condition* (London: Allen Lane / Penguin, 2000).
2. Aeschylus, *The Eumenides,* in *The Oresteia: Agamemnon, The Libation Bearers, The Eumenides,* trans. Robert Fagles (London: Penguin Classics, 1977; reprint, London: Penguin Classics, 1979), lines 663–666, p. 261.
3. Irigaray, in her work between the eighties and nineties insisted on women's legal representation; see especially "Each Sex Must Have Its Own Rights," in *Sexes and Genealogies,* trans. Gillian C. Gill (New York: Columbia University Press, 1993), pp. 1–5; and "Civil Rights and the Responsibilities for the Two Sexes," in *Thinking the Difference: For a Peaceful Revolution,* trans. Karin Montin (London: Athlone, 1994), pp. 65–88.
4. Julia Kristeva, "Women's Time," in *The Kristeva Reader,* ed. Toril Moi (Oxford: Blackwell, 1986), p. 203.
5. Irigaray, *Sexes and Genealogies,* p. 196.
6. Aeschylus, *Agamemnon,* in *The Oresteia,* lines 1440–1444, p. 162.
7. The law of Metis functions to undercut the male omnipotent phantasy and forces him to recognize a limit between himself and the other whose properties and capacities he envies.

13. Iphigenia Becomes Metis

1. Claude Lévi-Strauss, "The Structural Study of Myth," in *Structural Anthropology,* trans. Claire Jacobson and Brooke Grundfest Schoepf (London: Penguin, 1963), 1:229. The French original was published by Plon in 1958.
2. Ibid., p. 228.
3. The deer only appears in Euripides' version of the myth, whereas in Aeschylus the story of Iphigenia is told without mention of her disappearance and replacement by the deer.
4. Euripides, *Iphigenia in Aulis,* in *Orestes and Other Plays,* trans. Philip Vellacott (London: Penguin Classics, 1972), line 1609, p. 426.
5. Freud has identified the displacement from vagina to throat as a frequent trick of the dream work and in hysterical symptoms; see "Fragment of an Analysis of a Case of Hysteria" (1905), *SE* 7:30. Further, Jean-Pierre-Vernant and Nicole Loraux have identified this displacement in Greek myth wherein the head, face, neck, throat, and mouth of the female have a "genitalized" meaning. See Nicole Loraux, *Tragic Ways of Killing a Woman,* trans. Anthony Forester (Cambridge: Harvard University Press, 1991), chaps. 1 and 3; and Jean-Pierre Vernant, *Mortals and Immortals: Collected Essays,* ed. Froma Zeitlin (Princeton, N.J.: Princeton University Press, 1991), p. 138.
6. Euripides, *Iphigenia in Aulis,* lines 1618–1621, p. 426.
7. See Hanna Segal, *Dream, Phantasy and Art* (London: Routledge, 1991), p. 35.
8. Even Clytemnestra's reaction to the sacrifice of Iphigenia cannot be considered as mourning since in murdering her husband she acts rather than thinks/works through/mourns.
9. Euripides, *Iphigenia in Aulis,* lines 894–903, p. 399; my italics.

10. Primary identification is closely bound up with oral incorporation and is located in the undifferentiated primitive relation to the mother in the oral stage. See Jean Laplanche and J. B. Pontalis, *The Language of Psychoanalysis* (London: Karnac, 1988), p. 336, for a discussion of the relation between primary identification and oral incorporation.

14. Virginity and Sibling Incest

1. Aeschylus, *The Eumenides*, in *The Oresteia: Agamemnon, The Libation Bearers, The Eumenides*, trans. Robert Fagles (London: Penguin Classics, 1977; reprint, London: Penguin Classics, 1979), lines 752–753, p. 264; my italics.

2. Hermione is Helen and Menelaus's only daughter, who, according to Euripides in his tragedy *Electra*, was entrusted to Clytemnestra (Helen's sister) while the war with Troy was waged.

3. Jean-Pierre Vernant and Pierre Vidal-Naquet, *Myth and Tragedy in Ancient Greece*, trans. Janet Lloyd (London: Zone, 1988), pp. 99–100.

4. This is dramatized in Euripides' version of *Electra*.

5. Euripides, *Iphigenia in Tauris*, in *Alcestis/Hippolytus/Iphigenia in Tauris*, trans. Phillip Vellacott (London: Penguin Classics, 1953; reprint, London: Penguin Classics, 1974), lines 251–252, p. 137.

6. Sophocles, *Electra*, in *Electra and Other Plays*, trans. E. F. Walting (London: Penguin Classics, 1953), line 166, p. 74.

7. Ibid., lines 83–84, p. 72.

8. Euripides, *Orestes*, in *Orestes and Other Plays*, trans. Philip Vellacott (London: Penguin Classics, 1972), lines 318–319, p. 307.

9. As I pointed out in the text, the sacrifice of Iphigenia does not result in her death but in her disappearance.

10. Examples include Elizabeth Bronfen, *Over Her Dead Body: Death, Femininity and the Aesthetic* (Manchester: Manchester University Press, 1992); Nancy Sorkin Rabinowitz, *Anxiety Veiled: Euripides and the Traffic in Women*, (Ithaca, N.Y.: Cornell University Press, 1993); and Nicole Loraux, *Tragic Ways of Killing a Woman*, trans. Anthony Forster (Cambridge: Harvard University Press, 1991).

11. Iphigenia is always read in conjunction with the famous sacrificed virgins, for example, Polyxena, Antigone, Persephone, and Makaria.

12. Jean-Joseph Goux, *Oedipus, Philosopher*, trans. Catherine Porter (Stanford, Calif.: Stanford University Press, 1993), pp. 5–24.

13. Euripides, *Iphigenia in Tauris*, lines 177–178, p. 135.

14. See Clytemnestra's speech in Sophocles, *Electra*, lines 531–550, p. 84.

15. Euripides, *Orestes*, line 325, p. 310.

16. Ibid., lines 1074–1078, p. 337.

17. Ibid., lines 1079–1084, p. 337.

18. Aeschylus, *The Libation Bearers*, in *The Oresteia*, lines 178–211, pp. 185–187.

19. Luce Irigaray, *Sexes and Genealogies*, trans. Gillian C. Gill (New York: Columbia University Press, 1993), p. 177.

Conclusion: The Question of Chrysothemis

1. Sophocles, *Electra*, in *Electra and Other Plays*, trans. E. F. Walting (London: Penguin Classics, 1953), lines 396–399, p. 79.

Bibliography

Abraham, Nicholas and Maria Torok. *The Shell and the Kernel: Renewals of Psycho-analysis.* Vol. 1. Trans. and ed. Nicholas T. Rand. Chicago: University of Chicago Press, 1994.

——. *The Wolfman's Magic Word: A Cryptonomy.* Trans. Nicholas T. Rand. Minneapolis: University of Minnesota Press, 1987.

Adams, Parveen and Elizabeth Cowie, eds. *The Woman in Question.* London: Verso, 1990.

Aeschylus. *The Complete Greek Tragedies 1.* Ed. Richard Lattimore and David Grene. Chicago: University of Chicago Press, 1958.

——. *The Oresteia: Agamemnon, The Libation Bearers, The Eumenides.* Trans. Robert Fagles. London: Penguin Classics, 1977. Reprint, London: Penguin Classics, 1979.

——. *Prometheus Bound and Other Plays.* Trans. Phillip Vellacott. London: Penguin Classics, 1961.

Anderson, Robin, ed. *Clinical Lectures on Klein and Bion.* London: Routledge, 1992.

Apollodorus. *The Library of Greek Mythology.* Trans. Robin Hard. Oxford: World Classics, 1997.

Baruch, Elaine Hoffman and Lucienne J. Serrano, eds. *Women Analyze Women: In France, England and the United States.* New York: New York University Press, 1988.

Benjamin, Jessica. *The Bonds of Love: Psychoanalysis, Feminism, and the Problem of Domination.* New York: Pantheon, 1988.

——. *Like Objects, Love Objects: Essays on Recognition and Sexual Difference.* New Haven: Yale University Press, 1995.

——. *Shadow of the Other: Intersubjectivity and Gender in Psychoanalysis.* New York: Routledge, 1998.

Benvenuto, Bice. *Concerning the Rites of Psychoanalysis; or, The Villa of the Mysteries.* Cambridge: Polity, 1994.

Benvenuto, Bice and Roger Kennedy. *The Works of Jacques Lacan: An Introduction.* London: Free Association Books, 1986.

Bettelheim, Bruno. *Symbolic Wounds: Puberty Rites and the Envious Male.* New York: Collier, 1962.

Bion, W. R. *Learning from Experience.* London: Maresfield, 1962.

——. *Second Thoughts.* London: Maresfield, 1967.

Bollas, Christopher. *Psychoanalysis and Self Experience.* London: Routledge, 1993.

Boothby, Richard. *Death and Desire: Psychoanalytic Theory in Lacan's Return to Freud.* London: Routledge, 1991.

Bott-Spillius, Elizabeth, ed. *Melanie Klein Today: Developments in Theory and Practice.* Vol. 1, *Mainly Theory.* London: Routledge, 1988.

Boulous-Walker, Michelle. *Philosophy and the Maternal Body: Reading Silence.* London: Routledge, 1998.

Bowie, Malcolm. *Lacan.* London: Fontana, 1991.

Breen, Dana, ed. *The Gender Conundrum: Contemporary Psychoanalytic Perspectives on Femininity and Masculinity.* London: Routledge, 1993.

Brennan, Teresa. *The Interpretation of the Flesh: Freud and Femininity.* London: Routledge, 1992.

——, ed. *Between Feminism and Psychoanalysis.* London: Routledge, 1989.

Britton, Ronald. *Belief and Imagination: Explorations in Psychoanalysis.* London: Routledge, 1998.

Bronfen, Elisabeth. *The Knotted Subject: Hysteria and Its Discontents.* Princeton, N.J.: Princeton University Press, 1998.

——. *Over Her Dead Body: Death, Femininity and the Aesthetic.* Manchester: Manchester University Press, 1992.

Buckley, Peter, ed. *Essential Papers on Object Relations.* New York: New York University Press, 1986.

Burgin, Victor, James Donald, and Cora Kaplan, eds. *Formations of Fantasy.* London: Methuen, 1986.

Burgoyne, Bernard and Mary Sullivan, eds. *The Klein-Lacan Dialogues.* London: Rebus, 1997.

Burke, Carolyn, Naomi Schor, and Margaret Whitford, eds. *Engaging with Irigaray: Feminist Philosophy and Modern European Thought.* New York: Columbia University Press, 1994.

Burke, Nancy, ed. *Gender and Envy.* London: Routledge, 1998.

Butler, Judith. *Antigone's Claim: Kinship Between Life and Death.* New York: Columbia University Press, 2000.

——. *Gender Trouble: Feminism and the Subversion of Identity.* London: Routledge, 1990.

——. *The Psychic Life of Power: Theories in Subjection.* Stanford, Calif.: Stanford University Press, 1997.

Campbell, Jan. *Arguing with the Phallus: Feminist, Queer and Postcolonial Theory. A Psychoanalytic Contribution.* London: Zed, 2000.

Chasseguet-Smirgel, Janine, ed. *Creativity and Perversion.* London: Free Association Books, 1985.

——. *Female Sexuality: New Psychoanalytic Views.* London: Karnac, 1985.

Chodorow, Nancy. *The Reproduction of Mothering: Psychoanalysis and the Sociology of Gender.* Berkeley: University of California Press, 1978.

Cixous, Hélène and Catherine Clément. *The Newly Born Woman* Trans. Betsy Wing. London: Tauris, 1996.

Clément, Catherine. *The Weary Sons of Freud.* Trans. Nicole Ball. London: Verso, 1987.

Cornell, Drucilla. *Beyond Accommodation: Ethical Feminism, Deconstruction and the Law.* London: Routledge, 1991.

Culler, Jonathan. *Structuralist Poetics: Structuralism, Linguistics and the Study of Literature.* London: Routledge, 1975.

De Lauretis, Teresa. *Alice Doesn't: Feminism, Semiotics, Cinema.* London: Macmillan, 1984.

——. *The Practice of Love: Lesbian Sexuality and Perverse Desire.* Bloomington: Indiana University Press, 1994.

Deleuze, Gilles. *Essays Critical and Clinical.* Trans. Daniel W. Smith and Michael A. Greco. London: Verso, 1998.

Derrida, Jacques. *Writing and Difference.* Trans. Alan Bass. London: Routledge, 1978.

Doane, Janice and Devon Hodges. *From Klein to Kristeva: Psychoanalytic Feminism and the Search for the "Good Enough" Mother.* Ann Arbor: University of Michigan Press, 1992.

Doane, Mary Ann. *The Desire to Desire: The Woman's Film of the 1940s.* Bloomington: Indiana University Press, 1987.

Dowden, Ken. *The Uses of Greek Mythology.* London: Routledge, 1992.

Eisenstein, Hester and Alice Jardine, eds. *The Future of Difference.* Jersey City, N.J.: Rutgers University Press: 1987.

Elliott, Anthony. *Freud 2000.* Cambridge: Polity, 1998.

Elliott, Anthony and Stephen Frosh, eds. *Psychoanalysis in Contexts: Paths Between*
——. *Theory and Modern Culture.* London: Routledge, 1995.

Euripides. *Alcestis/Hippolytus/Iphigenia in Tauris.* Trans. Phillip Vellacott. London: Penguin Classics, 1953. Reprint, London: Penguin Classics, 1974.

——. *The Bacchae and Other Plays.* Trans. Philip Vellacott. London: Penguin Classics, 1973.

——. *The Complete Tragedies.* Vols. 1–4. Eds. David Greene and Richard Lattimore. Chicago: Chicago University Press, 1958.

——. *Medea and Other Plays.* Trans. Phillip Vellacott. London: Penguin Classics, 1963.

——. *Orestes and Other Plays.* Trans. Philip Vellacott. London: Penguin Classics, 1972.

Evans, Dylan. *An Introductory Dictionary of Lacanian Psychoanalysis.* London: Routledge, 1996.

Evans, Mary, ed. *The Woman Question.* London: Sage, 1994.

Feldstein, Richard and Judith Roof, eds. *Feminism and Psychoanalysis.* Ithaca, N.Y.: Cornell University Press, 1989.

Felman, Shoshana. *Jacques Lacan and the Adventure of Insight: Psychoanalysis in Contemporary Culture.* Cambridge: Harvard University Press, 1987.

——. *What Does a Woman Want? Reading and Sexual Difference.* Baltimore: Johns Hopkins University Press, 1993.

Finzi, Silvia Vegetti. *Mothering: Toward a New Psychoanalytic Construction.* Trans. Katherine Jason. New York: Guilford, 1996.

Flax, Jane. *Thinking Fragments: Psychoanalysis, Feminism, and Postmodernism in the Contemporary West.* Berkeley: University of California Press, 1990.

Foley, Helen, ed. *The Homeric Hymn to Demeter*. Princeton, N.J.: Princeton University Press,1984.

Freud, Sigmund. *The Standard Edition of the Complete Psychological Works of Sigmund Freud*. Trans. and ed. James Strachey. Vols 1–24. London: Hogarth, 1951–1973.

Fuss, Diana. *Essentially Speaking: Feminism, Nature and Difference*. London: Routledge, 1989.

——. *Identification Papers*. London: Routledge, 1995.

Gallop, Jane. *The Daughter's Seduction: Feminism and Psychoanalysis*. Ithaca, N.Y.: Cornell University Press, 1982.

Gatens, Moira. *Imaginary Bodies: Ethics, Power and Corporeality*. London: Routledge, 1996.

Gilligan, Carol. *The Birth of Pleasure: A New Map of Love*. New York: Vintage, 2002.

——. *In a Different Voice: Psychological Theory and Women's Development*. Cambridge: Harvard University Press, 1982.

Girard, René. *To Double Business Bound: Essays on Literature, Mimesis and Anthropology*. Trans. Patrick Gregory. London: Athlone, 1978.

——. *Violence and the Sacred*. Trans. Patrick Gregory. London: Athlone, 1988.

Goux, Jean-Joseph. *Oedipus, Philosopher*. Trans. Catherine Porter. Stanford, Calif.: Stanford University Press, 1993.

Graves, Robert. *Greek Myths*. Vols. 1 and 2. London: Penguin, 1955.

Green, André. *The Dead Mother: The Work of André Green*. Ed Gregorio Kohon. London: Routledge, 1999.

——. *On Private Madness*. London: Rebus, 1996.

——. *The Tragic Effect: The Oedipus Complex in Tragedy*. Trans. Alan Sheridan. Cambridge: Cambridge University Press, 1979.

Grosz, Elizabeth. *Jacques Lacan: A Feminist Introduction*. London: Routledge, 1990.

——. *Space, Time and Perversion*. London: Routledge, 1995.

H.D. *Tribute to Freud*. Manchester: Carcanet, 1970.

Hatab, Lawrence J. *Myth and Philosophy*. New York: Open Court, 1990.

Herman, Nini. *Too Long a Child: The Mother-Daughter Dyad*. London: Free Association Books, 1989.

Hesiod. "Theogony." In *Hesiod and Theognis*. Trans. Dorethea Wender. London: Penguin Classics, 1973.

——. *The Works and Days, Theogony, The Shield of Heracles*. Trans. Richard Lattimore. Ann Arbor: University of Michigan Press, 1991.

Hinshelwood, R. D. *A Dictionary of Kleinian Thought*. London: Free Association Books, 1989.

Hirsch, Marianne. *The Mother-Daughter Plot: Narrative, Psychoanalysis, Feminism*. Bloomington: Indiana University Press, 1989.

Homer. *The Iliad*. Trans. Robert Fagles. London: Penguin, 1990.

——. *The Odyssey*. Trans. Robert Fagles. London: Penguin, 1990.

Huffer, Lynne. *Maternal Pasts, Feminist Futures: Nostalgia, Ethics, and the Question of Difference*. Stanford, Calif.: Stanford University Press, 1998.

Ian, Marcia. *Remembering the Phallic Mother: Psychoanalysis, Modernism, and the Fetish*. Ithaca, N.Y.: Cornell University Press, 1993.

Irigaray, Luce. *Elemental Passions*. Trans. Joanne Collie and Judith Still. London: Athlone, 1992.

——. *An Ethics of Sexual Difference*. Trans. Carolyn Burke and Gillian C. Gill. London: Athlone, 1993.

——. *I Love to You: Sketch of a Possible Felicity in History.* Trans. Alison Martin. London: Routledge, 1996.

——. *Je, Tu, Nous: Toward a Culture of Difference.* Trans. Alison Martin. London, Routledge, 1993.

——. *Marine Lover of Friedrich Nietzsche.* Trans. Gillian C. Gill. New York: Columbia University Press, 1991.

——. *Sexes and Genealogies.* Trans. Gillian C. Gill. New York: Columbia University Press, 1993.

——. *Speculum of the Other Woman.* Trans. Gillian C. Gill. Ithaca, N.Y.: Cornell University Press, 1985.

——. *Thinking the Difference: For a Peaceful Revolution.* Trans. Karin Montin. London: Athlone, 1994.

——. *This Sex Which Is Not One.* Trans. Catherine Porter. Ithaca, N.Y.: Cornell University Press, 1985.

Kaufmann, Walter. *Tragedy and Philosophy.* Princeton, N.J.: Princeton University Press, 1968.

Kemp, Sandra and Judith Squires, eds. *Feminisms.* Oxford: Oxford University Press, 1997.

King, Pearl and Riccardo Steiner, eds. *The Freud–Klein Controversies, 1941–45.* London: Routledge, 1991.

Klein, Melanie. *Envy and Gratitude and Other Works: 1946–1963.* London: Virago, 1988.

——. *Love, Guilt and Reparation and Other Works: 1921–1945.* London: Virago, 1988.

——. *The Psychoanalysis of Children.* London: Vintage, 1997.

Knapp, Bettina. *Women in Myth.* Albany, N.Y.: State University of New York Press, 1977.

Kofman, Sarah. *The Enigma of Woman: Woman in Freud's Writings.* Trans. Catherine Porter. Ithaca, N.Y.: Cornell University Press, 1985.

Kohon, Gregorio, ed. *The British School of Psychoanalysis.* London: Free Association Books, 1986.

Kristeva, Julia. *The Black Sun: Depression and Melancholia.* Trans. Leon S. Roudiez. New York: Columbia University Press, 1989.

——. *Powers of Horror: An Essay in Abjection.* Trans. Leon S. Roudiez. New York: Columbia University Press, 1982.

——. *Visions Capitales.* Paris: Editions de la Reunion des Musées Nationaux, 1998.

Lacan, Jacques. *Écrits: A Selection.* Trans. Alan Sheridan. London: Routledge/Tavistock, 1977.

——. *The Ethics of Psychoanalysis, 1959–1960: The Seminar of Jacques Lacan. Book 7.* Ed. Jacques-Alain Miller. Trans. Dennis Porter. London: Routledge, 1992.

——. *The Four Fundamental Concepts of Psychoanalysis.* Trans. Alan Sheridan. London: Penguin, 1964.

Laplanche, Jean. *Essays on Otherness.* Ed. John Fletcher. London: Routledge, 1999.

——. *New Foundations for Psychoanalysis.* Trans. David Macey. Oxford: Blackwell, 1989.

Laplanche, Jean and J. B. Pontalis. *The Language of Psychoanalysis.* London: Karnac, 1988.

Leach, Edmund. *Lévi-Strauss.* London: Fontana, 1970.

Lebeck, Ann. *"The Oresteia": A Study in Language and Structure.* Cambridge: Harvard University Press, 1971.

Lennon, Kathleen and Margaret Whitford, eds. *Knowing the Difference: Feminist Perspectives in Epistemology.* London: Routledge, 1994.

Lévi-Strauss, Claude. *Myth and Meaning: The Massey Lectures.* London: Routledge, 1978.

——. *The Raw and the Cooked: Introduction to a Science of Mythology.* Trans. John Weightman and Doreen Weightman. London: Penguin, 1986.

——. *Structural Anthropology.* Vol. 1. Trans. Claire Jacobson and Brooke Grundfest Schoepf. London: Penguin, 1968.

Lichtenberg-Ettinger, Bracha. Interview. *Women's Art Magazine,* no. 56 (1994): 2–5.

——. *The Matrixial Gaze.* Leeds: University of Leeds Feminist and Art Histories Network Press, 1994.

Limentani, Adam. "To the Limits of Male Heterosexuality: The Vagina Man." In *The Gender Conundrum: Contemporary Psychoanalytic Perspectives on Femininity and Masculinity,* ed. Dana Breen. London: Routledge, 1993.

Loraux, Nicole. *The Experiences of Tiresias: The Feminine and the Greek Man.* Trans. Paula Wissing. Princeton, N.J.: Princeton University Press, 1995.

——. *Tragic Ways of Killing a Woman.* Trans. Anthony Forester. Cambridge: Harvard University Press, 1991.

Lorraine, Tamsin. *Irigaray and Deleuze: Experiments in Visceral Philosophy.* New York: Columbia University Press, 1999.

Lupton, Mary Jane. *Menstruation and Psychoanalysis.* Chicago: University of Illinois Press, 1993.

McDougall, Joyce. *The Many Faces of Eros: A Psychoanalytic Exploration of Human Sexuality.* London: Free Association Books, 1995.

Macksey, Richard and Eugenio Donato, eds. *The Structuralist Controversy: The Language of Criticism and the Sciences of Man.* Baltimore: Johns Hopkins University Press, 1970.

Marks, Elaine and Isabelle De Courtivron, eds. *New French Feminisms.* Brighton, U.K.: Harvester, 1981.

Matte Blanco, Ignacio. *The Unconscious as Infinite Sets.* London: Duckworth, 1975.

Mens-Verhulst, Janneke van, Karlein Schreurs, and Liesbeth Woertman, eds. *Daughtering and Mothering: Female Subjectivity Reanalysed.* London: Routledge, 1993.

Minsky, Rosalind. *Psychoanalysis and Culture: Contemporary States of Mind.* Cambridge: Polity, 1998.

——. *Psychoanalysis and Gender: An Introductory Reader.* London: Routledge, 1996.

Mitchell, Juliet. *Mad Men and Medusas: Reclaiming Hysteria and the Effects of Sibling Relations on the Human Condition.* London: Allen Lane / Penguin, 2000.

——. *Psychoanalysis and Feminism: A Radical Reassessment of Freudian Psychoanalysis.* London: Allen Lane, 1974.

——. *Psychoanalysis and Feminism: A Radical Reassessment of Freudian Psychoanalysis.* Rev. ed. London: Penguin, 1999.

——. "Sexuality, Psychoanalysis and Social Changes." In *The Institute of Psychoanalysis News,* p. 3. London: Institute of Psychoanalysis, 1998.

——. *Siblings: Sex and Violence.* London: Polity, 2003.

——. "Twenty Years On." *New Formations* 26 (Autumn 1995): 54–62.

——. *Women: The Longest Revolution. On Feminism, Literature, and Psychoanalysis.* New York: Pantheon, 1984.

——. *Women's Estate.* London: Penguin, 1971.

——, ed. *The Selected Melanie Klein.* London: Penguin, 1991.

Mitchell, Juliet and Jacqueline Rose, eds. *Jacques Lacan and the École Freudienne: Feminine Sexuality*. Trans. Jacqueline Rose. London: Macmillan, 1982.

Moi, Toril. *Sexual/Textual Politics: Feminist Literary Theory*. London: Methuen, 1985.

——, ed. *French Feminist Thought*. Oxford: Blackwell, 1987.

——. *The Kristeva Reader*. Oxford: Blackwell, 1986.

Mortley, Raoul, ed. *French Philosophers in Conversation: Levinas, Schneider, Serres, Irigaray, Le Doeuff, Derrida*. London: Routledge, 1991.

Nicholson, Linda, ed. *The Second Wave: A Reader in Feminist Theory*. London: Routledge, 1997.

O'Connor, Noreen and Joanna Ryan. *Wild Desires and Mistaken Identities: Lesbianism and Psychoanalysis*. London: Virago, 1993.

Olson, A. Gary and Elizabeth Hirsh, eds. *Women Writing Culture*. Albany: State University of New York Press, 1995.

Parker, Rozsika. *Torn in Two: The Experience of Maternal Ambivalence*. London: Virago, 1995.

Phillips, Adam. *Winnicott*. London: Fontana, 1988.

Phillips, John and Lyndsey Stonebridge, eds. *Reading Melanie Klein*. London: Routledge, 1999.

Phillips, Shelley. *Beyond the Myths: Mother-Daughter Relationships in Psychology, History, Literature and Everyday Life*. London: Penguin, 1991.

Pound, Ezra and Rudd Flemming. *Elektra*. Ed. Richard Reid. Princeton, N.J.: Princeton University Press, 1989.

Quinodoz, Jean-Michel. "Dreams that Turn Over a Page: Integration Dreams with Paradoxical Regressive Content." *International Journal of Psychoanalysis* 80, part 2 (April 1999): 225–239.

Rabinowitz, Nancy Sorkin. *Anxiety Veiled: Euripides and the Traffic in Women*. Ithaca, N.Y.: Cornell University Press, 1993.

Racine, Jean. *Iphigenia/Phaedra/Athaliah*. Trans. John Cairncross. London: Penguin Classics, 1963.

Raphael-Leff, Joan and Rosine Jozef Perelberg, eds. *Female Experience: Three Generations of British Women Psychoanalysts on Work with Women*. London: Routledge, 1997.

Rickels, Lawrence. A. *The Vampire Lectures*. Minneapolis: University of Minnesota Press, 1999.

Riviere, Joan, ed. *Developments in Psychoanalysis*. London: Karnac, 1989.

Rose, Jacqueline. "Of Knowledge and Mothers: On the Work of Christopher Bollas." *Gender and Psychoanalysis* 1, no. 4 (1996): 411–427.

——. *Sexuality in the Field of Vision*. London: Verso, 1986.

——. *Why War? Psychoanalysis, Politics and the Return to Melanie Klein*. Oxford: Blackwell, 1993.

Roustang, François. *Dire Mastery: Discipleship from Freud to Lacan*. Trans. Ned Lukacher. Washington, D.C.: American Psychiatric Press, 1986.

——. *Psychoanalysis Never Lets Go*. Trans. Ned Lukacher. Baltimore: John Hopkins University Press, 1983.

Rubin-Suleiman, Susan, ed. *The Female Body in Western Culture: Contemporary Perspectives*. Cambridge: Harvard University Press, 1985.

Rukeyser, Muriel. *Collected Poems*. New York: McGraw-Hill, 1982.

Sandler, Joseph, ed. *Projection, Identification, Projective Identification*. London: Karnac, 1989.

Schützenberger, Anne Ancelin. *The Ancestor Syndrome: Transgenerational Psychotherapy and the Hidden Links in the Family Tree.* Trans. Anne Trager. London: Routledge, 1998.

Segal, Hanna. *Dream, Phantasy and Art.* London: Routledge, 1991.

——. *Klein.* London: Karnac / Institute of Psychoanalysis, 1989.

Seneca. *Four Tragedies and Octavia.* Trans. E. F. Walting. London: Penguin Classics, 1966.

Seu, Bruna I. and M. Colleen Heenan. *Feminism and Psychotherapy: Reflections on Contemporary Theories and Practices.* London: Sage, 1998.

Slater, Philip. *The Glory of Hera: Greek Mythology and the Greek Family.* Princeton, N.J.: Princeton University Press, 1968.

Soper, Kate. "Feminism, Humanism and Postmodernism." In *The Woman Question,* ed. Mary Evans, 2d ed., pp. 10–21. London: Sage, 1994.

Sophocles. *Electra and Other Plays.* Trans. E. F. Walting. London: Penguin Classics, 1953.

——. *Oedipus the King.* Vol. 1 of *The Complete Tragedies.* Trans. David Greene and Richard Lattimore. Chicago: University of Chicago Press, 1954.

Sprengnether, Madelon. *The Spectral Mother: Freud, Feminism, and Psychoanalysis.* Ithaca, N.Y.: Cornell University Press, 1990.

Stern, Daniel. *The Interpersonal World of the Infant: A View from Psychoanalysis and Developmental Psychology.* New York: Basic, 1985.

Stoller, Robert. *Sex and Gender: On the Development of Masculinity and Femininity.* New York: Science House, 1968.

Swindells, Julia and Lisa Jardine. *What's Left? Women in Culture and the Labour Movement.* London: Routledge, 1990.

Vernant, Jean-Pierre. *Mortals and Immortals: Collected Essays.* Ed. Froma Zeitlin. Princeton, N.J.: Princeton University Press, 1991.

Vernant, Jean-Pierre and Marcel Detienne. *Cunning and Intelligence in Greek Culture and Society.* Trans. Janet Lloyd. Chicago: University of Chicago Press, 1991.

——. *Myth, Religion and Society: Structuralist Essays.* Trans. Janet Lloyd. Cambridge: Cambridge University Press, 1981.

Vernant, Jean-Pierre and Pierre Vidal-Naquet. *Myth and Tragedy in Ancient Greece.* Trans. Janet Lloyd. New York: Zone, 1988.

Ward, Ivan, ed. *Is Psychoanalysis Another Religion? Contemporary Essays on Spirit, Faith and Morality in Psychoanalysis.* London: Freud Museum Publications, 1993.

Warner, Marina. *Six Myths of Our Time: Managing Monsters. The Reith Lectures.* London: Vintage, 1994.

Weed, Elizabeth and Naomi Schor, eds. *Feminism Meets Queer Theory.* Bloomington: Indiana University Press, 1997.

Weedon, Chris. *Feminist Practice and Poststructuralist Theory.* Oxford: Blackwell, 1987.

Welldon, Estela V. *Mother, Madonna, Whore: The Idealization and Denigration of Motherhood.* New York: Guilford, 1988.

Whitebrook, Joel. *Perversion and Utopia: A Study in Psychoanalysis and Critical Theory.* Cambridge, Mass.: MIT Press, 1996.

Whitford, Margaret. "Doing Feminist Research—Making Links." *Women's Philosophy Review,* no. 16 (1996): 33–41.

——. *Luce Irigaray: Philosophy in the Feminine.* London: Routledge, 1991.

——, ed. *The Irigaray Reader.* Oxford: Blackwell, 1991.

Wieland, Christina. "Matricide and Destructiveness: Infantile Anxieties and Technological Culture." *British Journal of Psychotherapy* 12, no. 3 (1996): 300–313.

——. *The Undead Mother: Psychoanalytic Explorations of Masculinity, Femininity and Matricide*. London: Rebus, 2000.

Wilson, Elizabeth, with Angela Weir. *Hidden Agendas: Theory, Politics and Experience in the Women's Movement*. London: Tavistock, 1986.

Winnicott, D. W. *Playing and Reality*. London: Routledge, 1971.

——. *Through Paediatrics to Psychoanalysis: Collected Papers*. London: Tavistock, 1958. Reprint, London: Karnac, 1975.

Woolf, Christa. *Cassandra: A Novel and Four Essays*. Trans. Jan Van Heurck. London: Virago, 1984.

——. *Medea: A Novel*. Trans. John Cullen. London: Virago, 1998.

Woolf, Virginia. *A Room of One's Own and Three Guineas*. London: Vintage, 1996.

Wright, Elizabeth, ed. *Feminism and Psychoanalysis: A Critical Dictionary*. Oxford: Blackwell, 1992.

Zanardi, Claudia, ed. *Essential Papers on the Psychology of Women*. New York: New York University Press, 1990.

Index

oedipal complex (*continued*)
86–87; Oresteian myth as other side
of, 95–96
oedipal structure, 17; alternatives to, 45–
46; Orestes myth and, 33; psychosis in,
96–97; role of phallus in, 27–28
Oedipus myth, 194n8; blindness, role of,
56–57; at level of intellect, 58–59; matricidal phantasy structures in, 58–59,
62; Orestes within, 129
Oedipus tragedy (Sophocles), 46–47
Olivier, Christiane, 196n12
"On Negation" (Green), 38
oppression, 3–5, 11–12
orchestral score metaphor, 17, 47–48,
51–52, 193n14
Oresteian myth, x, 19–20, 55–60, 193n1;
ambivalence of, 84–85; Clytemnestra's dream, 77–79; cultural imaginary organized by, 99–100; daughter
excluded from, 152–153; deer motif,
158–160, 165, 201n3; defensive function of, 45–46; differentiation in,
173–177; Electra's role, 143–147; function of sisters/daughters in, 129–147;
Green's view, 94–106; Irigaray's
view, 32–33, 68–69, 75, 99–100;
Klein's view, 76–77, 80–82, 83–93,
101–102, 195n6; marriages proposed
in, 170–172; Metis myth related to,
60–71, 72, 86, 158, 181–182; mother-
daughter structures in, 59–60; murder of Agamemnon, 56, 109–114, 153;
oedipal complex and, 33, 95–96, 129;
parental couple in, 111–112; potential
as structural model, 33, 72; recognition scene, 173–174; red rug imagery,
110–111; reparation foreclosed in, 82,
87; reworkings of, 43, 55; sacrifice
of Iphigenia, 56, 83, 109, 153–155,
158–162; spectator role, 111–112, 158;
structures of, 175–176
Orestes: Electra, relationship with,
144–147, 169–172; infantilization
of, 113; Oedipus within, 129; return of,
56, 113, 169; sisters, relation to, 130–131,
143–147, 148–149; trajectory of, 129,
143

paranoid schizoid position, 79–80, 83–84,
101–103, 145–146, 196n9
Parker, Rozsika, 188n28
parthenogenesis phantasies, 60–61, 86;
daughter and, 133, 154–155; incorporation linked with, 61, 63, 123–126; Law
of Metis prohibits, 123–124, 148–150;
in Zeus/Metis/Athena myth, 62–71,
99, 134, 148
patriarchal order, 6; exclusion of mother-
daughter relation, 131–132; failure of,
175–177
patricide, 34, 104
performativity, 4, 10–14
Persephone, 137
phallogocentrism, 29–30
phallus, 7–10, 27–28
phantasies: of dominant order, 18–19; as
screens against reality, 73–74
phantasy, defined, 183n1
phantom effect, 88–93, 105–106; Clytemnestra's daughters and, 133–134;
matricide and, 99–101; of Metis,
89–90, 92–93, 104, 106, 118–119, 134,
152–153
phobic hallucinations, 117–120
Powers of Horror: An Essay on Abjection
(Kristeva), 117–119
prescriptive approach, 8, 131, 135, 180
presence/absence binary, 41–42, 99,
116–119, 159–161
projection, 103; mother-daughter relation
and, 138–139, 145–147; onto mother,
103, 106, 107–108, 142–143
psychoanalysis, x; blindness of, 56–57; as
conservative, 12–14; deviation from
Oedipus as psychotic, 50–51; feminist
object-relations, 24–25; language of,
89–90; monolithic approach to myth,
46–48, 50, 185n16, 10, 192nn5; need
for alternative theorization, 49–52;
occlusion of matricide from, 33–34;
paternal third term, 6–7, 96; reproduction of already-known, 49–51
Psychoanalysis and Feminism (Mitchell),
142–143
psychosis, 8, 13. *See also* madness; deviation from Oedipus as, 50–51; in